A Discovery
of the True Causes
Why Ireland Was Never
Entirely Subdued

Sir John Davies

A Discovery
of the True Causes
Why Ireland Was Never
Entirely Subdued

[And] Brought Under
Obedience of the Crown of
England Until the Beginning of
His Majesty's Happy Reign
(1612)

Edited by James P. Myers, Jr.

The Catholic University of America Press
Washington, D.C.

Copyright © 1988
The Catholic University of America Press
All rights reserved
Printed in the United States of America

LIBRARY OF CONGRESS CATALOGING-IN-PUBLICATION DATA

Davies, John, Sir, 1569–1626.

A discovery of the true causes why Ireland was never
entirely subdued and brought under obedience of the
crown of England until the beginning of His Majesty's
happy reign (1612).

Bibliography: p.
Includes index.
1. Ireland—History—1172–1603.   2. Ireland—Foreign
relations—Great Britain.   3. Great Britain—Foreign
relations—Ireland.   I. Myers, James P., 1941–
II. Title.
DA933.D25   1988   941.506   87-25595
ISBN 0-8132-0652-9

Contents

Preface

AMONG THE SCORES of Elizabethan and Jacobean tracts on Ireland, Sir John Davies's *A Discovery of the True Causes Why Ireland Was Never Entirely Subdued . . .* (1612) occupies a unique position. Coming near the end of a literary-polemical legacy dating from the twelfth-century writings of Gerald of Wales, it summarizes, indeed climaxes, the tradition of which it is so integral a part. More significantly, the *Discovery* preserves for us as accurate an expression of official policy toward the Ireland of the Jacobean settlement as we are likely to find among the essays of its author's contemporaries, for Davies, an accomplished Elizabethan poet, wrote as Ireland's highest legal officer, a fact stressed by the tract's dedicatory page, identifying him not by name but by title—"By his Maiesties Atturney Generall, of Ireland."

The *Discovery* has been reprinted in full several times (see Bibliography), most recently in a photographic facsimile of the 1612 edition. No editor, however, has endeavored to present a text satisfying to a modern reader, who, although interested in the record of England's presence in Ireland, might lack the diverse scholarly resources required to appreciate the semantic, legal, and historical complexities of Davies's important discussion. It is to supply such a need that I have prepared this text. Accordingly, I have modernized spelling and punctuation, glossed obsolete and archaic terms, clarified historical allusions, and translated Davies's extensive quotations from classical and medieval sources. The textual note concluding this preface details more fully the ways I have sought to make the *Discovery* more accessible to the modern reader, while also preserving those features Davies, as a scholar and legal historian, deemed essential.

With pleasure, I acknowledge my great indebtedness to the individuals and institutions which over the years have supported my inquiry into Anglo-Irish relations during the Renaissance, and especially into the curious roles enacted by poet Sir John Davies: to the Folger Shakespeare Library and the Henry E. Huntington Library, for access to their excellent collections; to my colleagues in the Department of English at Gettysburg College, particularly to Mary Margaret Stewart, James D. Pickering, and Edward J. Baskerville, for listening to me; to David B. Quinn, for reading parts of this study and offering several helpful suggestions; to Kathleen Crapster and Nellie Heller of the Gettysburg College Library, for assistance in obtaining hard-to-find materials; to Carl A. Rubino of the University of Texas and Jay Lees of North Iowa University, for translating the text's very difficult, error-riddled classical and medieval quotations, respectively. To the Gettysburg College Research and Development Fund, which provided several substantial grants permitting acquisition of rare materials, leave time, and travel to Ireland, I am also deeply grateful. I wish also to single out two individuals for very special notice. I have profited greatly from my epistolary friendship with F. W. Harris, whose thorough investigations into Davies's guiding influence during the Jacobean settlement both confirmed and contributed appreciably to my understanding of the historical significance of the *Discovery*. Finally, I return particular thanks to Jerrold Casway, for his encouragement and support, for his contagious excitement for Renaissance Ireland, and for his availability.

The Present Text

In preparing this edition, I have endeavored to provide an attractive and readily accessible text for the nonspecialist reader possessing a historical interest in modern Ireland's turbulent beginnings. I have, at the same time, preserved all those features that distinguish the *Discovery* as a scholarly work.

As I suggest in the Introduction, the *Discovery* exists in a hur-

riedly printed and very probably hastily written form, only partially corrected at the time of printing. Inversion of letters, errors
in pagination, occasional omissions of text, lapses in paragraph-
ing, and inconsistencies in punctuation and spelling—all these
abound. Following the lead provided by Jaggard's incomplete
page of *errata* in the 1612 edition, I have silently corrected the
inversions and accidental errors, restoring without comment
such substantive readings as the *errata* page notes. Notwithstanding the probability of authorial and compositorial haste, the text
of the *Discovery* seems otherwise relatively free of substantive
errors. The handful of emendations required I have duly noted
in Appendix I.

Because the present text is offered to the modern, nonspecialist, but historically interested reader—however much an ideal
projection of the editor's imagination he or she may be—I have
modernized and made consistent spelling and capitalization.
Some uncertainty still exists concerning the rhetorical purposes
expressed by seventeenth-century pointing; and an author's practices were, in addition, always subject to modification through
the whim of the compositor. When possible, I have tried to preserve Davies's apparent intention in respect to pointing, altering
punctuation when required by our conventions or for the sake
of clarity.

On the issue of Davies's extensive Latin and occasional French
quotations I have proceeded in two different ways, possibly
opening myself to criticism for inconsistency. As a scholar
inspired by the new principles advanced by Camden and the
Society of Antiquaries (of which Davies was a member), Davies reinforces his argument with considerable textual citation.
Drawn from original historical documents (many now lost), copies thereof, and, occasionally, memorial reconstructions, these
lengthy quotations in medieval legal Latin and French, further
transmuted by an uncomprehending compositor, pose great difficulties for even a modern reader with background in Latin. I
have therefore relegated Davies's original citations (altering only

the u/v, i/j usage) to Appendix I notes, substituting English translations in the text. The classical quotations, intended to create a literary appeal, present a different problem. Because they are not as intrusive, in number or length as the legal citations, and because their inclusion speaks to certain artistic expectations favored by Davies's contemporary readership, I have retained them, providing translations and attributions (when possible) in the footnotes.

In dating laws, proclamations, and administrative memoranda, Davies sometimes employs the style which later came to prevail in historical documentation, for example, "1 Henry VII" to indicate 1485, the first year of King Henry VII's reign. More often, his practice seems to have no consistency: for example, "the seventeenth year of King Henry the Second," or "the 29. of Edward the First." I have silently regularized all such references to conform with contemporary usage.

Textual Notes

In 1612, following contemporaneous practice, John Jaggard printed the book with extensive marginal notes. These are of two orders: sectional headings and source documentation. In addition to being difficult to justify in a modern text, such marginal notations detract from the appearance and clarity of the page. I have therefore eliminated them, placing the sectional titles at their appropriate positions within the body and moving the source notes, as the 1612 text presents them, to Appendix I (deleting only those which duplicate references in the body, or sometimes incorporating a few into the text in places where Davies already employs that convention).

Those marginal notes signaling section headings I have incorporated into the body of the *Discovery*, sometimes, and without comment, making new paragraphs where these seem indicated by the headings and occasionally combining consecutive headings where it appeared logical and convenient to do so. In a few instances, Davies or Jaggard attempted numerical sequencing for the sectional titles; but because the effort was neither sustained nor complete, I have eliminated these rather than try to reconstruct the numbering throughout. Source notes are listed in Appendix I by page and line numbers (separated by a point). An asterisk in the outer page margin of the text of the *Discovery* signals a source note, to be found in Appendix I.

I have used square brackets within the text to indicate all other substantive emendations, both interpolations and deletions (as in the case of the incomplete numbering of section headings). The list in Appendix II records my emendations, showing: (1) the page where each occurs in the present text; (2) the new reading; and (3), following the left square bracket, the original reading.

Abbreviations

CSPI	*Calendar of State Papers, Relating to Ireland, 1509–1670*, 24 vols. (London, 1860–1912).
Carew MSS	*Calendar of the Carew Manuscripts, Preserved . . . at Lambeth, 1515–1624*, 6 vols. (London, 1867–73).
HMC *Hastings*	*Report on the Manuscripts of the Late Reginald Rawdon Hastings . . .* , ed. Francis Bickley, Historical Manuscripts Commission, 4 vols. (London, 1928–47).
HMC *Salisbury*	*Calendar of the Manuscripts of the . . . Marquess of Salisbury . . . Preserved at Hatfield House*, Historical Manuscripts Commission, 23 vols. (London, 1883–1973).
IHS	*Irish Historical Studies* (Dublin, 1938–).
OED	*The Oxford English Dictionary*, 13 vols. (Oxford, 1933).
SPI	State Papers, Ireland, Public Record Office, London.

Introduction

Introduction

THE PUBLICATION IN 1612 of Sir John Davies's *A Discouerie of the true causes, why Ireland was neuer entirely subdued, and brought vnder Obedience of the Crowne of England, vntill the beginning of his Maiesties happy raigne* marked the completion of the first phase of its author's energetic and successful administrative career, which began in 1603 as solicitor-general for Ireland, even as his tenure as Speaker in the Irish Parliament of 1613–15 initiated him into the second, less spectacular, stage that would extend until 1619. In significant ways, the *Discovery* offered its reader a succinct, articulate survey of the bewildering administrative and military difficulties the English Crown had encountered in the course of its four-hundred-year endeavor at subjugating Ireland and went on to review the vital, if fateful, political reformation haltingly begun under Henry VIII, continued with more enduring effect under Elizabeth I, and dramatically consummated during the reign of James I, the monarch to whom Davies dedicated his tract. At a time when the Crown had already taken several tentative steps and was now catching its breath before fully plunging into the largely uncharted administrative terrain of regulating the newly pacified commonwealth, the *Discovery*, conspicuous with the facile optimism distinctive of its author, intimated to its readers that, with Ireland's most perplexing problems resolved, they had every cause to anticipate that the island would "from henceforth prove a land of peace and concord. . . . [and] will hereafter be as fruitful as the land of Canaan." Borrowing the title of a document Davies prepared in

1610, we might conveniently appreciate the *Discovery* as "Observations on the State of Ireland in 1612" by that commonwealth's highest legal administrator.

In no small way, the policies executed from 1603 on owed their inspiration and immediate success to Davies's legal brilliance and subtlety. Hence, although Davies remains remarkably self-effacing in surveying the reforms instituted during James I's reign, his celebration of his monarch's political wisdom, along with that of James's principal councillors, may also be taken implicitly to reflect the author's own self-esteem. It was, of course, an esteem well garnered. But that John Davies's political star would ascend so auspiciously would probably not have occurred to many of those who, in 1603, weighed his chances for succeeding in a land that had proved a nemesis to so many earlier Englishmen.

Assessing the Davies of 1603, one might well wonder what in his character inspired Sir Charles Blount, Lord Mountjoy and lord deputy, later lord lieutenant, of Ireland, to urge his appointment as solicitor-general. Although he had secured a measure of recognition, and therefore patronage, because of his poems (most notably, the *Orchestra* and the *Nosce Teipsum*), Davies still moved within the shadow of official disgrace. Banished from the Middle Temple and disbarred from the practice of law for assaulting his friend and fellow lawyer Richard Martin on 9 February 1597/8, and having been restored to the practice of law only in October of 1601, he seems an unlikely candidate for the post. Moreover, as extant records witness, Davies was vigorously and conspicuously seeking to repair his reputation, sometime in ways which provoked ridicule and scorn from his contemporaries, even those for whom the maneuver for power was a daily spectacle. On the death of Queen Elizabeth in 1603, for example, when many scrambled for the notice of the king-to-be, Davies joined those who lost no time in rushing north to Scotland. Writing on 30 March 1603, six days after Elizabeth's death, the gossip John Chamberlain recorded, "There is much posting that way and many run thither of their own errand, as if it were nothing else but first come first served, or that preferment were a goal to be got by footmanship: among whom ... [is] John Davies, the poet."[1] He succeeded in attracting the royal eye; Anthony Wood recalls: "The King inquired the names of those gentlemen who were in the company of the said lord [Hunsdon], and he naming John Davies ... the King straightway asked, whether he was *Nosce Teipsum?* and being answered that he was the same, he graciously embraced him, and thenceforth had so great a favor for him, that soon after he made him his solicitor and then his attorney-general in Ireland."[2]

In pursuing advancement, Davies tirelessly courted the sponsorship of several powerful statesman: Sir Thomas Egerton, lord keeper of the great seal (later Lord Ellesmere, the lord chancellor); Henry Percy, ninth earl of Northumberland; Henry Howard, earl of Northampton; Edward Coke, attorney-general; Thomas Sackville, Lord Buckhurst, the lord treasurer; and Sir Robert Cecil (later earl of Salisbury), Elizabeth's and James's principal secretary. But at this time his most strategically placed advocate seems to have been Lord Mountjoy, who had earlier advised Davies to dedicate his long philosophical poem *Nosce Teipsum* to Queen Elizabeth and, as viceroy, recommended him to the post of solicitor-general for Ireland.[3] Very possibly, Mountjoy perceived in Davies something of a kindred spirit, whose deepest need would be to succeed by fulfilling expectations entertained by the officials to whom he would be directly responsible.

1. John Chamberlain, *The Letter of John Chamberlain*, ed. Norman E. McClure (Philadelphia, 1939), 1:189.

2. Anthony Wood, *Athenae Oxoniensis* ... , ed. Philip Bliss, 5 vols. (London, 1813–30), 2:401. Hans Pawlisch, however, argues plausibly that Wood's account is apocryphal and that James's praise of *Nosce Teipsum* dates from 1594, when Davies accompanied an embassy to Scotland (see *Sir John Davies and the Conquest of Ireland: A Study in Legal Imperialism,* [Cambridge, Eng., 1985], pp. 21–33).

3. Bodleian MS. Carte, Fol. 590ʳ.

Sir Charles Blount, Lord Mountjoy, the conqueror of Ireland, had only recently succeeded in redeeming his own reputation and unambiguously establishing his loyalty to the Crown. Early in life, Mountjoy had dedicated himself to refurbishing his family's fortune and much-decayed name.[4] Rising in Elizabeth's favor and following the meteoric career of Robert second earl of Essex, Mountjoy had been seriously implicated in the earl's impetuous insurrection in 1601. But though other conspirators had been duly punished, Mountjoy was appointed lord deputy of Ireland, a surprising reversal because he had never repudiated his friendship with Essex and had remained faithful to his mistress, Penelope Rich, the sister of Essex. Yet he had also remained loyal to the queen, and even though he anticipated being arrested at any moment during the troubles, it appears that she and Cecil intuited the direction of his higher allegiance, probably apprehending, as Mountjoy's biographer Frederick M. Jones has observed, that "Mountjoy's was not the character to stand out in defiant independence or to be prepared to lose all in a heroic attachment." A military leader of intelligence and proved skill, and therefore potentially valuable for helping to resolve the rapidly worsening crisis in Ireland, Mountjoy, eager to please, was willing to allow himself to become "the tool of Mr. Secretary."[5] Identifying and hoping to exploit this disposition, Elizabeth and Cecil stood by him even during the grimmest hours of the siege of Kinsale when others questioned his competence and called for his replacement. With the defeat of Hugh O'Donnell and Hugh O'Neill at Kinsale in 1601 and the making of peace in 1603, Mountjoy vindicated their faith, redeemed his name, and found himself the recipient of great honors, acclaim, and wealth.

His recent experiences, then, could well have made him sympathetic to a subordinate of similar character and inclination.

4. See Cyril Falls, *Mountjoy: Elizabethan General* (London, 1955); and Frederick M. Jones, *Mountjoy, 1563–1606: The Last Elizabethan Deputy* (London, 1958).

5. Jones, *Mountjoy*, p. 42.

Davies's letters show him bent on making his fortune by convincing those in power of his trustworthiness and usefulness. But aside from his apparent readiness to labor faithfully under the direction of others, additional qualities might have arrested Mountjoy's attention.

During the period of his disbarment, Davies had become active in the Society of Antiquaries, an intellectual circle which included such notables as William Camden, Sir Robert Cotton, John Stow, and Sir Francis Thynne. Inspired by the historical methodology of Camden's *Britannia,* (1586), the Society of Antiquaries was formed to investigate the origins of England's political and social institutions. By recovering and examining the original documents and evaluating evidence, the members developed and refined new methods of historical inquiry, sharing the fruits of their investigations with one another by means of learned papers. Beyond satisfying the curiosity of its members, however, the society, as recognized by Linda Peck, "shaped a new role for the historian" and defined "a new relationship between the government and the antiquary, not merely the administrator or the propagandist but the 'expert.' For this scholarly community represented a pool of easily accessible information about traditional solutions to public problems." Examining the productive relationship between Cotton and the earl of Northampton, Peck observes how Cotton "used his antiquarian skills both to support government policy and to reform government practice."[6]

As a member of the Society of Antiquaries, Davies presented several papers, including one on epitaphs (November 1600) and another entitled "Antiquity, Authority, and Succession of the High Steward of England" (June 1603). Throughout his career, he was fascinated with historical and legal precedents, particularly those bearing on parliamentary history. And the *Discovery* itself consistently reveals how his mind delighted in tangling

6. Linda Levy Peck, *Northampton: Patronage and Policy at the Court of James I* (London, 1982), pp. 101–4, offers an account of the society's origins; quotations on pp. 102 and 104.

with the intellectual puzzles posed by history and in endeavoring the resolve contemporary difficulties by uncovering and appreciating their historical origins.

Significantly, Mountjoy himself disclosed similar scholarly inspiration. The earl of Essex, when maneuvering for the viceroyalty of Ireland, had employed the argument of Mountjoy's presumed bookishness and speculative, rather than practical, experience to challenge the latter's suitability for the post. Later, in 1603, when several of the southern towns rebelled on religious grounds, Mountjoy, brandishing a volume of St. Augustine, debated Father James White, vicar-apostolic of Waterford and Lismore, in his field camp, on the issue of obedience due kings by their subjects. And when his marriage to the recently divorced Penelope Rich brought down on him and his wife disgrace and banishment from the court in 1606, Mountjoy wrote his *Discourse or Apology ... in Defense of His Marriage with the Lady Rich*, described by Cyril Falls as "a notable piece of casuistical argument, forcible and pregnant," and by Frederick M. Jones as "obscure and ponderous."[7] The lawyer's fondness for debate, his profound fascination with historical patterns and broad cultural concerns, and his keen intellectual vision would have impressed Mountjoy as highly compatible with his own character and, more significantly, as evidence of Davies's special scholarly capability for the office.

Finally, Mountjoy would have realized that Davies, candidate for high legal office in Ireland, would bring with him invaluable parliamentary experience. Sitting in the Commons for Corfe Castle, Dorset, in 1601, in Elizabeth's last Parliament, Davies had achieved renown as a parliamentarian by promoting the authority of the Parliament. Later events conspired to single Davies out precisely because of his unique, pragmatic knowledge of the mechanics of holding a parliament and thrust him into the very center of the procedural deliberations which preceded the Irish Parliament of 1613–15.

7. Falls, *Mountjoy*, p. 227; Jones, *Mountjoy*, p. 181.

Superficially, then, Davies's personality and recent history might compel the modern inquirer to question Mountjoy's judgment in selecting him for the position of solicitor-general, second most important legal officer in the Irish administration. Closer examination suggests, however, the felicitousness of his choice and further reminds us how little we appreciate the subtle complexities of the client/patron relationship in Jacobean England.[8] Davies's obsession to procure preferment, together with his eagerness to please would-be benefactors, his acclaimed literary achievements, his fascination with social issues and historical complexities, his proven legislative aptitude, and his overall compatibility with the viceroy's own character—all these would have persuaded Mountjoy that in John Davies he could depend upon a reliable, supple, effective instrument for assisting Ireland's demoralized, war-torn society along the painful path to becoming a commonwealth modeled on the English ideal. And the following decade and a half indeed confirmed the deputy's intuition and wisdom.

Anticipating his appointment as solicitor-general, Davies went to Dublin in November 1603, where on 18 December he was knighted. Even before receiving this honor, however, the new legal officer commenced his correspondence with Cecil. Until the latter's death in 1612, Davies was to maintain a fairly constant flow of letters (essays, actually) to the secretary, outstanding for their length, attention to legal detail, and cogent, often witty descriptions of Ireland and its people. It appears as though he had turned away totally from his poetic activities—at least, little of literary interest remains from this period[9]—to channel his lit-

8. For discussions of the Tudor-Stuart patronage system, see Wallace MacCaffrey, "Place and Patronage in Elizabethan Politics," in S. T. Bindoff, J. Hurtsfield, and C. H. Williams, eds., *Elizabethan Government and Society: Essays Presented to Sir John Neale* (London, 1961), pp. 95–126; J. E. Neale, "The Elizabethan Political Scene," in *Essays in English History* (London, 1958), pp. 59–84; G. E. Aylmer, *The King's Servants* (London, 1961); and Peck, *Northampton*.

9. For appreciations of Davies's poetry, see Alexander B. Grosart, "Memorial-Introduction," in Grosart, ed., *The Complete Works of Sir John*

erary energies into penning these highly informative and lively epistles.

From the opening sentence of his first letter, dated 1 December, it becomes clear that one of the more important responsibilities delegated to Davies involved supplying Cecil with the intelligence he required as principal formulator of the Crown's policies. "It were too much presumption in me to interrupt and trouble your Lordship with my trifling advertisements," he begins, with the studied, though time-honored, humility of the client, "but that I perform my duty therein and obey your Lordship's own commandment."[10]

Wasting no time, Davies observes how "the pestilence and famine which rageth in this town" have cast a miserable aspect upon "the face of things." Never one to linger over bleaker realities, however, Davies expresses the great comfort he soon felt at seeing "so many [legal] causes depending, and such good forms of proceeding" in the courts—proof positive that once even a presumably wild people like the Irish have been "over-assubjected, and their swords over-mastered, they appeal . . . willingly to the seats of justice and become the most litigious of all other." Noting how the inhabitants, particularly those in Ulster, still "subject to oppression and misery" by their native chieftains, "prayed . . . upon their knees" for the king's justice, he conceived "a very good hope that, after a parliament wherein many mischiefs may be removed and prevented, and after the people are acquainted with the forms of justice . . . this kingdom will grow humane and civil, and merit the name of a 'commonwealth,' which at this time may properly be termed a 'common-misery.'"[11]

Davies, 3 vols. (London, 1869–76); Robert Krueger, "General Introduction," in Krueger, ed., *The Poems of Sir John Davies* (Oxford, 1975), pp. xix–xvii; and James L. Sanderson, *Sir John Davies* (Boston, 1975).

10. Davies to Cecil, 1 December 1603, SPI, 215:114; repr. in Grosart, ed., *Works of Davies*, 3:xliii.

11. Ibid.; Grosart, ed., *Works of Davies*, p. xliv.

The extant state papers immediately preceding 1611 do not record much examination of the precedents for holding a parliament. Yet with the peace established and no parliament having been called since Sir John Perrot's in 1585–86, the necessity for convening one had impressed itself on the Crown.[12] Certainly Davies registers his own concern, perhaps also confirming for us that his recent parliamentary experience was indeed a major criterion for his being selected for the post. In another letter to Cecil, dated 20 February 1603/4, Davies refers at greater length to this issue, stressing that the urgency of holding a parliament was a shared concern among the Crown's administrators: "Touching the Parliament *which we expect shortly shall be summoned here*," he explains to Cecil, "I have sent your Lordship the copy of Poynings' Act (which directs the manner of holding the Parliament here), together with the copies of all the other acts which have either superseded that Act or expounded it." One of the cumbersome provisions of Poynings' Act required that all legislation to be proposed to the Irish Parliament must first be sent to England for approval by the Crown. Accordingly, Davies elaborates, "It is time that the Council here had instructions to consider what acts are fit to be passed, *for by that time they be certified to and fro the year will be almost passing*."[13]

Clearly, Davies energetically assisted the Crown to prepare for convening an Irish parliament as soon as possible. But as the resourceful and perceptive solicitor-general acclimatized himself to the bureaucratic weather, he perceived a number of issues requiring immediate rectification. And as if these were insufficient to postpone the summoning of a parliament, several events beyond the control of the lawyers and administrators laboring industriously in the Pale seemed to conspire to delay the summoning even further. Continuing plague ("another thorn in the

12. See T. W. Moody, "The Irish Parliament under Elizabeth and James I," *Royal Irish Academy Proceedings* 45 (1939): 49–53.

13. Davies to Cecil, 20 February 1603/4, SPI, 216:114; repr. in Grosart, ed., *Works of Davies*, 3:liii; my emphasis.

foot of the law");[14] an overtaxed, undersized judiciary; an econ-
omy, fueled by debased metal, skidding to ruin; a chaos of claims
and counterclaims regarding land ownership; the legal position
of the country's huge Catholic majority to be resolved; imprecise
land surveys; the flight of Ulster's last remaining native
chieftains; Cahir O'Dougherty's and Shane Carragh O'Cahan's
rebellions; the depredations of pirates infesting the southern
coasts; sheer inexperience and ignorance in holding a parliament—these problems so absorbed the attention of the Dublin
administration that the parliament, perceived in 1603 to be so
desirable, was repeatedly postponed until May 1613.

In his letters of 1 December 1603, 20 February 1603/4, and 7
March 1603/4, Davies apprised Cecil of the economic dangers
deriving from a debased coinage; of the need to reform the
realm's extensive religious "abuses and enormities"; of the losses
to "His Majesty in point of profit" because his exchequer was so
ill-served by its minor officers; of the offenses committed to "the
public peace and security" through "the facility in obtaining the
King's pardon"; of the desperate need to increase the number of
judges "both in the King's Bench and Common Pleas." Although we might infer that the solicitor's reports, enhanced with
analyses and proposed solutions to the problems anatomized,
were providing Cecil with the information he required, Davies
seems not to have felt secure that his endeavors were accomplish-
ing anything. Apart from the customary belittling of his efforts
as a subordinate, we detect a sincere uncertainty. Concluding the
20 February epistle, for example, Davies apologizes for "the
length as well as the rudeness of" his news and then promises
that "when hereafter I understand things better, I shall make
shorter relations and more material." Still apprehensive whether
his letters were reaching a sympathetic, appreciative eye, he begins his 19 April 1604 missive with an even more extended pro-

---

14. Davies to Cecil, 7 March 1604/5, SP1, 216:9; repr. in Grosard, ed., *Works
of Davies*. 3:lvi.

fession of his good intentions: "I am not certain that my letters do come to your Lordship's hands; yet I presume they do, and therefore I presume [to] continue this duty. Yet as often as I write, I do wish and pray that your Lordship may receive my letters in an instant of good leisure, for otherwise they cannot but be tedious and troublesome to your Lordship."[15]

For all the apparent evidence to the contrary, Davies seems to have been an insecure individual. His reiterated declarations of eagerness, industriousness, unworthiness, faithfulness, and so on may be interpreted as beyond the stylistic posturings of a client advancing his own cause to his patron: rather, he seems to be angling for assurance and approval from those whom he served so loyally. Very occasionally, he permitted this need to surface. In a letter of autumn 1606,[16] for example, he nakedly discloses both the pain of feeling rejected and his yearning for some expression of support from Cecil, then earl of Salisbury.[17] Describing the reaction in Dublin to the Crown's hardening policy on continuing religious nonconformity, Davies exclaims that "I am more maliciously hated and ill-spoken of than all the rest, because they think the proclamation was procured only by my solicitation when I was in England." He goes on to remind Salisbury that, anticipating his response, he had communicated his fear to the secretary, who, it would seem, brushed aside Davies's apprehension. Notwithstanding Salisbury's earlier assurance, he again laments that "I have been less respected by the State here than ever I was in former time." Catching himself and trying to modulate beyond the subject of his own unpopularity, he con-

15. Davies to Cecil, 20 February 1603/4, SPI, 216:114; repr. in Grosart, ed., *Works of Davies*, 3:liv; Davies to Cecil, 19 April 1604, SPI, 216:15; repr. in Grosart, ed., *Works of Davies*, 3:lvii.

16. For the dating of this letter, see G. A. Hayes-McCoy, "Sir John Davies in Cavan in 1606 and 1610," *Breifne* 1 (1960): p. 181, n. 24.

17. Sir Robert Cecil, having already been advanced by James I to Baron Essendine (in 1603) and Viscount Cranborne (in 1604), became the first earl of Salisbury on 4 May 1605.

cludes the digression with a plea: "I only beseech your Lordship
upon the next occasion to give me some little sunbeam or reflec-
tion of grace or countenance out of England, to revive my reputation somewhat amongst them."[18]

A willing creature of Cecil and his other supporters on the
Privy Council in England, Davies felt himself uncomfortably
isolated during the short administration of Lord Deputy Sir
George Carey (1603–5). Inexperienced in his new position, he
frequently seems unclear about what his benefactors expected of
him. He may also have been feeling the consequences of his own
occasionally tactless personality. A complaint voiced by Sir
Charles Calthorpe in 1605/6 intimates that Davies was scheming
conspicuously for the attorney-generalship: "There has been and
is a plotting by Mr. Solicitor Davies's friends to prefer him to my
place, and that I should be removed to be some second judge,
with an augmentation of my fee, without any assurance thereof
or my consent thereunto. . . . It is fully 22 years since my coming
into this realm, and so long have I continued as attorney to her
late Majesty."[19] It is doubtful that Davies's "friends" would have
undertaken this campaign without his active encouragement.

Later evidence, some circumstantial, also suggests that Davies's tactlessness and indiscretion continued to dog his strug-
gle to obtain advancement. Humphrey May, writing from London, relays to Davies news of James I's high estimation of him,
adding that the king "knows you will be careful in passing particulars which are not in charge, to avoid clamor and disturbance
of any of his subjects, by dealing with the owners of lands
with their own consents"[20]—very possibly, a pointed, albeit
diplomatic, caution to desist while such behavior might still be
overlooked. In 1615, he apparently misrepresented or divulged to
the Irish Council criticism of it confided by the king—missing

18. Davies to Cecil, undated, SPI, 217:94,96; repr. in Grosart, ed. *Works of
Davies*, 3:lxxxviii.
19. Calthorpe to Salisbury, 4 January 1605/6, HMC *Salisbury*, 18:5–6.
20. May to Davies, 3 April [1609?], HMC *Hastings*, 4:5.

documents obscure the actual situation. In a strongly worded protest, the English Privy Council, charged by James, admonishes "that Sir John Davies has failed both in duty and discretion, whereof when time shall be convenient he is to render an account for making his report, with whom at no time he [the king] has had any such language which might tend to the disreputation of any person of quality, neither gave him direction to deliver any such message, holding now charge in that realm, or to the disgrace of the present Government."[21]

Though his indiscretions hardly served him well, they do not seem seriously to have eclipsed the esteem with which his superiors typically viewed his work. But it is reasonable to infer that his ostentation and impetuousness, his failure to foresee how others might respond to his occasional excesses—and here we might recall his physical assault in public upon Richard Martin in 1597/8—and his apparent need to create intimacy by sharing privileged information are symptoms of a smoldering insecurity.

With his communication of 19 April 1604, Davies strikes out into unexplored epistolary, as well as legal, regions, for the letter records the experiences he and Chief Baron Edmund Pelham encountered on a "circuit or progress over the greatest part of Leinster, as justices of assize and gaol delivery."[22] The form eventually proved to be a happy one. Davies found that within the formal boundaries of narrative structure, he could expand or contract his legal exposition, draw his conclusions, or simply concentrate on details of gossip, physical description, or dramatic moment, and further, that he could admix these in almost any combination to edify and delight his powerful benefactors. It is

21. English Privy Council to the lord deputy and Irish Privy Council, December [?] 1615, *CSPI*, 5:107. Earlier in his career Davies's tactlessness and lack of discipline climaxed in his attack on Richard Martin in 1598. Hans Pawlisch (*Davies*, pp. 16–21) presents additional evidence of Davies's boisterousness from the records associated with Davies's earlier years.

22. Davies to Cecil, 19 April 1604, SPI, 216:15; repr. in Grosart, ed., *Works of Davies*, 3:lvii.

doubtful that any but a mind as supple as that of the author of *Nosce Teipsum* could have so expressively married the felicities of narrative art to the strict niceties of legal inquiry and exposition. These long narrative letters are unique, and several stand as minor epistolary masterpieces, preserving not only priceless eye-witness descriptions by a poet-bureaucrat of Jacobean Ireland but also invaluable testimony of many of the crucial judicial inquiries that successfully prepared the island for plantation.

Very possibly, his report to Salisbury, dated by G.A. Hayes-McCoy as November/December 1606, describing the circuit through Monaghan, Fermanagh, and Cavan, excels all the narrative letters. Following an elaborately contrived apology for most certainly duplicating "frequent dispatches from the Lord Deputy and Council here," Davies discovers his justification in the way he "may sometimes add a circumstance which may give light to the matter of substance, and make it the clearer unto your Lordship"[23]—a vindication offered, in view of the narrative's encyclopedic thoroughness, not without a good measure of humorous understatement.

The "most unsettled and unreformed parts of" Ulster—Monaghan, Fermanagh, and Cavan—confronted the Crown with challenging problems in "settling" the territories so that they might be brought effectively within the compass of the administration's jurisdiction. After briefly touching upon the roots of the problems unique to each county, creating thereby a tripartite framework for his narrative, Davies details events of the first stage of the circuit, but not before first relieving his legal exposition with a short, entertaining, carefully selective description of the commissioners' journey from Mellifont Abbey, Garret Moore's great house near Drogheda, to the town of Monaghan, "which doth not deserve the name of a good village, consisting of divers scattered cabins, or cottages, whereof the most part are

23. Davies to Cecil, 1604–5 [?], Sloane MS. 4793; repr. in Grosart, ed., *Works of Davies*, 3:119–20.

possessed by the cast [discharged] soldiers of that garrison." Yet even here, Davies remains alive to his patron's expectations: descriptions of countryside and hamlet serve pragmatic ends. He pointedly observes that "albeit we were to pass through the wastest and wildest parts of all the north, yet had we only for our guard six or seven score foot, and fifty or three score horse," whereas even in the most peaceful of former times, "no Lord-Deputy did ever adventure himself into those parts without an army of eight hundred or one thousand men."[24]

In the village itself, the commissioners found the platform for a new castle, construction on which had been suspended for two years. This, too, prompts the observant correspondent to draw his moral: "The chief lords of the country are pleased and comforted therewith; because if it were erected and finished in that form as was intended, it would at all times be a bridle unto their insolency: for the M'Mahouses [MacMahons] undoubtedly are the most proud and barbarous sept among the Irish; and do ever soonest repine and kick and spurn at the English government."[25]

Settled in their camp outside the hamlet, the commissioners set about the principal task of establishing the legality of claims and titles to Monaghan's five baronies and the holdings therein, a chore particularly difficult because so many of the MacMahons, fierce supporters of Tyrone's insurrection, had been killed while in rebellion, thereby forfeiting their lands. After disposing of temporal and church lands, the commission appointed juries to try the criminal cases. But when the juries acquitted the prisoners irrespective of the testimony and evidence, judging instead the degree of relationship within the sept or the coercive power of friends of the accused, the commissioners resorted to their own form of intimidation, punishing "one jury with good round fines and imprisonment, for acquitting some prisoners,

24. Ibid.; Grosart, ed. *Works of Davies*, 3:127–28.
25. Ibid.; Grosart, ed., *Works of Davies*, p. 128.

contrary to direct and pregnant evidence."[26] Once the Irish perceived how it was to be, they began returning the judgments the Crown demanded.

The commission concluded its business by issuing "several orders" to foster the secure establishment of the church and the civil government. It next proceeded from Monaghan "through ways almost impassable for our carriages, by reason of the woods and bogs," to the island of Devenish in Fermanagh (at least parts of which Davies later appropriated for himself under dubious circumstances).[27] There, the commission followed the same pattern as it had in Monaghan. Different historical circumstances, however, demanded different procedures, for great numbers of freeholders had survived the rebellion and later received royal pardon, whereas the demesne lands of Hugh Maguire, Fermanagh's earlier chieftain, had been forfeited with his death during the rebellion.

Each county confronted the land commissioners with unique problems, and as they labored through the tangle of precedents, conflicting practices of brehon and common law, historical occurrences, and genealogical claims, Davies carefully recorded the deliberations and judgments, thereby creating a body of contemporary precedents for his successors. Yet even in the midst of the most abstruse legal expositions, he often interpolated episodes remarkable for their narrative or descriptive skill, intended to vary and enliven the analyses. These letters are more than prosaic reporting, and the episode involving the brehon O'Breslin is outstanding for exhibiting Davies's playfulness.

To resolve questions pertaining to Maguire's original mensal lands—demesne lands set aside for provisioning the chieftain with such foodstuffs as butter and grain—the commissioners

26. Ibid.; Grosart, ed., *Works of Davies*, p. 137.

27. See the petition of James Spottiswood, bishop of Clogher, 26 February 1633/4, requesting restoration of lands to the bishopric of Clogher, which had been "dispossessed by Sir John Davies" during the time of his tenure as attorney-general (HMC *Hastings*, 4:53–4).

sent for the O'Donnells' principal chronicler and brehon (judge of Irish law), one O'Breslin, who was said to possess an ancient legal document relevant to their inquiry. But O'Breslin, "so aged and decrepit, as he was scarce able to repair unto us," claimed that the document had been "burned among other of his papers and books by certain English soldiers" during the war, contrary to general testimony:

> Thereupon my Lord Chancellor . . . did minister an oath unto him, and gave him a very serious charge to inform us truly what was become of the roll. The poor old man fetching a deep sigh, confessed that he knew where the roll was, but that it was dearer to him than his life, and therefore he would never deliver it out of his hands, unless my Lord Chancellor, would take the like oath, that the roll should be restored unto him again: my Lord Chancellor smiling, gave him his word and his hand that he should have the roll redelivered unto him.[28]

Translated and perused, the document clearly certified the extent of Maguire's mensal lands, which proved far less than he "made himself owner of . . . cutting [taxing] what he listed, and imposing as many bonaghtes, or hired soldiers, upon" his people as he wished. From this discovery, Davies moves on to conjecture how differently things might have fallen out "if the State here had in former times but looked into the state of this country, and had established the English laws and justice among them, whereby every man might have enjoyed his own": Maguire's power would have been appreciably less, possibly preventing him from becoming one of the mainstays of the rebellion. And so it might have been, he implies, with the other great chieftains: "Assuredly these Irish Lords appear to us like glow worms, which afar off seem to be all fire; but, being taken up in a man's hands, are but silly worms."[29]

Acknowledging that he has perhaps lingered overlong on this episode, he apologizes to Salisbury, but does so with the humor-

28. Repr. in Grosart, ed., *Works of Davies*, 3:148.
29. Ibid.

ous and self-abnegating irony of one who now exposes how slyly he has succeeded in informing in ways not anticipated by his reader, thus delighting him as well: "I have digressed a little too much in this place, for which I humbly crave pardon, if your Lordship shall not think it pertinent to this discourse, wherein I meant to set forth the quality and quantity of M'Guyre's mensall duties."[30]

With businesslike efficiency he completes his report on the commissioners' achievements in Fermanagh, going on to detail the work performed in Cavan. With so much of the procedural background already clarified in his descriptions of the earlier inquiries, Davies succinctly delineates the unique circumstances in Cavan and then expeditiously moves through the judgments and measures taken to ensure the future implementing of civil justice in the county and rounds off the section with his own recommendations.

The conclusion to the letter consists of two paragraphs, the first celebrating the Herculean energy expended by Lord Deputy Sir Arthur Chichester in cutting "off three heads of that hydra of the North, namely, M'Mahown, M'Guyre, and O'Relie," and then reiterating the numerous benefits to be expected as the rule of common law continues to be advanced into those parts of Ulster visited by the commission.[31]

The final paragraph shifts attention to Davies's professional and, I think, rhetorical self-consciousness. Perpetually concerned that he satisfy Salisbury's expectations, he here apologizes for any defects inhering in his report, particularly its episodic, uneven structure—disunity being the principal lapse for any writer. Yet Davies, with the subtlety and tongue-in-cheek irony of a literary gamester, turns this flaw—more imagined than real, I feel—into a device for further illuminating how tirelessly he continues to labor for the good of the state. "I have made unto

30. Ibid., p. 151.
31. Ibid., p. 161.

your Lordship a broken and disjointed relation," he laments, "for which I humbly crave pardon." Rather than conclude on such a flat, conventional plea, however, he embellishes the apology with a justification simultaneously self-pitying and self-congratulatory. His missive's unevenness resulted, he affirms, "because I was continually interrupted in the writing thereof, being employed . . . in a new commission of assize and nisi prius [trial before a single judge, not a full court] for the counties of Waterford, Wexford, and Wicklow; so as I have been enforced," he repeats, "to take fractions and starts, and almost instants of time, to finish the several periods of this rude discourse."[32]

The insecurity implicit in the letter has its roots both in the received rhetorical convention of letters addressed by a client to his patron and in Davies's own character. Significantly, as he earnestly labored to fulfill the trust of his benefactors, they reciprocated with the assurances he required. As early as 9 September 1604, Ellesmere, the lord chancellor, wrote encouragingly: "In the discourse which you have sent me, I find not only a very loving respect which you have towards me (for which I owe you hearty thanks), but also a very wise and judicious observation of the state of this wasted kingdom and the condition of the people."[33]

Ellesmere's warm tone and sentiments make it clear that he valued Davies as much as a friend as a client. Cecil's relationship with Davies was another matter. Clearly, Cecil was the most important of his patrons now, and his continuing support after 1606, when Mountjoy died, became critical. Davies, consequently, must have viewed most auspiciously the secretary's glowing encouragement to continue as he had been: "You have so perfectly described, or rather anatomized," Salisbury wrote late in 1606, "all those parts wherein you have traveled, and the disposition of the people, as will give me more light to direct my coun-

32. Ibid., pp. 161–62.
33. Ibid., p. cii.

sels upon many occasions than any other kind of advertisement ... [Do not] ... continue for my sake ... [but] for
increase of your good opinion with his Majesty.[34]

In confirmation of his good standing, in 1606 Davies was
appointed attorney-general for and serjeant-at-law in Ireland—
just in time for him to be in a position to assist in giving direction to the Dublin administration's endeavor to exploit a most
unexpected and consequential event, the effects of which continue to reverberate in contemporary Ireland.

To this day, historians do not agree why the last great native
chieftains Hugh O'Neill, earl of Tyrone; Rory O'Donnell, earl of
Tyrconnell; and Cuconaught Maguire, lord of Fermanagh, precipitately sailed for the continent with almost one hundred rela-
tives and retainers, never to return.[35] They do concur that these
leaders, perceiving the inevitable and not-too-distant destruction
of the native Irish culture and with it their own considerable autonomy, despaired and followed the path of flight marked out
earlier by several of the Irish nobility, most notably Donal
O'Sullivan Beare. Nicholas Canny has stressed that the year preceding the Flight of the Earls, 1606, was a time "of crisis for the
Ulster lords,"[36] for the Crown, implementing its proclamation of
March 1605, which enfranchised the inhabitants of Ulster as subjects of the English king (thus denying the ultimate authority of
their chieftains over them), had begun extending the rule of English law into the Irish provinces by means of commissions
appointed to examine land claims and reallocate holdings. In effect, the Crown sought to strike at the very source of the chief-

34. Salisbury to Davies, November [?] 1606, HMC *Hastings*, 4:2–3.
35. See C. P. Meehan, *The Fate and Fortunes of Hugh O'Neill, Earl of Tyrone,
and Rory O'Donnel, Earl of Tyrconnel* ... (New York, 1868); Nicholas Canny,
"The Flight of the Earls, 1607," *IHS* 17 (1971):380–99; and F. W. Harris, "The
State of the Realm: English Military, Political and Diplomatic Responses to the
Flight of the Earls, Autumn 1607 to Spring 1608," *Irish Sword* 14
(1980):47–65.
36. Canny, "Flight of the Earls," p. 389.

tains' power, for once deprived of land, their accustomed and necessary income would also disappear.

Already deeply in debt, their holdings drastically reduced, Maguire and O'Donnell may have concluded that they had little to lose by joining the Irish regiment serving in the Low Countries with the archduke of Austria—O'Neill's son Henry already held the rank of colonel in the Irish regiment—possibly biding their time until they could secure military assistance from Spain to recover their inheritances.[37]

Hugh O'Neill's circumstances in Tyrone were different from those of Maguire and O'Donnell, even as his more experienced, more mature personality distinguished him from his impetuous fellow chieftains. Although he, too, faced strategic legal assaults on the territorial sources of his sovereignty and had lost one of his foremost friends and allies in the government with the death of Mountjoy in 1606, he still nurtured the hope that he could persuade the London administration, particularly James I, who had supported him in the past, of the legality of his claims and prerogatives. Anticipating his intended journey to England, as Canny has remarked, "defeat . . . was far from his mind"; whereas, by abandoning his ancestral lands, it appeared that he had everything to lose. Consequently, he surprised everyone when he joined O'Donnell and Maguire. Davies, for one, exclaimed, "It were strange that he should quit an earldom and so large and beneficial a territory for smoke and castles in the air; and . . . should leave the possession to try if he could win it again by force."[38]

Most probably, as Canny has conjectured, O'Neill panicked.[39] Unprepared for the appearance of Maguire's escape ship in

37. For an account of the founding of the Irish Regiment, see Jerrold Casway, "Henry O'Neill and the Formation of the Irish Regiment in the Netherlands, 1605," *IHS* 18 (1973): 481–88.

38. Canny, "Flight of the Earls," p. 395; Davies to Ellesmere, 12 September 1607, in John Payne Collier, ed., *The Egerton Papers* (London, 1840), p. 415.

39. Canny, "Flight of the Earls," pp. 398–99.

Lough Swilly at the very moment he was preparing to plead his case before James and for O'Donnell's decision to flee immediately, and realizing further how the Crown would interpret his remaining behind as part of the trio's apparent conspiracy to foment yet another Spanish-supported rebellion, O'Neill probably concluded that his position was untenable. Instead of journeying on to London, whence he might never be allowed to return, he precipitately turned about, gathered what family and retainers he could in Dungannon, and embarked with the other fugitives waiting at Lough Swilly.

Even though the flight caught the Crown off balance, it brought Dublin the undreamed-of opportunity to bring Ulster within the widening compass of its administrative power. Davies, already one of the most aggressive legal strategists for toppling the supremacy of the native Ulster leadership, immediately identified the promise now offered:

As for us that are here, we are glad to see the day wherein the countenance and majesty of the law and civil government hath banished Tyrone out of Ireland, which the best army in Europe and the expense of two millions of sterling pounds did not bring to pass.

And we hope His Majesty's happy government will work a greater miracle in this kingdom than ever St. Patrick did: for St. Patrick did only banish the poisonous worms, but he suffered the men full of poison to inhabit the land still; but His Majesty's blessed genius will banish all those generations of vipers out of it and make it ere it be long a right fortunate island.[40]

In the confusion and uncertainty left in the wake of Maguire's escape ship, Dublin promptly endeavored both to stabilize the potentially anarchical situation and to exploit an invaluable opportunity. F. W. Harris, one of the most recent commentators to investigate the immediate consequences of the Flight,[41] has detailed the government's responses, and his painstaking re-

---

40. Davies to Ellesmere, 12 September 1607, in Collier, ed., *The Egerton Papers*, p. 416.
41. Harris, "State of the Realm"; Harris, "Matters Relating to the Indict-

search reinforces C. Litton Falkiner's seminal insight that Davies "was in a large degree the guiding spirit of the Irish administration" during these formative years.[42]

To protect Ulster from the invasion the administration expected at any moment, as well as to squelch local rebellions and at the same time smooth the way for colonization, Lord Deputy Chichester and the Irish Council overhauled the government of Ulster, putting the affairs of Tyrone, Tyrconnell, and Armagh securely under the jurisdiction of a specially appointed commission. With an essentially civil mandate, this commission administered oaths of allegiance and dealt with unlawful assemblies and threats to the peace. In addition, Dublin provided for a system of military governorships to handle the more overtly military tasks of enforcing its will. The civil-military apparatus thus established and set into motion was, as summarized by Harris, largely "concerned with maintaining tranquility and calm within the province while awaiting orders for the plantation which everyone expected, and for which the first plans were being drawn up when the earls were barely out of sight of the lands in question."[43]

Extant records show Davies centrally involved in the deliberations and proceedings in the years following the Flight of the Earls. In communications to Secretary Salisbury and Lord Chancellor Ellesmere (virtually identical and both dated 12 September 1607),[44] he summarized the recent known events leading

---

ments of 'The Fugitive Earls and Their Principal Adherents,' " *Irish Jurist* 18 (1983): 344–59; Harris, "The Rebellion of Sir Cahir O'Doherty and Its Legal Aftermath," *Irish Jurist* 15 (1980): 298–325; Harris, "The Commission of 1609: Legal Aspects," *Studia Hibernia* 20 (1980): 32–55 (includes a previously unpublished letter of Davies to Salisbury relating to the 1609 commission, dated 4 September 1609).

42. C. Litton Falkiner, *Essays Relating to Ireland: Biographical, Historical, and Topographical* (London, 1909), p. 33.

43. Harris, "State of the Realm," p. 58.

44. Davies to Salisbury, 12 September 1607, *CSPI*, 2:270–74; Davies to Ellesmere, 12 September 1607, in Collier, ed., *The Egerton Papers*, pp. 410–16.

up to the Flight and guardedly speculated on the possible desti-
nations of the fugitive earls. In addition, the attorney-general
drafted the articles under which the absconded chieftains could
be indicted for treason and stage-managed the separate grand
jury indictments taken at Lifford in Donegal and at Strabane in
Tyrone.[45]

The indictments of O'Donnell, O'Neill, and, to a lesser degree, Maguire, were particularly fundamental to the Crown's
unfolding design for Ulster. Davies, in Canny's words, apparently "had no scruples about bringing a trumped-up charge [of
treason] against the exiles." Inspired by brazenly pragmatic
motives, his indictments instigated the legal momentum essential
for forfeiting the great holdings of the trio and eventually sup-
planting native institutions with English. Harris has described
the statutory urgency of the indictments: "Charges decided upon
by the Crown regarding the disposition of forfeited lands would
thus have both the appearance and substance of legal validity.
The stability of Ulster, and so of the whole of Ireland, would be
seen to rest upon a foundation of English law and justice. Oppo-
nents of any such change would clearly have placed themselves
outside the law and, as rebels and enemies of the Crown, could
be dealt with summarily."[46] Subsequent developments indeed
established that "rebels and enemies of the crown" would be
handled with dispatch—lessons given and lessons heeded.

In April 1608, Sir Cahir O'Dougherty, lord of Inishowen,
feeling the Crown had reneged on its promises to ratify his
claims to Inishowen and the Isle of Inch in Lough Swilly, went
into rebellion, seizing the English fort at Culmore and destroying much of the settlement at the Derry. O'Dougherty's rising
inspired other minor insurrections in Ulster, the most notable
being that of Shane Carragh O'Cahan, whose sept lands were

45. See Harris, "Matters Relating to the Indictments," pp. 344–47.
46. Canny, "Flight of the Earls," p. 381; Harris, "Matters Relating to the
Indictments," p. 358.

centered in what is now known as Coleraine. Disorganized, spontaneous, and lacking any genuine long-range objectives, the rebellions were expeditiously crushed by the Crown's armies under Marshal Sir Richard Wingfield, their leaders either killed, or if captured, tried for treason and executed. O'Dougherty's lands, moreover, were forfeited under the laws of treason. In this way, extensive territories about Lough Foyle were securely brought under the Crown's control.

In his study of O'Dougherty's rebellion and its aftermath, Harris postulates five stages which led to the subjugation of Ulster. In the first stage, the government simply endeavored to administer Ulster as a native enclave. After the Flight of the Earls in 1607, however, the Crown, having confiscated Tyrone, Tyrconnell, and parts of Fermanagh, was able to enforce its will summarily. In the third phase, O'Dougherty's and its attendant rebellions permitted the Crown to expunge "the second level of Gaelic leadership within the province." Native opposition to its program thus effectively eliminated, the government was free to concentrate on the bureaucratic implementation of the colonization of Ulster by loyal English and Scots planters. This, the fourth stage, it achieved by way of three commissions (in 1608, 1609, and 1610) charged with surveying the province, gathering and evaluating testimony on land holdings, and arraigning and trying criminals. Coupled with the trials and executions of the traitors, these exhibitions of legal maneuvering and manipulation, in which Davies played a leading hand, unequivocally brought home to the native inhabitants the grim reality of their postflight lives: "Recourse to law as a means of thwarting the plantation would avail . . . little because the law was being utilized as a device to produce" the plantation.[47] For all of its pious pleading that English government would ensure a rule of law under which citizens, Irish and English alike, would be protected equally from the depredations of arrogant, self-serving,

---

47. Harris, "Rebellion of Sir Cahir O'Doherty," pp. 299–301, 317.

land-hungry chieftains, the Crown imperiously brushed aside all but the pretense of enforcing justice in favor of a policy of expediency and expropriation. It remained only for Dublin and London to sanction its executive and judicial actions by means of legislative decree, and this, in what became the fifth and final phase, it sought to achieve through a parliament.

The last commission, held during the summer of 1610, completed the bureaucratic preparation of Ulster for plantation by means of wholesale expropriation of native holdings and approving of patents for prospective undertakers or colonists. With the disbanding of the commission, Davies apparently felt that his tenure as attorney-general had been fulfilled, and he now yearned for recall. Writing to Salisbury while in England in 1610, he reminds the secretary that he has "served a 'prenticeship of seven years in Ireland, and [that] His Majesty has said that Ireland should be but a place of probation to servitors of their robe, so that, after a competent time of trial, they should be recalled to serve His Majesty here."[48] Accordingly, he hopes to obtain from the secretary "some hope and comfort touching his recall." Buttressing his petition, he appended a seven-point catalog of difficulties and business "reduced and settled," crucial matters wherein he had played a shaping role. In 1611, in an even more self-pitying tone, he reminds Salisbury that despite the king's having rewarded him with a legal appointment as serjeant-at-law, he has had no opportunity to exercise the honor. He hopes, therefore, that His Majesty may "revoke him hence before he be so broken with years and painful journeys as to become unfit and unable to practice" law.[49] Later that same year, he reaffirmed his desire, pointedly recollecting that he has "now served eight years, which is double the time that the two servitors of his profession, who are already revoked, have spent in this kingdom, for neither of them continued here above four years."[50]

48. Davies to Salisbury, May[?] 1610, *CSPI*, 3:451.
49. Davies to Salisbury, 19 February 1611, *CSPI*, 4:13.
50. Davies to Salisbury, 29 July 1611, *CSPI*, 4:91.

Having brilliantly proven his usefulness, Davies wanted to return to England, doubtless to continue his ascent toward a position of power in a more salutary, lucrative environment. The *Discovery*, published in 1612, may well have been part of his campaign to obtain recall, for again and again the tract belabors how Ireland now stands poised between the chaotic darkness of its earlier history and the bright promise of its newly acquired identity as a civil commonwealth. As solicitor- and attorney-general, Davies had accomplished his part in bringing this about, and he implies that new potentials merit new personalities to help realize them.

But officials in Dublin—apparently supported by their counterparts in London—had other plans for their restless, aspiring legal officer. The State Papers often mention Dublin's uncertainty on the procedure for holding a parliament, for the simple fact was that Ireland's long history of turmoil had prevented the evolution of an established parliamentary tradition. Over the forty-five-year reign of Elizabeth, for example, Irish parliaments had been called but three times (in 1560, 1569–70, and 1585–86), yet ten had been held in England during the same period.[51] The last Irish parliament, moreover, had been convened so long ago that few then living recalled much of its deliberations and enactments; a month's search even failed to produce a list of those who had sat during 1585–86.[52] Lord George Carew, former lord president of Munster,[53] sent in 1610 by James on a special fact-finding mission, captured Dublin's anxiety when he wrote:

51. For accounts of the 1613–15 Parliament, see Richard Bagwell, *Ireland under the Stuarts and during the Interregnum*, 3 vols. (London, 1909–16), 1:108–38; Moody, "Irish Parliament"; and Brian Farrell, ed., *The Irish Parliamentary Tradition* (Dublin, 1973).

52. Moody, "Irish Parliament," p. 55.

53. George Carew (1555–1629), later earl of Totnes, not to be confused with Sir George Carey, briefly lord deputy under Mountjoy's lieutenancy from 30 May 1603 to 3 February 1603/4. (The forms *Carew* and *Carey* were interchangeable, both having a pronunciation approximately represented by the modern *Carey*.)

"The long forbearance of Parliament in Ireland will be an occasion for want of experience of many errors in both the houses, the form and order (used in them) being almost forgotten. The Lower House by reason of many English gentlemen that have been burgesses in England will err less than the other, for of 44 Lords Ecclesiastical and Temporal within that realm, there are not ... above eight that ever saw more than one short Parliament."[54]

Davies grappled with the new challenges. The Irish Calendar preserves from 1610 a notice of his "Motives of Importance for the Holding of a Parliament in Ireland."[55] This curious document sets forth his "considerations ... for a Parliament," emphasizing particularly that that body should be "summoned to supply divers defects of law, and to establish matters of importance which are now unsettled" and going on to list ten specific concerns to be dealt with. He also expresses apprehension, shared by his colleagues, that a majority of "Popish recusants" sitting in the proposed parliament would "distaste and reject such Bills" as were deemed for "the benefit of the Crown and kingdom."[56]

Ironically, these notes immediately precede his petition for recall in the published State Papers. This placement intimates that, although he may have desired to return to England, Davies, perceiving the direction of the Crown's need, had resigned himself to continuing on in Ireland; indeed, it is clear from extant comments that he had been singled out to fill the important position of Speaker of the Irish Parliament. In 1611 Carew wrote that "the choice of the Speaker ... is very material. Of Irish birth there are none to be trusted, and if there were, there is none liv-

54. "Remembrances to Be Thought of Touching the Parliament" [1611], *Carew MSS.*, 5:148.
55. *CSPI*, 3:451. (The editors note that the document duplicates, "apparently word for word," item 99, *Carew MSS.*, 5:164ff., where it has been incorrectly placed under November 1611.)
56. "Motives of Importance," *Carew MSS.*, 5:166, 168.

ing meet for that place, by reason of their many years and little experience. The best choice which I can think of is the King's Attorney-General, who has been a burgess in many Parliaments in England."[57] One wonders where Carew had heard that Davies had "been a burgess in many Parliaments in England"—actually, he seems to have sat but once, in 1601—but no less a personage than Lord Deputy Chichester concurred with Carew's recommendation: "In the choice of a speaker for the Parliament, it will please his Lordship [Salisbury] to think of" Sir John Davies.[58]

The Crown acknowledged early on that a parliament summoned to ratify and promote further the subjugation and plantation of Ulster would have to be constituted of a Protestant majority whose vested interests reflected official policy. As we have seen, Davies recorded his fear that a preponderance of "Popish recusants" would obstruct the passing of "such Bills as shall be transmitted out of England . . . although they be for the benefit of the Crown and kingdom," thus reduplicating the government's earlier frustrations over Perrot's Parliament of 1585–86, "when the Lower House did obstinately refuse to pass divers good Bills containing matter of civil government, only out of a froward and perverse affection to the State."[59]

Davies's concern was shared by others. Carew introduced his own recommendations "touching the Parliament" by suggesting that all members of the Lower House "should take the oath of supremacy . . . otherwise not to be admitted." Rightly anticipating objections to administering the oath, he went on to urge that circulating "a rumor that it is required will be a means to increase the number of Protestant burgesses and knights, and deter the most spirited Recusants from being of the house."[60]

57. "Remembrances," ibid., p. 140.
58. Chichester to Salisbury, 23 February 1612, *CSPI*, 4:248.
59. "Motives of Importance," *Carew MSS.*, 5:168.
60. "Remembrances," ibid., p. 146.

The government's virtually unassailable position, however, inspired it to employ another, more certain, albeit arrogant, strategy. In a maneuver deriving from the same political motive that later produced "gerrymandering," it simply created enough new constituencies to guarantee the safe Protestant edge it desired. Thus, trenchantly summarized by T. W. Moody, "the work of permanently swamping the catholics in the house of commons was boldly and rapidly executed."

Three fundamental facts are illustrated by these results. In the first place, they completely falsified the numerical distribution of the two religions in the country. Secondly, they corresponded roughly with the new distribution of landed property between the native Irish and the Anglo-Irish on the one hand, and the new British adventurers, mostly of Elizabethan and Jacobean importation, on the other. Thirdly, they indicate the regional distribution of these two landed classes: of the 100 catholic members, only one was returned from Ulster; of the 135 protestant members, 63.[61]

With a Protestant majority of thirty-two in the Commons and eleven in the House of Lords, Dublin had every reason to expect the painless ratification of its program. What it seems not to have foreseen was the spirited, resourceful opposition mounted by the Catholic minority and its feisty champion Sir John Everard.

The stormy opening sessions of this Parliament have been recounted often, and with good reason, for the challenge offered the Protestant majority by the Catholics exhibits many of the qualities of good theater: the unexpected skill, ingenuity, indeed, combativeness demonstrated by an underdog mistakenly taken for granted as overawed and toothless; the frustrations, embarrassments, and reversals endured by a bully whose arrogance and unabashed self-interest are unmasked; the sudden, suspenseful modulations of mood through assurance, frustration, elation, anger, pathos, even comedy; and the ultimate recognition by

61. Moody, "Irish Parliament," pp. 54, 57.

both adversaries that compromise, though rather lopsided, was a more fruitful solution than strong-headed belligerency.

In the resistance laid down by the Anglo-Irish Catholics we might recognize intimations of the legislative obstruction-ism employed so adroitly in the nineteenth century by Daniel O'Connell. Even before the opening of Parliament, a number of the Anglo-Irish recusant lords—including Gormanston, Slane, Fermoy, Trimelston, Mountgarret, Buttevant, Delvin, Louth, and Cahir—reiterated in a petition several of their complaints already sent to Chichester on 25 November 1612 but ignored. This time the deputy replied, but hardly to their satisfaction.[62] When the Parliament met on 18 May, the Catholic lords refused to attend.

In the Commons, the election of the Speaker catalyzed the conflict. The Catholics there proposed their candidate, Sir John Everard, a former justice of the King's Bench who had resigned rather than take the oath of supremacy. Since the Catholics resisted attempts to have their numbers tallied, the Protestants withdrew to count their own numbers, determining that their 127 votes provided their candidate, Davies, with the needed majority. But the Catholics, maintaining that the Protestants had withdrawn while the Commons (that is, the Catholics who remained) elected Everard, disallowed Davies and, crying out "An Everard! An Everard!" "intruded Sir John Everard into the Speaker's chair." Even after being informed that the Protestants had a clear majority, Everard "refused to come forth" from the chair, turning aside a further attempt to remove him: "Where-upon Mr. Treasurer and Mr. Marshal . . . took Sir John Davies by the arms and lifted him from the ground and placed him in the chair upon Sir John Everard's lap, requiring him still to come forth of the chair; which he obstinately refusing, Mr. Treasurer, the Master of the Ordnance, and others whose places

62. See Nobility to Chichester, 18 May 1613 [?], *Carew MSS.*, 5:265–67.

were next the chair, laid their hands gently upon him and removed him out and placed Sir John Davies quietly therein."[63]

Thwarted, the Catholic faction "in contemptuous manner
departed out of the House," spurning all appeals to join with
those within and promising instead to appeal to the lord deputy
concerning the election. In the following days, the contestants
played out their games, the opposition parties in both Houses
launching a volley of petitions, the Crown's supporters endeavoring to carry on parliamentary business and at the same time
appealing, futilely, to the recusants to participate. As Richard
Bagwell has observed, the administration's, particularly Chichester's, patience and restraint were remarkable, but perhaps
the majority party was studiously avoiding any further action
which might be used to invalidate the subsequent proceedings.[64]

As it was, the Catholics were already complaining formally to
Dublin and London. The petition by the recusant lords may be
taken as typical. The petitioners remind Chichester of their earlier objections to fraudulent elections whereby some members
"were falsely returned by the sheriffs, although not duly elected"
and others "were returned for the new corporations which are
mere villages with hardly any population." They also recall that
the Parliament was held "contrary to ancient usage in the castle
and under the control of a garrison newly increased in number."
Anticipating that abuses would arise, they draw attention to two
enormities: first, to the great number of members ("above a hundred") "unduly returned" who have failed to show by what
authority they claim "a voice in the Parliament," and second, to
these same members who "in a disorderly manner ... created Sir
John Davies, Speaker of the Parliament, and afterwards ...
violently ejected him [Everard] from the chair and imprisoned
for a whole hour the residue of the members." In consequence of

63. "A True Statement of the Protestants," ibid., pp. 272–73.
64. Bagwell, *Ireland under the Stuarts*, 1:116.

these alleged illegalities and outrages, the signatories conclude by requesting a leave of absence from Parliament and the liberty "to repair to England to lay the matter before His Highness."[65]

Although the State Papers reveal Chichester endeavoring to meet with patience the flurry of objections descending on him, a minute appended to a second petition of the same date from the recusant lords intimates the depth of his irritation: "This is but a mere cavil, not fit to be answered."[66] Clearly, the Catholic minority had succeeded in penetrating the public display of control maintained by such as the lord deputy.

Throughout the hubbub, Davies exhibited the same unflappable character that allowed him to react with comparative dispassion during the fateful days following the earls' flight. At least in the execution of his official duties, he usually seems to have preserved a degree of impersonal detachment from events which otherwise so fired the passions of colleagues and adversaries. He invariably checked his personal insecurities, and this disengagement enabled him to grasp and master circumstances that inflamed others, often to their detriment. Occasionally, however, the image he projects approaches the comical. When we recreate the scene of the portly, and presumably grave and silent, Davies being hoisted by Mr. Treasurer (Sir Thomas Ridgeway) and Mr. Marshal (Sir Richard Wingfield) into the air and dropped into Sir John Everard's lap, the effect cannot be anything but one of broad, if unintended, comedy introduced into this scene of high seriousness. The same humorous potential may be seen in descriptions of his attempting to perform his speakerly role as though nothing untoward had occurred. With the obdurate minority waiting outside to see the majority's reaction to its obstructive withdrawal from the proceedings, "the Speaker, sitting in the chair, began a speech declaring (as the matter is) his disability and unwillingness to accept the place"—having been

---

65. Recusant Lords to Chichester, 21 May 1613, *CSPI*, 4:348.
66. Ibid., p. 347.

physically deposited there by his friends, could he have missed the broad irony of his words?—"in the midst of which Sir W[illiam] Burke and Sir Chr[istopher] Nugent [of the Catholic faction] came in without any reverence and interrupted, calling for the keys of the outer door; and being commanded by the Speaker to take their places, they contemptuously refused so to do." With that, "Sir John Everard and all party departed out of the castle, affirming they would not return any more."[67] The account does not record whether Mr. Speaker Davies ever finished his speech that first day.

On 21 May, the same date as the petitions of the recusant lords, the Speaker was officially presented to the lord deputy, who represented the authority of the House of Lords. The protracted and heated deliberations prologuing the presentation, with Davies apparently standing or sitting silently throughout the contention, continued the spectacle of the first day. But it is Davies's acceptance speech that compels our recognition of potentially comic ironies. Prepared, of course, well before the beginning of the Parliament,[68] his speech surveys parliaments in general and traces parliamentary history, "and by way of comparison did show how much this Parliament did *excel all the former* as well in respect of the *felicity of the time wherein it is called as of the number and worthiness of the persons that are called into it*."[69] Granted Davies's peacemaking intent, one may speculate nonetheless on why he did not moderate his pro forma flattery a bit to conform with the recent foot-dragging by the Catholics and the raucous, abusive clashing of personalities.

Such is the portrait recorded of Davies during these tempestuous days; a man at times so passive that he barely seems more than a puppet; a man so mechanically inflexible in his need to

---

67. "A True Declaration," *Carew MSS.*, 5:274.

68. See Davies's preliminary notes for his acceptance speech in "Motives of Importance," ibid., pp. 164–70, which *CSPI*, 3:451, dates as May [?] 1610.

69. "A True Declaration," *Carew MSS.*, 5:275.

perform as expected that he does not, or cannot, adapt to the bewildering fluctuations in the political wind and temperature; a man so disengaged from the turmoil enveloping him that his tactlessness seems at times Jonsonian. Admittedly, this disquieting portrait might have resulted unintentionally from writers whose attention was concentrated more upon detailing the events of the conflict than on delineating the character of any one of the actors; but it is an image confirmed in many ways by the pages of the *Discovery*.

The minority party achieved its immediate end: Parliament was adjourned so that deputations representing the factions could present their petitions, objections, and declarations to the king himself. In August 1613, James appointed a special commission to examine both the alleged illegalities in the parliamentary elections and the turbulent opening sessions. Partly in consequence of the commission's findings, the king issued a royal proclamation that resulted in the Protestant faction's losing 24 members, the Catholics losing 2 and gaining 4, leaving the former with a much-diminished working majority of 108 to 102[70]—and because the Protestants proved more lax in attending sessions than the Catholics, the latter often held the legislative edge. The Crown, furthermore, withdrew its proposed anti-Catholic legislation. Deliberations and further delays caused by Poynings' Law (which mandated that all bills be submitted to and approved by the king and the English Privy Council before introduction into the Irish Parliament) delayed the reconvening of Parliament until 11 October 1614. Four bills—recognizing the king's title, attainting the fugitive earls and others, abolishing benefit of clergy in cases of burglary and rape, and establishing machinery for trying pirates—all passed smoothly.

Very possibly, the king's withdrawal of the pending anti-Catholic legislation did much to allay the fears of the minority

70. Moody, "Irish Parliament," p. 60.

party. And, too, urged on by Everard, the Anglo-Irish recusants closed ranks with the Protestants in attainting the Ulster chiefs.[71] The emergence of this new conciliatory mood in Parliament merited recognition and praise by Mr. Speaker Davies in his congratulatory speech at its reconvening. Employing a favorite musical metaphor, he observes how "His Majesty . . . , finding the strings of his harp of Ireland in discord and out of tune, hath not by hard wresting broken them, but by gentle and easy winding brought them to a concord; and though in the tuning of this instrument there hath been a little jarring and harshness at the first, yet now the strings are set right by so happy and skilful a hand, we hope the music that shall follow shall be the sweeter."[72]

His poet's imagination reaches out for other metaphors, discovering apt similarities first in platitudes about weather—"I . . . did never doubt but that of that stormy beginning there would come a calm end, and that after our blustering forenoon we should have a fair afternoon"—and next in geography: "Now it cannot be otherwise when two rivers do meet and fall in together, but that their waters should be at first a little troubled, though when they have struggled a little together they easily come to be one stream, and run on along smoothly in the same channel. And so (I trust) shall we do now, hold one fair course together at the end."[73]

Davies's confident reading of Parliament's temperament, of course, proved accurate, and thus, at the end of October, he was happy to relay to the earl of Somerset details of its newly emergent spirit. After the committees for returns and privileges agreed that all their questions be put aside during the present Parliament, Davies observed how dramatically the attitudes of the members became transformed: "For whereas before they looked sadly and strangely one upon the other, there was now

71. Bagwell, *Ireland under the Stuarts*, 1:133.
72. "Speech of Sir John Davies," 11 October 1614, *CSPI*, 4:517–18.
73. Ibid., p. 518.

observable a serenity and clearness in every one's aspect, which argued that all parties were well pleased and contented." Playing out his role as peacemaker, Davies graciously invited the principal leaders of the recusant faction to his house "and gave them the best entertainment he could, and they accepted his entertainment cheerfully and friendly."[74]

Procedural difficulties over the important subsidy desired by the Crown resulted in several more prorogations, but once the subsidy was passed (on 28 April 1615), the Parliament went on to give speedy approval to five more bills, among them enactments repealing statutes treating the Irish as enemies, repealing the law against introducing Scots into Ireland and intermarrying with them, providing for a general pardon, and providing for highway repair and the clearing of passes. With only ten of the Crown's once ambitious and extensive list of proposed laws passed, James resolved that Parliament should be disbanded. It was an unpopular action, this dissolving of the long-planned Parliament, which, stormy at first, now functioned smoothly and to the satisfaction of more than might reasonably be expected. But the Crown had its subsidy and, moreover, had obtained legislative sanction for the Ulster Plantation. And very probably, as Bagwell suspected, "the King thought Irish Parliaments dangerous and unmanageable as he learned to regard English ones, and he had no great appetite for legislation when the prerogative was strong enough to carry out the most pressing reforms."[75] Hence Chichester was authorized to proclaim the dissolution of Parliament, which he did on 24 October 1615.

Compared with the years 1603–15, the remainder of Davies's tenure (1615–19) as attorney-general appears uneventful. In 1615, however, he published his *La Primer Discours des Cases et Matters in Ley.*[76] Dedicated to his long-standing benefactor

74. Davies to Somerset, 31 October 1614, ibid., p. 514.
75. Bagwell, *Ireland under the Stuarts*, 1:138.
76. Translated as *A Report of Cases and Matters in Laws* . . . (Dublin, 1762); repr. in Grosart, ed., *Works of Davies*, vol. 2.

Ellesmere, the lord chancellor, the collection, Davies says, provided "the first report of cases arising in Ireland and ruled in the courts of justice there, that ever was made and published to the world since the laws of England were first established in this kingdom."[77]

The year 1615 was also the year Davies fell afoul of the king. Returning from England in November, he evidently reported to Chichester and the council some confidences James had shared with him concerning "their misgovernment in the administration of the affairs of that kingdom" of Ireland—either that, or he rashly fabricated tales. In any case, the Irish Council "declared their grievance for the relation which Sir John Davies . . . has made." In response, James directed his Privy Council "to return them this answer: that Sir John Davies has failed both in duty and discretion, whereof when time shall be convenient he is to render an account for making his report, with whom at no time he [the king] has had any such language which might tend to the disreputation of any person of quality, neither gave him direction to deliver any such message, holding now charge in that realm, or to the disgrace of the present Government."[78] Additional references imply allegations of financial mismanagement, but because the original letter of the Irish Council has been lost or suppressed, the particulars alluded to remain unknown.[79]

Still longing for recall, on 21 June 1619 Davies wrote to George Villiers, marquess of Buckingham reiterating his plea and recommending a relative as his successor—"he is of near alliance unto me"—Sir William Reeves. He also hoped for some "retribution, to recompense the charge of transporting my fam-

77. Grosart, ed., *Works of Davies*, 2:285.
78. English Privy Council to the lord deputy and Irish Privy Council, December [?] 1615, *CSPI*, 5:107.
79. See *CSPI*, 5:107–8, nos. 197–99.

ily from thence, and of settling it here in this kingdom, where I am become almost an alien by reason of my long absence."[80]

These allusions to his personal feelings and circumstances suggest Davies's desire to settle his family once and for all safely in England. In 1609, this son of a tanner from Tisbury, Wiltshire, who had risen to knighthood and a position of legal renown, married Eleanor Touchet, third daughter of George Lord Audley, later earl of Castlehaven.[81] They had three children—two sons, Richard and John (a mute and possibly retarded),[82] both of whom died young, and a daughter, Lucy, destined to be married into the prestigious Hastings family and become sixth countess of Huntingdon. Having earlier expressed fear over the unhealthy effects that service in Ireland might produce on him and having already lost his two male children, it is reasonable to assume that the future welfare of his remaining family also reinforced his wish to return to England.

His request was granted. Living at Englefield in Berkshire or his townhouse in the Strand, he continued to practice law as king's sergeant-at-law. In addition, he sat for Newcastle-under-Lyme in the Parliament of 1621. Producing two more legal works,[83] he also revised his poetry, publishing his major works in 1622. In 1626, Davies was to assume duties as lord chief justice when he suddenly died on 8 December, at the age of fifty-seven.

The year 1612, which saw the first publication of the *Discov-*

80. Davies to Buckingham, 21 June 1619; repr. in Grosart, ed., *Works of Davies*, 3:cix–cx.

81. Eleanor Davies (later Douglas) was a spirited, rebellious, and, depending on one's perceptions, eccentric woman. For an account of her life and writings, see C. J. Hindle, "A Bibliography of the Printed Pamphlets and Broadsides of Lady Eleanor Douglas, the Seventeenth-Century Prophetess," *Edinburgh Bibliographical Society Transactions* 1 (1935–38): 69–75.

82. See Sir Robert Jacobs to Davies, 13 May 1617, HMC *Hastings*, 4:16–17, wherein Jacobs movingly writes of Davies's afflicted son.

83. *The Question Concerning Impositions, Tonnage, Poundage, Prizage, Cus-*

ery, was a vital one in Davies's life. Late in February, the Irish
Council empowered him to represent its interests in London
during the consultations pertaining to the convening of Parliament. Applying himself with characteristic energy, he increased
"the high opinion already entertained of his merit and suffi-
ciency," so impressing the king that he was rewarded with an appointment as serjeant-at-law in England.[84] Yet even during these
busy months, he attempted to recover his position among
London's brotherhood of lawyers: on 20 April he petitioned
Salisbury for leave to "make some use of his calling and practice
here" because the great amount of unfinished business would
delay the convening of Parliament until November.[85]

This request suggests that Davies had free time, at least during the spring months of 1612. Perhaps his relative inactivity inspired him to complete work on the *Discovery*. That it was
largely written in Ireland but added to in England is clear from
internal evidence: throughout the essay, Davies employs, as
would be expected of one writing in Ireland, such phrases as
"this land," *"this* realm," and *"here"* in referring to Ireland; but
occasionally, in whole paragraphs and other short sections, he
slips into using *"that* kingdom," *that* realm," *"that* country," and
"there," demonstratives implying distance.[86] Always the antiquary, the attorney-general might well have used his leisure to
prepare this authentication of Ireland's new, hard-won status
within the community of civil nations and therefore of her pre-
paredness for the much-discussed and long-postponed parlia-

---

toms and an *Abridgement* of Sir Edward Coke's *Reports*, neither published during his lifetime.

84. Privy Council to Chichester, 25 September 1612, *CSPI*, 4:285.

85. Davies to Salisbury, 20 April 1612, ibid., p. 263.

86. See particularly pp. 73, 118, 174, 195, 210–12 for passages suggesting
that he was in Ireland at the time of writing and pp. 69, 72, 194, 198 for
indications of his distance. (The latter frequently seem to occur in transitional
passages hurriedly inserted in England.)

ment, a historical survey buttressed by the extensive body of facts his research into that nation's troubled past had recovered from the English and Irish archives.

But as always, he might have had another, more personal motive for publishing the *Discovery* at this time. From at least 1610 on he had been endeavoring to obtain his recall. He must have foreseen that a widely distributed printed review of the Crown's success in bringing Ireland to heel—a discussion that would also provide oblique testimony to his own scholarly, legal, and administrative genius—might well win him the recognition he sought. At this terminal point in his Irish career—or so he had protested to Salisbury—what more cogent device for advertising his achievements than a scholarly examination of England's conquest of Ireland by one who had played a not insignificant role in the postwar years?

Salisbury's death on 24 May might have reinforced his decision to publish in 1612. He still enjoyed the favor of both Lord Chancellor Ellesmere and the king, but his prospects for remaining in England cannot have been anything but dim, especially with Salisbury's death. Dublin relied upon him increasingly, and so, too, would London, for giving personal, on-the-scene definition and impetus to its Irish policy now that Salisbury was gone. In the years immediately following the secretary's death, moreover, Henry Howard, earl of Northampton, emerged at court as the pivotal political force. A curious and obscure figure, Northampton never achieved the close relationship Mountjoy, Ellesmere, and Salisbury had with Davies, even though the two shared antiquarian, legal, and scholarly interests.[87] His principal benefactor—the man he had flattered in his 19 February 1611 epistle as "the *primum mobile* of his promotion"—now gone, it behooved Davies to secure new sources of patronage, which he sought to do by finishing his tract and dedicating it to the king-

---

87. See Peck, *Northampton*.

dom's ultimate source of Irish policy and, more important, its seemingly inexhaustible wellspring of bounty—the king himself.

We do not know with certainty that the *Discovery* was published after Salisbury's death on 24 May. But these new frustrations make it seem most likely. If indeed Davies undertook to publish his essay at this time, he probably came to regret the decision, for the *Discovery* is too often repetitious and uneven in its treatment, too lacking in smooth integration of many of its parts.[88] It is also a carelessly printed, poorly proofread book. With a great many typographical errors (even for a seventeenth-century London printshop such as John Jaggard's), faulty pagination, and a very incomplete *corrigenda*, it is not the work that Davies would presumably have allowed to circulate had he been available to perfect it and correct copy himself. The relatively idle days of spring apparently gave way to a busier summer and early autumn. The State Papers suggest that London wanted to retain him as long as it could and that Dublin urged his return.[89] Pressured by business from both centers, knowing he must soon leave, Davies cannot have had the leisure he required to refine his book. Departing from London near the end of September, he might have planned to revise it later; or he might already have turned his manuscript over to Jaggard and whatever uncertain fate awaited it.

An entry in the Stationers' Register establishes that the tract was printed sometime after his return to Dublin, probably between 25 March 1612 and 24 March 1613, which period would have been reckoned by the Jacobeans, still calculating time by the old Julian calendar, as 1612. The entry records the following for 15 December 1612: "John Jaggard. Entred for his copie vnder

88. Pages 85–7, 124, 176, 187 reveal especially abrupt transition. Also, the monotonously recurring phrase near the end "as is before remembered" implies awkward organization.

89. See particularly *CSPI*, 4:285–86, nos. 523, 524.

th[e h]ands of master D[octor] Mockett and th[e] wardens, *A booke called A Description of the estate of Ireland as nowe it standes vnder the government of King James.*"[90]

This entry, which ignores the author (even as the book's title page fails to cite Davies by name), must be for Davies's book, its title casually formulated by the printer. When Jaggard reissued the tract later in 1613, using surplus copy remaining from the printing of 1612—the printed texts are virtually identical[91]—he provided it with a new title page bearing a title more closely echoing that recorded in the Stationers' Register: *A Discoverie of the State of Ireland: with the true Causes why that Kingdom was neuer entirely subdued . . . . The state of Ireland* recalls the Stationers' Register's wording *the estate of Ireland*; neither phrase was included in the 1612 published title. All three titles (the Stationers' Register's and those of the 1612 printing and 1613 reissue) give similar, final verbal emphasis to Ireland during the reign of King James—*vntil the Beginning of his Maiesties happie Raigne* (1612 title), and *vnder the Government of King James.*

By having his ownership of the copy-text recorded at Stationers' Hall, Jaggard in effect announced his intention to print and publish it at some future date, and he received license from his guild to do so. Registration with the Stationers' Company implied a kind of copyright, but one protecting the printer/publisher, not the author. Because the long Christmas season was about to begin, however, it is unlikely that the work was offered for sale before 6 January, and most probably Jaggard did not begin setting print until after the end of the Christmas holidays. In addition, if he wanted to have the book out before, or to coincide with, the beginning of the Irish Parliament, now postponed

90. E. Arber, ed., *A Transcript of the Registers of the Company of Stationers, 1554–1640,* 5 vols. (London, 1874–94), 3:509.
91. The reissue of 1613 even reproduces the *errata* noted in the printing of 1612. It does, however, correct some (but not all) of the earlier printing's faulty pagination, for example, that running from pages 52 to 57.

until February,[92] he would have had to set copy with speed and thereby risk all the associated errors and sloppiness that compositorial haste brings.[93] Even the most cursory examination of the book suggests that he did not surmount these hazards.

The conjectural circumstances related to the book's publication, then, are as follows. Endeavoring to exploit the English fascination with Ireland, an interest perhaps made more timely in consequence of the coming Parliament, Davies published his *Discovery* in 1612, drawing upon his extensive recent archival investigations into Irish history, military and civil. Possibly prompted by the death of Salisbury, he dedicated it to King James in a bid to obtain new sources of patronage and to enlist sympathy for the recognition of his desire for recall. Although he might have long intended publication, the decision to do it in 1612 seems to have been a sudden and not altogether happy one, resulting in several suggestions of hurry: the unassimilated passages written in England; an awkward amount of repetition;

92. James I to Sir Arthur Chichester, 26 September 1612, *CSPI*, 4:286.

93. The evidence for hasty printing rests upon faulty pagination and a list of *errata* included with some, but apparently not all, copies of the book. Many copies misnumber the following pages: 139 (as 143), 142–43 (as 146–47), 146 (as 150), 168 (as 166), 187 (as 189; with the page numbers 188 and 189 being dropped altogether), and 236 (as 220). In some other copies additional mispagination is left uncorrected: pp. 52, 53, 56, and 57 (as 54, 51, 58, and 55, respectively). In addition, some copies leave the final pages 285, 286, and 287 unnumbered. Consistent with early seventeenth-century printing practice, the *Discovery* was apparently proofread and corrected as it came off the press, with faulty sheets, to save time and expense, being included and sold along with the more perfect copies.

This practice may help to explain why many copies of the *Discovery* carry no page of *errata* (though some of the original sheets, of course, could have been lost). But even the *errata* page bears evidence of rush work in both its incompleteness and inaccuracies. The following irregularities should be noted: (1) "fol. 18. for *regnem*, read *regnum*" (p. 18 gives the form "*Regem*"); (2) "fol. 86. for Gliun, Clinn" (on p. 86 some copies show "Cliuu," others, interestingly, "Cliun"); (3) "fol. 103. for Clandalkin, Clan-dalkan" (the text carries the inverted *n*, "*Claudalķin*"; the *errata* page notes and otherwise emends several other inversions); (4) "fol. 183. . . . for the Archdeacon; *Archdeacon*" (text: the "Arch-Deacon"); and (5) "fol. 191. for mightely; nightly" (text: "mightily").

and the poorly executed, only partially corrected edition brought out when he, having returned to Ireland, was unavailable to revise and correct text. Jaggard's own evident haste, which further compromised the book's quality, might well have resulted from the printer's rush to have it ready for the convening of Parliament.

Coming as it does near the end of a firmly rooted tradition of Elizabethan and Jacobean writings on Ireland, the *Discovery* shares with its antecedents a number of definitive attitudes and conventions. These writings constitute a kind of subgenre which might be termed "the Elizabethan-Jacobean essay on Ireland," and they inhere within and in turn help to give dimension to a literary tradition profoundly shaped by Gerald of Wales, whose *Topography of Ireland* and *Conquest of Ireland* date from the 1180s.[94] Briefly, and recognizing that there do exist exceptions, the Elizabethan-Jacobean Irish essay may be identified by the following shared characteristics: the essays were generally authored by writers who had obtained personal experience in Ireland as soldiers, colonists, or administrators; they express an ethnocentric, arrogant rejection of Irish culture, even as they paradoxically exhibit a fascination with their subject; the tracts, voicing bewilderment, often indignant bafflement, over the failure of the English crown to complete and make good the conquest initiated by Henry II, purport to offer solutions to the impasse; and the essays endeavor to give substance to their resolutions by examining the four-hundred-year-old record of England's failure to secure control over the island.

94. For further discussions of some of these points, see Margaret Mac-Curtain, "The Roots of Irish Nationalism," in Robert O'Driscoll, ed., *The Celtic Consciousness* (New York, 1981), pp. 371–82; Brendan Bradshaw, "Sword, Word and Strategy in the Reformation in Ireland," *Historical Journal* 21 (1978): 475–502; and James P. Myers, Jr., "Introduction," in Myers, ed., *Elizabethan Ireland: A Selection of Writings by Elizabethan Writers on Ireland* (Hamden, Conn., 1983), pp. 1–21. Nicholas P. Canny, "Edmund Spenser and the Development of an Anglo-Irish Identity," *Yearbook of English Studies* 13 (1983): 1–19, discusses the influence of Spenser's essay on subsequent writers.

Although the *Discovery* rests securely within this tradition, unique cultural differences which nurtured the author also set it apart from its predecessors. For the work was written not only well after the Elizabethan conquest but at a time when the Jacobean settlement had been successfully initiated; and its author, though intimately acquainted with Irish life, had avoided the anguish and tragic reversals which befell those writers who had participated in the ferocious wars and near anarchy of the years before 1603. More than any of the other Elizabethan-Jacobean writings on Ireland, the *Discovery's* optimism and proud consciousness of historical achievement distinguish it. And further, Davies's own legal training and neoclassical affinities of style and his facility for discovering continuities within the seeming chaos of history aided him in shaping his materials into an argument of point and logical coherence far excelling the earlier writings from which he, in part, drew his inspiration.[95]

The general structure of the *Discovery* is so transparent that it may be summarized with surprising ease. Following a preliminary tribute to Ireland and her people, whom he finds "endued with extraordinary abilities of nature," Davies presents the question that both firmly links his tract with the tradition of the Irish essay and provides it with thematic unity: "What were the true causes why this kingdom ... for the space of four hundred and odd years ... was not ... thoroughly subdued and reduced to obedience of the Crown of England, although there hath been almost a continual war between the English and the Irish? and why the manners of the mere Irish are so little altered since the days of King Henry II? ... albeit there have been since that time

95. Krueger, ed., *Poems of Sir John Davies*, pp. liv–lxvii, explores Davies's neoclassical style.

In his discussion of Davies's historical mastery, J. G. A. Pocock writes of the *Discovery* that "it remains perhaps the most outstanding piece of historical writing achieved by an Englishman in James I's reign" (*The Ancient Constitution and the Feudal Law* [New York, 1967], p. 62; pp. 59–63 explore Davies's analysis of the conflict between common and brehon law.)

so many English colonies planted in Ireland." His hypotheses derive from his investigations into Irish history since 1169, the date of the Anglo-Norman invasion, and, though they overlap untidily at times, the answers cluster about one of two major themes: defects in the execution of martial affairs and errors in the managing of civil proceedings. To present his interpretations cogently, he traces under each of his many subheadings the history of the Crown's endeavors. This historical technique, though often persuasive and clearly assisting him to integrate his materials more smoothly than some of his predecessors, produces redundancy and an awkward predictability, a suggestion of his outline readily at hand, that prompts one to wonder why he did not seek to integrate his several chronologies with one another by examining two or three issues simultaneously. The answer, of course, may lie in his training as a lawyer, the rhetorical ideal of which profession stressed point and clarity over broader esthetic motives: one thesis, one marshaling of historical proof.

Because to him, as a legal administrator, civil matters presumably proved more absorbing and more accessible, as well as more important than military, he first deals with the crown's "faint prosecution of the war" of conquest, dividing his subject into two subheadings. The first of these argues that the English forces were ill-paid and poorly led; in short, that they were invariably too weak to accomplish anything more than a conquest "piece and piece, by slow steps and degrees, and by several attempts in several ages." Too often, the archives document small bands of private soldiers carving out veritable principalities for themselves and accepting the Irish chieftains whom they defeated as tributary princes, not conquering them as subjects of the Crown. Only when he comes to the end of Elizabeth's reign does he find a force powerful enough to subject the island— a well-paid, large army, professionally commanded by Lord Mountjoy.

Davies also discovers that the English kings, rather than concentrating all their resources on subjugating Ireland, allowed themselves to be diverted. From Henry II's rebellious children, Richard I's crusade and French campaigns, the Barons' Wars of John's time, down on through the Scots' invasion of Ireland and the Wars of the Roses, some other business always deflected the kings of England from the task of reducing the island totally. Once more, only when he surveys the reign of Elizabeth does he find a prince willing, even though beset with insurrections, armadas, and armies across the Channel, to release resources sufficient to conquer Ireland. Unlike her predecessors, she reacted decisively to the dangers posed by a partially subdued Ireland; she fought "to save, not to gain, a kingdom." Intrigued by the paradox of a woman's completing what centuries of male kings had not, Davies earlier had insinuated into his otherwise pragmatically conceived essay a fundamental note of mystery, which he traces back to the inscrutability of providential design: "Who can tell whether the Divine Wisdom, to abate the glory of those kings, did not reserve this work to be done by a queen, that it might rather appear to be His own immediate work?" Similar queries direct the reader's attention to an order of meaning not accessible to mundane comprehension.

In the following section, Davies explores "the defects of the civil policy and government, which gave no less impediment to the perfection of this conquest." Working now with materials of greater familiarity, he is more analytic and expansive than in the part on military history. The skeleton of his outline does not obtrude as noticeably here. But his greater relaxation and acquaintance with the bureaucratic terrain also have their dangers, and he becomes bogged down in detail or leads us along digressions that are but tributaries to the mainstream of his argument. And because civil government was so frequently subordinate to the exigencies of martial law, he often backtracks to recover and investigate military details he might have done better to have disposed of earlier. Although more thorough perhaps than the earlier sections, this part is at once repetitious, more discursive, and not so well unified. It creates a disproportion between the two parts of the essay, an expository subtlety and digressiveness that are inconsistent with the simpler complexity of linear detail in the earlier survey.

For Davies, the outstanding flaw in the Crown's policy was its refusal to accord the Irish status as subjects, despite the ample documentary evidence he recovered that they desired citizenship. Rather, from the first the English regarded the Irish as aliens and enemies unprotected by the law. And since the English lacked sufficient strength to crush them decisively, the four-hundred-year history of the occupation was marked by an almost "perpetual war between the nations."

The second error in civil government proceeded from the creation of large palatinates, or virtually independent principalities, within the island. To reward the conquistadors who privately undertook to seize territory from the Irish, English kings granted these warlords huge tracts of land and liberties and privileges "too great for subjects." The consequences of establishing these palatinates were numerous, far-reaching, and ultimately destructive of the Crown's intent to extend its rule over the whole island. Davies's analysis of the interlocking complexities here reveals him at his best, even if it also exhibits how arbitrarily he has divided up his impediments to the conquest into martial and civil affairs.

The virtual, unchecked autonomy enjoyed by these lords invited them to declare total control over the Irish (whom they refused to admit to the status of subjects and kept in serfdom), as well as the English, within their demesnes. Laying claim to one another's land, they made war (and concluded peace) on each other virtually at will. In this way, they so weakened themselves that they were forced into making alliances with the Irish chieftains to strengthen themselves against one another. Instead of continuing the conquest, they actually lost ground to the Irish, who had commenced to reconquer their land. In the long run, the Old English aristocracy began to lose its identity, "degenerately" adopting Irish customs (such as the detested coyne and livery, fosterage, and gossipred),[96] language, even names. The record proved to Davies clearly that this Hibernization commenced near the end of Edward II's reign and the beginning of Edward III's, in response to Edward Bruce's Scottish invasion, and that more than anything the adoption of coyne and livery, an Irish form of arbitrary taxation on the tenants, to pay and provision the impoverished English armies was the root cause of much ill. In a four-page digression, he describes how the initial reliance on coyne and livery lifted the FitzGerald earls of Desmond to a level of unmatched power and then how the evil repercussions of this abuse reflexively destroyed that same dynasty.

Davies identifies as his third impediment a form of absenteeism, the reluctance or refusal of the English nobility, from king down, to attend in person to the island's problems. Only three English kings (Henry II, John, and Richard II) ever undertook journeys to Ireland, and yet on each occasion they demonstrated how the royal presence could overawe the Irish. Conversely, the absence of most of the kings and the great landowners only served to weaken the English authority in the land.

Throughout the discussion, Davies traces the Crown's attempts to reverse the degeneration of the Anglo-Irish and carry on the conquest. Citing the outstanding viceroys who strengthened the English cause, he devotes special attention to the Statutes of Kilkenny (1366), Poynings' Laws (1494), and the numerous advances made during Elizabeth's reign. But all of these fell short of completing the conquest, which had to wait until King James's "happy reign."

96. *Coyne and livery* denotes the billeting of soldiers and their horses upon private individuals and is also used more generally to described the commandeering of food and other provisions for the maintenance of soldiers and horses. *Fosterage* refers to the Irish practice of sending children away from their own families to be raised and educated by others. *Gossipred* defines the Irish custom contracting "spiritual affinity with another by acting as a sponsor at a baptism" (*OED*).

At the very same moment England and Scotland became propitiously united under a single crown, the Irish wars ended, enabling James and his eager administrators to draw Ireland into the community of Europe's civilized commonwealths. Following the king's proclamation of a general pardon establishing the public peace, the Crown's agents moved out beyond the Pale, settling land disputes, certifying new holdings, establishing counties, opening the forests and passes, advancing the rule of common law to embrace all English and Irish subjects, and— setting in place the brightest, most luminous jewel in James's Hibernian crown—transforming long intractable Ulster into a ripe territory for loyal English and Scots undertakers.

For all of its perceptiveness and historical methodology, the *Discovery* remains, expectedly, a promotional document, for the Crown as well as for Davies. It is political propaganda concealing a history of atrocity and injustice, whitewashing the record of greed, cupidity, self-righteousness, cruelty, and arrogance that more truly define the English presence in Ireland. In this polemical emphasis it is certainly one with the tradition of writing that nurtured it. Davies shares with Richard Stanihurst, John Hooker, Edmund Campion, Sir Philip Sidney, Edmund Spenser, John Derrick, and Barnabe Rich an unchecked colonial impulse. And yet, for all that the *Discovery* rests securely within a coherent political and literary convention, it differs profoundly from its antecedents in its perception and tone. Rather than with Draconian, vindictive passion born of suffering and loss, Davies's essay speaks with a voice distinctly forgiving, dispassionate, disengaged, even gamesome.

A lawyer attuned to the ritualized theatricality of the legal process and a professional code which as often as not affirmed the priority of written codes and judicial precedents over what most people call reality, the attorney-general would understandably apprehend his materials differently from a secretary—say, an Edmund Spenser or a Fynes Moryson—who had followed his lord deputy through the grim verities of Irish warfare, or from a soldier such as Barnabe Rich or Thomas Churchyard. Distant from the world of raids, ambushes, sieges, dangerous military thrusts through a hostile countryside of bog, forest, and mountain, finding his materials rather in the archives of the Bermingham Tower of Dublin Castle or in the Tower of London, Davies is at once aloof, disengaged, occasionally even Olympian.

The very nature of his task and its methodology partake of the convention of a game—to discover in the extant historical record why England's conquest of Ireland had been for over four hundred years thwarted and what factors enabled Elizabeth and particularly James to complete what Henry II's restless barons had inaugurated. Except when he discusses the accomplishments of the Crown's commissions of 1608, 1609, and 1610, he writes awkwardly removed from the events, or even kindred experiences, so central to his thesis and analyzes them from within the strict formalities regulating the presenting of legal and historical proof. Not for him heartrending, Spenserian meditations on Munster's "anatomies of death" crawling forth from their forests to scratch open graves as though they were larders; nor Moryson's haunting recollections of homeless scarecrows crowding Ulster's few roads, by the sides of which might be found entire families starved to death, their swollen lips lividly stained green from watercress and nettles. Nor no impassioned, righteous vindication of the survivor of Glenmalure and the victor of Smerwick for his slaughter of eight hundred Continental mercenaries because it was the most expedient solution available to him. Indeed, the long, anguished history of conquest, ambush, defeat, massacre, and reconquest becomes a game for the attorney-general—"a game at Irish," to use his own metaphor: "But when the civil government grew so weak and so loose as that the English lords would not suffer the English laws to be put in execution within their territories and seigniories, but in place thereof both they and their people embraced the Irish customs, then the estate of things, like a game at Irish, was so turned about as the English, which hoped to make a perfect conquest of the Irish, were by them perfectly and absolutely conquered."

The Irish game, a variation of backgammon, was characterized by a rapid sequence of back-and-forth reversals for the players, so that the apparent winner-to-be could easily lose during the final moves. Davies appropriated an apt metaphor indeed for describing the paradox wherein so often the nation with the greater resources and superior material culture too often found itself confronting disaster.

Davies's quick mind, however, perceived more subtle, revealing comparisons between the game of Irish and the long Anglo-Irish conflict. Charles Cotton, writing of Irish in *The Compleat Gamester*, emphasizes the need for intelligence in what might otherwise be but a game of chance: "Irish is an ingenious game and requires a great skill to play it well, especially the after-game. It is not to be learned otherwise than by observation and practice." He cautions against moving too rapidly and too aggressively, against being too intent on "hitting every blot." Rather, by playing slowly, "with discretion and consideration . . . though your adversary have filled his tables . . . and you by hitting him enter, you may win the game; nay, sometimes though he hath born his men to a very few."[97]

It was precisely by applying "observation and practice" to the after-game, from the later 1590s on, that the Crown effected the decisive reversal and carried the victory. By strategically, and with no undue haste, extending the force of common law into the pacified Irish counties, it gradually wrought its long-sought transformation of the Irish soul, causing the Irish "to conform themselves to the manner of England in all their behavior and outward forms . . . and in every way else [to] become English, so as there will be no difference or distinction but the Irish Sea betwixt us." For so long, and especially after the English defeat at the Yellow Ford in 1598 and the hellish months marking the

97. Charles Cotton, *The Compleat Gamester* . . . (London, 1674), pp. 154–55.

siege of Kinsale in 1601, the English cause appeared impossible, if not altogether lost, but intelligently conceived and applied countermeasures ultimately turned the tables about, giving the Crown the entire game: "And thus we see a good conversion, and the Irish game turned again."

Davies's apparent fondness for the game metaphor may have its roots in his legal training—it is instructive in this respect that Luke Gernon, another lawyer, initiates his *Discourse of Ireland* (1620) with an extended analogy turning on the card game post and pair and employs several game strategies throughout his essay.[98] More significantly, however, the metaphor discloses a deeper motive lurking beneath Davies's proclaimed intent to "discover the true causes," for beyond deepening the essay's urbane feel for its materials, it also conceals several morally objectionable realities and misrepresents certain equally dubious cultural developments. By imaging the four-hundred-year war, which at times achieved genocidal magnitude, as an innocuous game of tables, Davies flatteringly, if not altogether intentionally, reshapes the record so as to enhance the Crown's identity. This instance is not isolated; it is one of a cluster of rhetorical strategies employed to celebrate England's policies and the administration's recent successes.

Consonant with the poetic genius that eulogized Queen Elizabeth by way of the extended musical conceits of the *Orchestra*, Davies's intent led him to appropriate less elaborate musical metaphors in the *Discovery*. In one section, for example, he observes of Poynings' Laws that they "were like good lessons set for a lute that is broken and out of tune, of which lessons little use can be made till the lute be made fit to be played upon." But in the course of time the instrument of civil harmony was indeed restored to working order. Thus, near the conclusion of his essay,

---

98. Gernon's *Discourse* was first printed in C. L. Falkiner, ed. *Illustrations of Irish History and Topography, Mainly of the Seventeenth Century* (London, 1904), and was reprinted in Myers, ed., *Elizabethan Ireland*.

he compares vanquished Ireland with, appropriately, a harp, the stings of which, now fingered by the "civil magistrate . . . are all in tune . . . and make a good harmony in this commonweal."[99]

Aptly, Davies hit upon this metaphor through the one immediately preceding it, which depended upon the mechanical regularity and predictability of an accurately tuned timepiece: "The clock of the civil government is now well set, and all the wheels thereof do move in order."

Glossily covering over the tensions and unresolved conflicts that were to erupt with traumatic violence in the rising of 1641, these figures of speech glibly anticipate Davies's concluding hope that Ireland "will from henceforth prove a land of peace and concord . . . . [and] will hereafter be as fruitful as the land of Canaan." In stressing Ireland's great agricultural promise by means of the Old Testament simile involving Canaan, the fabled land of milk and honey, he ties the culminating knot, as it were, in a strand of agricultural conceits that threads back through the essay to the very beginning, thus helping to unify the tract.

More than any other, the agricultural simile indelibly colors his, and his reader's, perceptions of the matters explored. To elaborate and illustrate his thesis that the Crown failed in its colonial responsibility by faintly prosecuting the war and insufficiently administering the territory already within its power, he recollects how "the husbandman must first break the land before it be made capable of good seed; and when it is thoroughly broken and manured, if he do not forthwith cast good seed into it, it will grow wild again and bear nothing but weeds." Appealing to his readers with this practical, if commonplace, bit of wisdom, the astute attorney-general presses on with his analogy: "So a barbarous country must be first broken by a war before it will be

99. This was a favorite metaphor of Davies; the author of *Orchestra* had already employed the musical figure with effect in several addresses in the Irish Parliament. See his second speech accepting the Speakership, reprinted in Grosart, ed., *Works of Davies*, 3:223.

capable of good government; and when it is fully subdued and conquered, if it be not well-planted and governed after the conquest, it will eftsoons return to the former barbarism."

Kindred enterprises, both the planting of seed and the planting of colonies must needs be prepared for by analogous acts of violence, plowing, and war.[100] The comparison, of course, works to the advantage of the colonial activity, for what could be more natural, wholesome, indeed, essential and praiseworthy, than sowing and harvesting crops? Assuredly, very little. Yet his fertile imagination essays one alternative figure. Leaving aside the agricultural commonplace for a moment, Davies explores an engineering conceit in the following passage: "But, as it falleth out many times that when a house is on fire, the owner, to save it from burning, pulleth it down to the ground, but that pulling down doth give occasion of building it up again in a better form, so these last wars, which to save the kingdom did utterly break and destroy this people, produced a better effect than was at first expected."

As in the earlier farming simile, this figure paradoxically affirms how a creative exploit must be initiated by a destructive act. Saving the kingdom by utterly breaking and destroying its people, however, reflects too starkly the true consequences of the Nine Years' War, and perhaps because he sensed that this analogy failed to serve his polemical end as usefully as the other, he never returns to it. More typically, he recovers and exploits the suggestive similarities between farming and colonizing. And, often, his critical vocabulary throughout the essay punningly evokes both these activities: *plantation*, expectedly, but also his verbs *plant, supplant, grow, root, uproot*, and *nourish* help to lay down an analogical base from which he can easily elaborate met-

100. Eamon Grennan, "Language and Politics: A Note on Some Metaphors in Spenser's *A View of the Present State of Ireland*," *Spenser Studies* 3 (1982): 99–110, discusses the rhetorical effect of metaphoric language in an earlier Irish tract.

aphoric language in accord with the requirements of his argument, as the following exemplifies: "If the English would neither in peace govern them [the Irish] by the law, nor could in war root them out by the sword, must they not needs be pricks in their eyes and thorns in their sides till the world's end?"

Davies's reshaping of the history of conquest and pacification is a whitewash, pure and simple, and metaphors like that of the Irish game and those drawn from agriculture and music assist him in promoting the image of benevolent and paternal concern expediently appropriated by his government. And his aloof, disengaged tone, sounded from the first pages on, performs a similar task. Avouching Ireland's beauty, bounty, and great political promise, even as he ignores the evidence of continuing turmoil,[101] the speaker urbanely and coolly finds that his observations "*hath bred in me some curiosity to consider*, what were the true causes" (my emphasis) for England's four-hundred-year failure at conquest. Logically, the connection between his generous praise of Ireland and his questioning of England's failure appears spurious. Implying a necessitous relationship, the lawyer Davies would admit that none exists. Rhetorically, however, this creation of a persona at once generous in his praise and earnest in his curiosity assists in erecting the perspective through which he would filter his arguments.

How consciously he manipulates his point of view remains debatable. The same tonal distinctiveness also permeates his correspondence, where it often seems modified through association with a more evident sense of humor. In addition, he had difficulty in redefining his role when the procedural expectations during the opening days of Parliament were upset by the recu-

101. In a passage criticizing the prideful blindness of the English lawyers who came to Ireland after the wars, Mountjoy's former secretary Fynes Moryson prophetically observed after he revisited the island in 1613 that "when Ireland should have enjoyed the fruits of the last war, in the due subjection of the mere Irish, these times threatened the next combustions from our degenerate English-Irish" (*Itinerary* ..., 3 pts. [London, 1617], 2.2.300).

sant members. When a firm, aggressive reaction to the recusants seemed needful, the Speaker apparently either remained silent or acted out the part he had prepared beforehand. The aloofness, urbanity, and dispassion that so indelibly color the facts in the *Discovery* seem to derive from Davies's habitual mind-set. Certainly these qualities also distinguish his poetry, particularly the *Orchestra* and the epigrams. They may also lead one to speculate on another possible reason for his being selected for the two administrative roles he filled: his patrons might have been impressed by his detached perception of matters and events with which so many others had had too intimate experience—and that so recently—thus rendering them ill-suited for a role requiring gamesomeness and histrionic virtuosity.

Yet for all his aloofness, he occasionally falters, at least twice voicing passionate involvement with his subject. The first of these instances occurs when he is defining Irish customs that the English have traditionally denounced as barbarous, particularly describing how he feels the descendants of the Anglo-Normans degenerately and perversely came to adopt them in place of English usages. The principal abuse Davies isolates is that "most wicked and mischievous custom" of coyne and livery, which he holds as the central cause for the rise of so many other ills: "This crying sin did draw down as great, or greater, plagues upon Ireland than the oppression of the Israelites did draw upon the land of Egypt." He expends a great many pages examining the dire consequences resulting from the wholesale appropriation of this abusive and lawless form of taxation, not the least of which was the rise and fall of the powerful and arrogantly autonomous House of Desmond, the history of which dynasty was for Davies a record of unqualified degeneracy, "which gave the greatest impediment to the full conquest of Ireland."

Davies's indignation over Hibernization of the Old English echoes that of the earlier writers. If anything, the energy with which the Anglo-Norman families took to Irish ways challenged the Elizabethan-Jacobean conception of England's cultural superiority. The earlier critics shrilly denounced Hibernization with all the vituperative hostility of a people whose cultural self-identity is under attack. Even though Davies avoids the extremely irrational outbursts of Campion and Spenser, he responds nonetheless with, for him, remarkable fervor. The Anglo-Normans' substitution of Irish names, implying a shameful rejection of their inheritance, evokes his special scorn. These defectors, he accuses, "grew to be ashamed of their very English names (though they were noble and of great antiquity) and took Irish surnames and nicknames"—this "in contempt and hatred of the English name and nation, whereof these degenerate families became more mortal enemies than the mere Irish."

This same impassioned, defensive contempt echoes throughout most of the earlier essays, indicating a pervasive ethnocentric insecurity. In the second instance of impassioned involvement, though, Davies's emotional heat has a more personal inspiration. Resulting from his profound conflict with Hugh O'Neill, it seems sincere. Of all the antagonists he had to contend with, O'Neill proved particularly elusive. Improvising, temporizing, resourcefully evading the pitfalls that snared Rory O'Donnell and Cuconaught Maguire; supported by Mountjoy and the king; and turning back most of Dublin's efforts to undermine the remnants of his much eroded authority, O'Neill used his intuition and diplomatic skill from 1603 to 1607 to overpower what resources Davies could muster against him. O'Neill, in addition, was the keystone in the native resistance to pre-Flight endeavors at opening Ulster, an enterprise very close to the attorney-general's heart. Hence Davies symbolically singles him out for ridicule and attack.

More than any other of the native Gaelic leaders who remained in position during the earlier years of Davies's tenure, O'Neill typified most reprehensibly the conniving, treacherous imperiousness Davies excoriated. But the native chieftains had not only preserved much of their former authority; they had also retained their prerogatives by means of the Crown's official pol-

icy of surrender-and-regrant.[102] Davies, consequently, was compelled to attack with emotion rather than with the assured disdain of a man who knew his law. These men, exceptions to
policy as Davies wanted it to be, defied England's ideal of
humane rulership under the pretense of already possessing royal
license. "And this was the fruit that did arise of the letters
patents granted of the Irish countries in the time of Queen
Elizabeth," he argues, "where before they did extort and oppress
the people only by color of a lewd and barbarous custom, they
did afterwards use the same extortions and oppressions by warrant under the Great Seal of the Realm." Virtually untouchable
by the law that had ratified their authority, these chieftains successfully obstructed the Crown's intent. No wonder Davies lauds
the supernatural intervention that seemed to drive them out of
Ulster: "The occasion of the disposing of those lands did not
happen without the special providence and finger of God, which
did cast out those wicked and ungrateful traitors who were the
only enemies of the reformation of Ireland."

The other native lords of Ulster, impetuous and insolvent,
were less threatening than O'Neill, whose experience and craft
seemed to draw a magic wall around Tyrone as well as Tyrconnell and Fermanagh. To Davies, O'Neill embodied all
that was barbarous and lawless in the Irish aristocracy, particularly its supreme indifference to English law. As he observed to
Ellesmere (and Salisbury) in 1607, after O'Neill's flight, "It is
certain that Tyrone, in his heart, doth repine at the English government in his country, where, until his last submission [in 1603]
... he ever lived like a free prince, or rather like an absolute
tyrant there." In the same letter, he adds that O'Neill "hath ever

102. Promoted first under Henry VIII, surrender-and-regrant was a policy
for assimilating the native Gaelic leadership into the English political hierarchy
by inviting the chieftains to "surrender" their Gaelic customs, privileges, and
claims to land in return for "grants" of privilege and the same land under
English law.

been noted to be subtle, fox-like, and craftily wise."[103] In his letter to Salisbury of 6 January 1607/8, he describes himself and O'Neill angrily baiting one another in a dispute originating over Donal O'Cahan's claim to the sovereignty of what is now Coleraine. Boasting, prophetically as it turned out, Davies told O'Neill "that he [Davies] was assured that he should live to see Ulster the best reformed province in the kingdom." The earl retorted "that he wished from his heart he might never live to see that day; and his reason was, because he would not have live so long a man that had entitled the King to so much of his land." To this, the attorney-general riposted, apparently moderating his earlier thrust, but in actuality directing it more accurately to the target of O'Neill's exposed ego, "that he might live to see him the best reformed subject in the kingdom."[104] Before O'Neill could make his reply, Chichester intervened, defusing the tension.

Their hostility was unequal. O'Neill had the decisive advantages of age and experience, and his position was reinforced by support from such men as Mountjoy and the king. He was, moreover, the product of a culture that had for centuries excelled at improvising stratagems for neutralizing the colonizers; of a people who had given their name to a fast-moving variation of backgammon distinguished by unexpected, last-minute reversals whereby the apparent winner could be defeated. Yet Davies must have scored against O'Neill often enough, prompting the chieftain's reciprocal dislike evidenced in this exchange. And later, too, O'Neill found opportunity for registering his contempt for Davies. At the conclusion to a long, twenty-article enumeration of indignities and outrages he maintained had driven him from Ulster, for example, O'Neill singles out Davies as "a man more fit to be a stage-player than a counsel to His Highness" and as

103. Davies to Ellesmere, 12 September 1607, in Collier, ed., *Egerton Papers*, pp. 413, 415.
104. Davies to Salisbury, 6 January 1607/8, SPI, 223:2; repr. in Grosart, ed., *Works of Davies*, 3:xcix.

a man who had given him "very irreverent speech before the Council table."[105] Even granted that he reproaches Davies from a sense of personal injury, it is nevertheless illuminating that he assails the attorney-general's histrionic temperament and impolitic behavior, two traits we have already identified.

The unresolved tension between the two helps to explain Davies's rancor toward O'Neill in the *Discovery*. It aids in recognizing the source of the misrepresentations, contradictions, distortions, and venom in such passages as the following, where, arguing that the Irish have always desired English citizenship, he scathingly denounces O'Neill for haughtily asserting special, unique privileges:

> That ungrateful traitor Tyrone, though he had no color or shadow of title to that great lordship, but only by grant from the Crown and by the law of England (for by the Irish law he had been ranked with the meanest of his sept) . . . in one of his capitulations with the state, he required that no sheriff might have jurisdiction within Tyrone and consequently by that the laws of England might not be executed there: which request was never before made by O'Neill or any other lord of the Irishry when they submitted themselves; but contrariwise they were humble suitors to have the benefit and protection of the English laws.

It also helps us appreciate Davies's smugness when he describes O'Neill's occasional setbacks. For example, in detailing how, under James, the Crown had finally penetrated the long-hidden native Irish fastnesses, he pointedly stresses the strategic utility of the newly available intelligence: "It is known, not only how they live and what they do, but *it is foreseen what they purpose or intend to do*" (my emphasis). He then continues his boast with barbed reference to O'Neill, relishing the earl's discomfort and indignation: "Insomuch as Tyrone hath been heard to complain that he had so many eyes watching over him as he could

105. O'Neill to James I ("The Earl of Tyrone's Articles"), 1607, *CSPI*, 2:382–83.

not drink a full carouse of sack, but the State was advertised thereof within few hours after."

The contempt and sneering disdain apparent in the *Discovery* are exceptions to Davies's more consistent dispassion, broad-mindedness, and tolerance, even if these latter are often patronizing. After its victory, the Crown could well risk being generous and conciliatory. With the enemy firmly under heel, its native leadership expunged or driven from the land, the administration would not have ignored, on the eve of Ireland's first parliament in twenty-six years, the opportunity for establishing a new, benevolent, paternal character. Among many other purposes, this also seems one of the principal intents of Davies's Irish tract. Playing out his role of peacemaker, the attorney-general for Ireland affirms for his readership a vision of what was, what is, and what ought to be. He looks into the seeds of time, purporting to say which grain will grow and which will not, and promises, if not a brave new world, then at least something approximating one. The former rebels, "absolutely reduced" to James's "immediate subjection," will happily continue as subjects of the king, "as long as they may be protected and justly governed, without oppression on the one side or impunity on the other . . . . [and] may have the protection and benefit of the law when upon just cause they do desire it." Envisioning the impartial execution of the law, Davies cannot but foresee that Ireland "will from henceforth prove a land of peace and concord." And had the Crown sincerely taken the lessons of history to heart and promulgated a rule of law equitable for English and Irish both, Sir John Davies's hope might well have come to be.

A Discovery
of the True Causes
Why Ireland Was Never
Entirely Subdued

Sir John Davies

A Discovery of the True Causes
Why Ireland Was Never Entirely Subdued
[And] Brought Under Obedience of the Crown of England
Until the Beginning of His Majesty's Happy Reign
(1612)

DURING THE TIME of my service in Ireland (which began in the first year of His Majesty's reign),[1] I have visited all the provinces of that kingdom in sundry journeys and circuits: wherein I have observed the good temperature of the air; the fruitfulness of the soil; the pleasant and commodious seats for habitation; the safe and large ports and havens lying open for traffic into all the west parts of the world; the long inlets of many navigable rivers, and so many great lakes and fresh ponds within the land, as the like are not to be seen in any part of Europe; the rich fishings and wildfowl of all kinds; and lastly, the bodies and minds of the people, endued with extraordinary abilities of nature.

The observation whereof hath bred in me some curiosity to consider, what were the true causes why this kingdom, whereof our kings of England have borne the title of "sovereign lords" for the space of four hundred and odd years (a period of time wherein divers great monarchies have risen from barbarism to civility and fallen again to ruin) was not in all that space of time thoroughly subdued and reduced to obedience of the Crown of England, although there hath been almost a continual war between the English and the Irish? and why the manners of the mere[2] Irish are so little altered since the days of King Henry II?

1. In 1603.
2. *mere*: pure (i.e., the native Irish).

—as appeareth by the description made by Giraldus Cambrensis[3] (who lived and wrote in that time), albeit there have been since that time so many English colonies planted in Ireland as that, if the people were numbered at this day by the poll, such as are descended of English race would be found more in number than the ancient natives.

And truly, upon consideration of the conduct and passage of affairs in former times, I find that the state of England ought to be cleared of an imputation which a vulgar error hath cast upon it in one point: namely, that Ireland long since might have been subdued and reduced to civility if some statesmen in policy had not thought it more fit to continue that realm in barbarism. Doubtless, this vulgar opinion, or report, hath no true ground, but did first arise either out of ignorance or out of malice. For it will appear by that which shall hereafter be laid down in this discourse that ever since our nation had any footing in this land, the state of England did earnestly desire, and did accordingly endeavor from time to time, to perfect the conquest of this kingdom, but that in every age there were found such impediments and defects in both realms as caused almost an impossibility that things should have been otherwise than they were.

Two Main Impediments of the Conquest

The defects which hindered the perfection of the conquest of Ireland were of two kinds and consisted, first, in the faint prosecution of the war, and next, in the looseness of the civil government. For the husbandman must first break the land before it be made capable of good seed; and when it is thoroughly broken and manured, if he do not forthwith cast good seed into it, it will grow wild again and bear nothing but weeds: so a barbarous

3. Giraldus Cambrensis, or Gerald of Wales (1146?–1220?), visited Ireland in 1183 and 1185 and wrote two influential works, the *Topographia Hiberniae* (ca. 1187) and the *Expugnatio Hiberniae* (ca. 1189).

country must be first broken by a war before it will be capable of good government; and when it is fully subdued and conquered, if it be not well-planted and governed after the conquest, it will eftsoons[4] return to the former barbarism.

The Faint Prosecution of the War

Touching the carriage of the martial affairs, from 17 King Henry II,[5] when the first overture was made for the conquest of Ireland (I mean the first after the Norman Conquest of England), until 39 Queen Elizabeth,[6] when that royal army was sent over to suppress Tyrone's Rebellion, which made in the end an universal and absolute conquest of all the Irishry, it is most certain that the English forces sent hither, or raised here from time to time, were ever too weak to subdue and master so many warlike nations, or septs,[7] of the Irish as did possess this island. And besides their weakness, they were ill-paid and worse governed. And if at any time there came over an army of competent strength and power, it did rather terrify than break and subdue this people, being ever broken and dissolved by some one accident or other before the perfection of the conquest.

What Is a Perfect Conquest?

For that I call a "perfect conquest" of a country which doth reduce all the people thereof to the condition of subjects; and those I call "subjects" which are governed by the ordinary laws and magistrates of the sovereign. For though the prince doth

4. *eftsoons*: soon afterward; forthwith.
5. The seventeenth year of the reign of Henry II, 1171, when Henry himself led a royal army into Ireland.
6. The date, 1597 or 1598, seems to refer to the beginning of Thomas Lord Burgh's deputyship, but Davies's reference to "that royal army" suggests that he intends the earl of Essex's expedition in 1599.
7. *septs*: clans; or divisions within clans, that is, subclans.

bear the title of "sovereign lord" of an entire country (as our kings did of all Ireland), yet if there be two-third parts of that country wherein he cannot punish treasons, murders, or thefts, unless he send an army to do it; if the jurisdiction of his ordinary courts of justice doth not extend into those parts to protect the people from wrong and oppression; if he have no certain revenue, no escheats or forfeitures out of the same, I cannot justly say that such a country is wholly conquered.

How the War Hath Been Prosecuted since 17 Henry II

First, then, that we may judge and discern whether the English forces in Ireland were at any time of sufficient strength to make a full and final conquest of that land, let us see what extraordinary armies have been transmitted out of England thither, and what ordinary forces have been maintained there, and what service they have performed from time to time, since 17 King Henry II.

In the Time of Henry II: The First Attempt but an Adventure of Private Gentlemen

In that year, MacMurrough,[8] lord of Leinster, being oppressed by the lords of Meath and Connaught, and expelled out of his territory, moved King Henry II to invade Ireland and made an overture unto him for the obtaining of the sovereign lordship thereof. The king refused to undertake the war himself, to avoid the charge[9] (as King Henry VII refused to undertake the discovery of the Indies for the same cause), but he gave license by his letters patents that such of his subjects might pass

8. Dermot MacMurrough, king of Leinster (1126–71), fled to England in 1166. He returned in 1167, having invited the earl of Pembroke, "Strongbow," to assist him in recovering his power in Leinster. Henry II himself invaded Ireland in 1171.
9. *charge*: burden, expenses.

over into Ireland as would at their own charge become adventurers in that enterprise.*

So as the first attempt to conquer this kingdom was but an adventure of a few private gentlemen. FitzStephen and FitzGerald[10] first brake the ice with a party of 390 men.

With What Forces the King Himself Came Over

The Earl Strongbow[11] followed them with 1,200 more, whose good success upon the seacoasts of Leinster and Munster drew over the king in person the next year after, "with 500 soldiers,"[12] as Giraldus Cambrensis reporteth, who was present in Ireland at that time: which, if they were but "500 soldiers," seemeth too small a train for so great a prince. But admit they were 500 knights, yet because in those days every knight was not a commander of a regiment or company, but most of them served as private men (sometimes a hundred knights under a spear),[13] as appeareth by the lists of the ancient armies,* we cannot conjecture his army to have been so great as might suffice to conquer all Ireland, being divided into so many principalities and having so many Hydra's heads,[14] as it had at that time.

For albeit Tacitus in the "Life of Agricola" doth report that Agricola,[15] having subdued the greatest part of Great Britain,

10. Robert FitzStephen landed in Wexford 1 May 1169, followed shortly by his half-brother Maurice FitzGerald.

11. "Strongbow" is the name erroneously applied by later historians to Richard FitzGilbert de Clare, earl of Strigoil and Pembroke, who landed near Waterford 23 August 1169. (Properly, the epithet belonged to Richard's father.)

12. "cum quingentis Militibus."

13. *spear*: lance bearing an ensign (designating a unit roughly corresponding to a company?).

14. In classical mythology, the Hydra was a poisonous water snake possessing many heads; when any one of these was cut off, several more would grow in its place.

15. Gnaeus Julius Agricola (A.D. 37–93) was a Roman governor of Britain. The historian Publius Cornelius Tacitus (ca. A.D. 55–ca. 117) was his son-in-law.

did signify to the Senate of Rome that he thought Ireland might also be conquered with one legion and a few aids, I make no doubt but that if he had attempted the conquest thereof with a far greater army, he would have found himself deceived in his conjecture. For a barbarous country is not so easily conquered as a civil, whereof Caesar had experience in his wars against the Gauls, Germans, and Britons, who were subdued to the Roman Empire with far greater difficulty than the rich kingdoms of Asia. And again, a country possessed with many petty lords and states is not so soon brought under entirely as an entire kingdom governed by one prince or monarch. And therefore the late king of Spain could sooner win the kingdom of Portugal than reduce the states of the Low Countries.[16]

What Manner of Conquest King Henry II Made of Ireland

But let us see the success of King Henry II: doubtless his expedition was such as he might have said with Caesar, *veni, vidi, vici.* For upon his first arrival, his very presence, without drawing his sword, prevailed so much as all the petty kings or great lords within Leinster, Connaught, and Munster submitted themselves unto him, promised to pay him tribute, and acknowledged him their chief and sovereign lord. Besides, the better to assure this inconstant sea-nymph (who was so easily won), the pope would needs give her unto him with a ring: *con[ub]io jungan stabili, propriamque dicabo.*[17] But as the conquest was but slight and superficial, so the pope's donation and the Irish submissions were but weak and fickle assurances. For, as the pope had no more interest in this kingdom than he which offered to Christ all

16. Philip II, king of Spain (1556–98), although he readily conquered the neighboring kingdom of Portugal (1579–81), could not subdue the independent territories of the Low Countries.

17. "I shall join them in a lasting marriage and call her his own" (Vergil, *Aeneid,* 4:126).

the kingdoms of the earth, so the Irish pretend that by their law a tanist[18] might do no act that might bind his successor. But this was the best assurance he could get from so many strong nations of people with so weak a power; and yet he was so well pleased with this title of the "Lordship of Ireland" as he placed it in his royal style before the duchies of Normandy and Aquitaine. And so, being advertised of some stirs raised by his unnatural sons in England,[19] within five months after his first arrival, he departed out of Ireland without striking one blow or building one castle or planting one garrison among the Irish. Neither left he behind him one true subject more than those he found there at his coming over, which were only the English adventurers spoken of before, who had gained the port towns in Leinster and Munster, and possessed some scopes of land thereunto adjoining, partly by Strongbow's alliance with the lord of Leinster, and partly by plain invasion and conquest.

And this is that conquest of King Henry II, so much spoken of by so many writers, which though it were in no other manner than is before expressed, yet is the entire conquest of all Ireland attributed unto him.

But the truth is, the conquest of Ireland was made piece and piece, by slow steps and degrees, and by several attempts in several ages. There were sundry revolutions, as well of the English fortunes as of the Irish, somewhiles one prevailing, somewhiles the other; and it was never brought to a full period till His Majesty that now is came to the Crown.

As for King Henry II, he was far from obtaining that monarchy royal and true sovereignty which His Majesty (who now reigneth) hath over the Irish. For the Irish lords did only promise to become tributaries to King Henry II. And such as pay only

18. *tanist*: from the Gaelic *tanaiste* ("next heir to an estate, or next chieftain of a clan"); the successor to a chieftain elected during the latter's lifetime by the electors of a clan.

19. Prince Henry, Richard ("the Lionhearted"), Geoffrey of Brittany, and John ("Lackland").

tribute, though they be placed by Bodin[20] in the first degree of subjection, are not properly subjects but sovereigns.* For though they be less and inferior unto the prince to whom they pay tribute, yet they hold all other points of sovereignty; and having paid their tribute which they promised, to have their peace, they are quit of all other duties, as the same Bodin writeth. And therefore, though King Henry II had the title of "Sovereign Lord" over the Irish, yet did he not put those things in execution which are the true marks and differences of sovereignty.

The True Marks of Sovereignty

For to give laws unto a people; to institute magistrates and officers over them; to punish and pardon malefactors; to have the sole authority of making war and peace, and the like, are the true marks of sovereignty, which King Henry II had not in the Irish countries, but the Irish lords did still retain all these prerogatives to themselves.

For they governed their people by the brehon law;[21] they made their own magistrates and officers; they pardoned and punished all malefactors within their several countries; they made war and peace one with another without controlment —and this they did not only during the reign of King Henry II, but afterwards in all times, even until the reign of Queen Elizabeth. And it appeareth what manner of subjects these Irish lords were by the concord made between King Henry II and Roderick O'Connor,[22] the Irish king of Connaught, in the year 1175, which is recorded by Hoveden[23] in this form:

20. Jean Bodin (1530–96), French political philosopher.
21. *Brehon law: brehon*, from the Gaelic *breitheamh* ("judge"); the native Irish legal code administered by the professional judges who were called *brehons*.
22. Rory O'Connor (d. 1199), the last high king of Ireland (1166–75).
23. Roger of Hoveden (fl. 1174–1201), English historian, was the author of the *Chronica*.

This is the accord and agreement between the Lord King Henry FitzEmperess of England and Roderick king of Connaught: namely, that the king of England grants to the aforementioned Roderick, his liegeman, [rule in Connaught] so that as king under him [i.e., Henry] he may be prepared to give him service as his liegeman, etc.[24]*

And the commission whereby King Henry II made William FitzAudelm[25] his lieutenant of Ireland hath this direction: "to the archbishops, bishops, kings, earls, barons, and all his loyal subjects in Ireland, greeting."[26] Whereby it is manifest that he gave those Irish lords the title and style of kings.

King John likewise did grant divers charters to the king of Connaught, which remain in the Tower of London.* And afterwards, in the time of King Henry III, we find in the Tower a grant made to the king of Thomond[27] in these words: "The king to the king of Thomond, greeting. We grant to you the land of Thomond which you held before, to hold from us throughout our life for a pledge of 130 marks."[28]* And in the Pipe Rolls remaining in Bremi[n]gham's Tower[29] in the Castle of Dublin, upon sundry accounts of the seneschal of Ulster (when that earldom was in the king's hands by reason of the minority of the earl), the entry of all such charges as were made upon O'Neill for

24. "Hic est finis et Concordia, inter Dominum regem Angliae Henricum, filium Imperatricis, et Rodoricum Regem Conactae, scilicet, quod Rex. Angliae concessit praedict' Roderico Ligeo homini suo, ut sit Rex sub eo paratus ad servitium suum, ut homo suus, etc."
25. William FitzAudelm (or fitz Audelin), viceroy in 1173.
26. "Archiepiscopis, Episcopis, Regibus, Comitibus, Baronibus, et omnibus fidelibus suis in Hibernia, Salutem."
27. Brian O'Brien, king of Thomond, executed in 1277 by Thomas de Clare.
28. "Rex Regi Tosmond salutem. Concessimus vobis terram Tosmond quam prius tenuistis, per firmam centum et triginta marcarum; Tenendum de nobis usque ad aetatem nostram."
29. In Davies's time, Bermingham's or Bremingham's (to use Davies's preferred form) Tower in Dublin Castle (which took its name from Richard de Bermingham) housed the principal legal documents pertaining to England's rule in Ireland.

rent-beeves[30] or for aids towards the maintenance of the king's wars are in this form: "Lord O'Neill returned 400 cows for rent; Lord O'Neill, £100 for aid of the king in support of his war in Gascony."[31] And in one roll (36 Henry III): "King O'Neill, £100 for aid of the lord king in support of his war in Wales"[32]*— which seemed strange to me that the king's civil officer should give him that style upon record unless he meant it in that sense as Maximillian the emperor[33] did when speaking of his disobedient subjects: "the title," said he, of *rex reg[n]um*[34] doth more properly belong to me than to any mortal prince, for all my subjects do live as kings—they obey me in nothing, but do what they list." And truly, in that sense these Irish lords might not unfitly be termed "kings." But to speak in proper terms, we must say with the Latin poet, *Qui rex est, regnum, maxime non habeat.*[35] But touching these Irish kings, I will add this note out of an ancient manuscript, the Black Book of Christ Church in Dublin:[36] "These kings were not ordained by the holy rite of any order, nor by the sacrament of unction, nor by hereditary law, nor by any succession of property; but with force over time each obtained his own kingdom."[37] And therefore, they had no just cause to complain when a stronger king than themselves became

30. *rent-beeves*: cattle for which rent is received, charged, or paid.
31. "Oneal Regulus 400 vaccas pro arreragio Reddit; Oneal Regulus, 100 li. de Auxilio Domini Regis ad guerram suam in [W]asconia sustinendam."
32. "Oneale Rex, 100 li. de auxilio domini Regis ad guerram suam in Wallia sustinendam."
33. Davies cites the Holy Roman Emperor Maximilian I ("the Dreamer"; 1459–1519), who struggled throughout his reign to increase the authority of the crown at the expense of the power possessed by the empire's numerous princelings.
34. "of king of the realm."
35. "He who is king may not have the greatest kingdom."
36. Bound collections of manuscripts were frequently designated, as here, by both the color of their bindings and their location or place of origin.
37. "Isti Regis non fuerunt ordinati solemnitate alicuius ordinis, nec unctionis Sacramento, nec jure haereditario, vel aliqua proprietatis successione, sed vi et annis quilibet Regnum suum obtinuit."

a king and lord over them. But let us return to our purpose and see the proceeding of the martial affairs.

How the War Was Prosecuted in the Time of King John

King Henry II, being returned into England, gave the lordship of Ireland unto the Lord John, his youngest son, surnamed before that time *Sans-terre* ["Lackland"].[38]* And the pope, confirming that gift, sent him a crown of peacock's feathers (as Pope Clement VIII sent the feather of a phoenix, as he called it, to the traitor Tyrone).[39] This young prince, the king's son, being but twelve years of age, with a train of young noblemen and gentlemen to the number of 300, but not with any main army, came over to take possession of his new patrimony, and being arrived at Waterford, divers Irish lords (who had submitted themselves to his father) came to perform the like duty to him. But that youthful company using them with scorn because their demeanors were but rude and barbarous, they went away much discontented and raised a general rebellion against him.* Whereby it was made manifest that the submission of the Irish lords and the donation of the pope were but slender and weak assurances for a kingdom.

Hereupon this young lord was revoked and Sir John de Courcy[40] sent over, not with the king's army, but with a company of voluntaries, in number 400 or thereabout. With these he

38. Pope Adrian IV had "donated," or given, Ireland to Henry II. With the approval of Pope Alexander III, Henry designated his favorite and landless (hence the nickname *sans terre*) son John as the "lord of Ireland" (*Dominus Hiberniae*) in 1177.

39. Early in 1600, following his campaign into the south to secure additional allies, Hugh O'Neill received needed support, principally money and arms, from Philip III of Spain. Perhaps in recognition that the church viewed O'Neill as the man destined to resurrect Catholic Ireland, Pope Clement VIII also sent him at this time a feather, it was asserted, from a phoenix (*penna phoenicis*), the mythical bird believed to rise newborn out of the ashes of its earlier life.

40. Justiciar, 1185–92.

attempted the conquest of Ulster, and in four or five encounters did so beat the Irishry of that province as that he gained the maritime coasts thereof from the Boyne to the Bann, and thereupon was made earl of Ulster.* So as now the English had gotten good footing in all the provinces of Ireland: in the first three provinces of Leinster, Munster, and Connaught, part by the sword and part by submission and alliance; and lastly in Ulster by the invasion and victories of Sir John de Courcy.

From this time forward until 17 King John (which was a space of more than thirty years), there was no army transmitted out of England to finish the conquest. Howbeit, in the meantime the English adventurers and colonies already planted in Ireland did win much ground upon the Irish: namely, the Earl Strongbow, having married the daughter of MacMurrough, in Leinster; the Lacys in Meath; the Geraldines and other adventurers in Munster; the Audleys, Gernons, Clintons, Russells, and other voluntaries of Sir John de Courcy's retinue in Ulster; and the Burkes (planted by William FitzAudelm) in Connaught. Yet were the English reputed but part-owners of Ireland at this time, as appeareth by the commission of the pope's legate in the time of King Richard I, whereby he had power to exercise his jurisdiction in "England, Wales, and those parts of Ireland in which John Earl of Morton holds power and dominion,"[41] as it is recorded by Matthew Paris.[42]*

King John, in the twelfth year of his reign,[43] came over again into Ireland: the stories of that time say with a great army, but the certain numbers are not recorded. Yet it is credible in regard of the troubles wherewith this king was distressed in England that this army was not of sufficient strength to make an entire conquest of Ireland; and if it had been of sufficient strength, yet

41. "in Anglia, Wallia, ac illis Hiberniae partibus, in quibus Iohannes Moretonii Comes potestatem habet et dominium."
42. Matthew of Paris (d. 1259), English monk who authored the important historical chronicle the *Chronica majora*.
43. John landed near Waterford on 20 June 1210.

did not the king stay a sufficient time to perform so great an action, for he came over in June and returned in September the same year.* Howbeit, in that time the Irish lords for the most part submitted themselves to him as they had done before to his father, which was but a mere mockery and imposture. For his back was no sooner turned but they returned to their former rebellion: and yet this was reputed a second conquest. And so this king, giving order for the building of some castles upon the borders of the English colonies, left behind him the bishop of Norwich[44] for the civil government of the land. But he left no standing army to prosecute the conquest: only, the English colonies, which were already planted, were left to themselves to maintain what they had got and to gain more if they could.

How the Martial Affairs Were Carried from 12 King John to 36 King Edward III

The personal presence of these two great princes, King Henry II and King John, though they performed no great thing with their armies, gave such countenance to the English colonies, which increased daily by the coming over of new voluntaries and adventurers out of England, as that they enlarged their territories very much. Howbeit, after this time the kings of England, either because they presumed that the English colonies were strong enough to root out the Irish by degrees, or else because they were diverted or disabled otherwise (as shall be declared hereafter), never sent over any royal army or any numbers of men worthy to be called an army into Ireland until 36 King Edward III, when Lionel duke of Clarence,[45] the king's second son, having married the daughter and heir of Ulster, was sent

44. John de Grey, bishop of Norwich, justiciar 1208–13.
45. Lionel duke of Clarence, Edward III's third son (not the second, as Davies says), was married to Elizabeth de Burgo, daughter and heiress to the last de Burgo earl of Ulster, William the Brown Earl. Lionel's lieutenancy extended 1 July 1361–69.

over with an extraordinary power in respect of the time (for the wars betwixt England and France were then in their heat),[46] as well to recover his earldom of Ulster, which was then overrun and possessed by the Irish, as to reform the English colonies, which were become strangely degenerate throughout the whole kingdom.

For though King Henry III gave the whole land of Ireland to Edward the Prince,[47] his eldest son, and his heirs, "so that it would not be separated from the Crown of England"[48]* (whereupon it was styled "the land of the Lord Edward, the kings eldest son," and all the officers of the land were called the "officers of Edward Lord of Ireland"); and though this Edward were one of the most active princes that ever lived in England, yet did he not either in the lifetime of his father or during his own reign come over in person, or transmit any army into Ireland. But on the other side, he drew sundry aids and supplies of men out of Ireland to serve him in his wars in Scotland, Wales, and Gascoigne.[49] And again, though King Edward II sent over Piers Gaveston[50] with a great retinue, it was never intended he should perfect the conquest of Ireland, for the king could not want his company so long a time as must have been spent in the finishing of so tedious a work.

So then, in all that space of time between 12 King John and 36 King Edward III, containing 150 years or thereabouts, although there were a continual bordering war between the English and the Irish, there came no royal army out of England to make an end of the war. But the chief governors of the realm, who were at first called *custodes Hiberniae*, and afterwards "Lords Jus-

46. The Hundred Years' War, 1337–1453.

47. Prince Edward's, later King Edward I's, tenure as lord of Ireland, 1254–1307, marked the beginning of the decline of the lordship of Ireland.

48. "ita quod non Separetur a co[ro]na Angliae."

49. Gascony, in southern France.

50. Piers Gaveston, or Peter de Gaveston, king's lieutenant, June 1308–July 1309.

tices," and the English lords, who had gotten so great possessions and royalties as that they presumed to make war and peace
without direction from the state, did levy all their forces within the land. But those forces were weakly supplied and ill-
governed, as I said before—weakly supplied with men and
money, and governed with the worst discipline that ever was
seen among men of war. And no marvel, for it is an infallible
rule that an army ill-paid is ever unruly and ill-governed. The
standing forces here were seldom or never reinforced out of
England, and such as were either sent from thence or raised here
did commonly do more hurt and damage to the English subjects
than to the Irish enemies by their continual cess[51] and extortion;
which mischief did arise by reason that little or no treasure was
sent out of England to pay the soldiers' wages: only the king's
revenue in Ireland was spent, and wholly spent in the public
service. And, therefore, in all the ancient Pipe Rolls in the times
of Henry III, Edward I, Edward II, and Edward III, between
the receipts and allowances, there is this entry: "Nothing in the
treasury."[52]* For the officers of the state and the army spent
all, so as there was no surplusage of treasure. And yet that *all* was
not sufficient, for in default of the king's pay, as well the ordinary forces which stood continually as the extraordinary which
were levied by the chief governor upon journeys and general
hostings were for the most part laid upon the poor subject
descended of English race. Howbeit this burden was in some
measure tolerable in the time of King Henry III and King
Edward I, but in the time of King Edward II, Maurice Fitz-
Thomas of Desmond,[53] being chief commander of the army
against the Scots, began that wicked extortion of coyne and liv-

---

51. *cess*: "the obligation to supply the soldiers and the household of the lord
deputy with provisions at prices 'assessed' or fixed by the government; hence
loosely used for military exactions" (*OED*).

52. "in Thesauro nihil."

53. Maurice FitzThomas, first earl of Desmond (1329–56).

ery,[54] and pay: that is, he and his army took horsemeat and mansmeat,[55] and money at their pleasure, without any ticket[56] or other satisfaction.* And this was after that time the general fault of all the governors and commanders of the army in this land. Only, the golden saying of Sir Thomas [Rokeby],[57] who was justice in 30 King Edward III, is recorded in all the annals of this kingdom: that he would eat in wooden dishes, but would pay for his meat, gold and silver.* Besides, the English colonies, being dispersed in every province of this kingdom, were enforced to keep continual guards upon the borders and marches round-about them; which guards, consisting of idle soldiers, were likewise imposed as a continual burden upon the poor English free-holders, whom they oppressed and impoverished in the same manner. And because the great English lords and captains had power to impose this charge when and where they pleased, many of the poor freeholders were glad to give unto those lords a great part of their lands to hold the rest free from that extortion. And many others, not being able to endure that intolerable oppression, did utterly quit their freeholds and returned into England.* By this mean, the English colonies grew poor and weak, though the English lords grew rich and mighty: for they placed Irish tenants upon the lands relinquished by the English; upon them they levied all Irish exactions; with them they married and fostered and made gossips. So as, within one age, the English, both lords and freeholders, became degenerate and mere Irish in their language, in their apparel, in their arms and manner of fight, and all other customs of life whatsoever.

By this it appeareth why the extortion of coyne and livery is

54. *coyne and livery*: the billeting of soldiers and their horses upon private individuals; food and exactions levied for the maintenance of soldiers and horses.

55. *horsemeat and mansmeat*: provender, food for horses and men.

56. *ticket*: voucher, receipt.

57. Justiciar, July 1349–July 1355.

called in the old statutes of Ireland a damnable custom, and the imposing and taking thereof made high treason.* And it is said in the ancient discourse, *Of the Decay of Ireland*,[58]* that though it were first invented in Hell, yet if it had been used and practiced there as it hath been in Ireland, it had long since destroyed the very kingdom of Beelzebub.[59] In this manner was the war of Ireland carried before the coming over of Lionel duke of Clarence.

The Army Transmitted with Lionel Duke of Clarence (36 Edward III)

This young prince, being earl of Ulster and lord of Connaught in right of his wife (who was daughter and heir of the Lord William Burke, the last earl of Ulster of that family, slain by treachery at Knockfergus),[60] was made the king's lieutenant of Ireland and sent over with an army in 36 King Edward III; the roll and list of which army doth remain of record in the King's Remembrancer's Office in England (in the press *De Rebus Tangentibus Hiberniam*)[61]* and doth not contain above 1,500 men by the poll; which because it differs somewhat from the manner of this age, both in respect of the command and the entertainment,[62] I think it not impertinent to take a brief view thereof.

58. This is the same tract Davies later attributes to Patrick Finglas (fl. 1535), baron of the exchequer (ca. 1520) and chief justice of the King's Bench in Ireland (1534–35); the title of the tract, as given in the *Carew MSS*, is "A Breviat of the Getting of Ireland, and of the Decay of the Same."

59. Beelzebub, another name for Satan, the ruler of Hell.

60. William de Burgo, the Brown Earl of Ulster, was murdered at Le Ford, now Belfast, by his own men on 6 June 1333. Knockfergus, the present-day Carrickfergus, is about twenty miles north of Belfast.

61. "of matters concerning Ireland."

62. *entertainment*: "provision for support of persons in service (*esp.* soldiers)" (*OED*); wages, pay.

The Lord Lionel was general, and under him Ralph earl of Stafford, James earl of Ormond, Sir John Carew, banneret, Sir William Windsor,[63] and other knights were commanders.

The entertainment of the general upon his first arrival was but 6s.8d., *per diem*, for himself; for 5 knights, 2s. apiece, *per diem*; for 64 esquires, 12d. apiece, *per diem*; for 70 archers, 6d. apiece, *per diem*. But being shortly after created duke of Clarence (which honor was conferred upon him being here in Ireland), his entertainment was raised to 13s.4d., *per diem*, for himself, and for 8 knights, 2s. apiece, *per diem*, with an increase of the number of his archers, viz., 360 archers on horseback out of Lancashire, at 6d. apiece, *per diem*, and 23 archers out of Wales, at 2d. apiece, *per diem*.

The earl of Stafford's entertainment was, for himself, 6s.8d., *per diem*; for a banneret, 4s., *per diem*; for 17 knights, 2s. apiece, *per diem*; for 78 esquires, 12d. apiece, *per diem*; for 100 archers on horseback, 6d. apiece, *per diem*. Besides, he had the command of 24 archers out of Staffordshire, 40 archers out of Worcestershire, and 6 archers out of Shropshire, at 4d. apiece, *per diem*.

The entertainment of James earl of Ormond was, for himself, 4s., *per diem*; for two knights, 2s. apiece, *per diem*; for 27 esquires, 12d. apiece, *per diem*; for 20 hoblers armed (the Irish horsemen were so-called because they served on hobbies),[64] 6d. apiece, *per diem*; and for 20 hoblers not armed, 4d. apiece, *per diem*.

The entertainment of Sir John Carew, banneret, was, for himself, 4s., *per diem*; for 1 knight, 2s., *per diem*; for 8 esquires, 12d. apiece, *per diem*; for 10 archers on horseback, 6d. apiece, *per diem*.

The entertainment of Sir William Windsor was, for himself, 2s., *per diem*; for 2 knights, 2s. apiece, *per diem;* for 49 squires,

---

63. Ralph de Stafford (1299–1372), first earl of Stafford; James Butler, second earl of Ormond (1338–82); Sir John Carew (d. 1362), king's escheator; Sir William Windsor (succeeded Lionel as king's lieutenant 1369–76); all came over with Lionel in 1361.

64. *hobbies*: small horses; ponies.

12*d*. apiece, *per diem*; for 6 archers on horseback, 6*d*. apiece, *per diem*.

The like entertainment[s], rateably, were allowed to divers knights and gentlemen upon that list, for themselves and their several retinues, whereof some were greater and some less, as they themselves could raise them among their tenants and followers.

The Manner of Levying Soldiers in Former Ages

For in ancient times, the king himself did not levy his armies by his own immediate authority or commission, but the lords and captains did by indenture covenant with the king to serve him in his wars with certain numbers of men for certain wages and entertainments, which they raised in greater or less numbers, as they had favor or power with the people. This course hath been changed in later times upon good reason of state: for the barons and chief gentlemen of the realm, having power to use the king's prerogative in that point, became too popular; whereby they were enabled to raise forces even against the Crown itself, which, since the statutes made for levying and mustering of soldiers by the king's special commission, they cannot so easily perform if they should forget their duties.

What Service Lionel Duke of Clarence Performed

This lord lieutenant with this small army performed no great service, and yet upon his coming over all men who had land in Ireland[65] were by proclamation remanded back out of England thither, and both the clergy and laity of this land gave two years' profits of all their lands and tithes towards the maintenance of the war here: only, he suppressed some rebels in low Leinster

---

65. Absentee landowners, of whom Lionel, as earl of Ulster, was one of the greatest.

and recovered the maritime parts of his earldom of Ulster.* But his best service did consist in the well-governing of his army and in holding that famous parliament at Kilkenny,[66] wherein the extortion of the soldier and the degenerate manners of the English (briefly spoken of before) were discovered and laws made to reform the same; which shall be declared more at large hereafter.

Sir William Windsor, Lieutenant (47 Edward III): His Forces and Service

The next lieutenant transmitted with any forces out of England was Sir William Windsor,[67] who in 47 King Edward III undertook the custody, not the conquest, of this land (for now the English made rather a defensive than an invasive war) and withal, to defray the whole charge of the kingdom for £11, 213.6s.8d., as appeareth by the indenture between him and the king remaining of record in the Tower of London.* But it appeareth by that which Froissart[68] reporteth that Sir William Windsor was so far from subduing the Irish as that himself reported that he could never have access to understand and know their countries, albeit he had spent more time in the service of Ireland than any Englishman then living.*

The State of the Revenue of Ireland in the Time of Edward III

And here I may well take occasion to show the vanity of that which is reported in the story of Walsingham[69] touching the rev-

66. In 1366 Lionel's parliament enacted the famous Statutes of Kilkenny, whereby the English endeavored to reverse Hibernization. See Davies below (pp. 154–6, 171–4).
67. Appointed king's lieutenant, 3 March 1369.
68. Jean Froissart (1338–1410?), French historian who authored the *Chronicle*.
69. Thomas Walsingham (d. 1422?), an English monk-historian.

enue of the Crown in Ireland in the time of King Edward III; for he, setting forth the state of things there in the time of King Richard II, writeth thus:

When the illustrious king of England, Edward III, had there set up his exchequer, as well as judges with the exchequer, he then took possession for the royal treasury the annual sum of £30,000. However, on account of the absence of his liegemen and the power of his enemies, nothing came from there. On the other hand, each and every year, the king paid from his purse 30,000 marks, to his shame and the serious detriment of his treasury.[70]

If this writer had known that the king's courts had been established in Ireland more than a hundred years before King Edward III was born, or had seen either the Parliament Rolls in England or the Records of Receipts and Issues in Ireland, he had not left this vain report to posterity, for both the benches and the exchequer were erected in 12 King John.* And it is recorded in the Parliament Rolls of 21 Edward III remaining in the Tower that the Commons of England made petition that it might be inquired why the king received no benefit of his land of Ireland, considering he possessed more there than any of his ancestors had before him. Now, if the king at that time, when there were no standing forces maintained there, had received £30,000 yearly at his exchequer in Ireland, he must needs have made profit by that land, considering that the whole charge of the kingdom in 47 Edward III (when the king did pay an army there) did amount to no more than £11,200 *per annum*, as appeareth by the contract of Sir William Windsor.*

Besides, it is manifest by the Pipe Rolls of that time, whereof many are yet preserved in Bremingham's Tower and are of bet-

---

70. "Cum Rex Angliae illustris, Edwardus tertius illic posuisset Bancum suum atque Judices, cum Scaccario, percepit inde ad Regalem Fiscum annuatim triginta millia librarum; modom propter absentiam ligeorum, et hostium potentiam, nihil inde venit: sed Rex per annos singulos, de suo Marsupio, terrae defensoribus soluit Triginta millia marcarum, ad regni sui dedecus et fisci gravissimum detrimentum."

ter credit than any monk's story,[71] that during the reign of King
Edward III the revenue of the Crown of Ireland, both certain
and casual, did not rise unto £10,000 *per annum*, though the
medium be taken of the best seven years that are to be found in
that king's time. The like fable hath Holinshed[72] touching the
revenue of the earldom of Ulster, which (saith he) in the time of
King Richard II was 30,000 marks by the year;* whereas in
truth, though the lordships of Connaught and Meath (which
were then parcel[73] of the inheritance of the earl of Ulster) be
added to the account, the revenue of that earldom came not to
the third part of that he writeth. For the account of the profits
of Ulster yet remaining in Bremingham's Tower, made by William FitzWarin, seneschal and farmer[74] of the lands of Ulster
seized into the king's hands after the death of Walter de Burgo,
earl of Ulster, from 5 Edward III until the eight[h] year do
amount but to nine hundred and odd pounds, at what time the
Irishry had not made so great an invasion upon the earldom of
Ulster as they had done in the time of King Richard II.*

As vain a thing it is that I have seen written in an ancient
manuscript touching the customs of this realm in the time of
King Edward III, that those duties in those days should yearly
amount to 10,000 marks,[75] which by mine own search and view
of the records here I can justly control.[76] For upon the late reducing of this ancient inheritance of the Crown, which had been
detained in most of the port towns of this realm for the space of
a hundred years and upwards, I took some pains (according to

71. Such as that chronicled by the monk Walsingham.
72. Rafael Holinshed (d. 1580?) compiled and partly authored the influential *Chronicles of England, Scotlande, and Irelande* . . . (1577; rev. ed. 1586–87).
73. *parcel*: part.
74. William FitzWarin, the king's seneschal (ca. 1271) in Ulster.
(*farmer*: "one who undertakes the collection of taxes, revenues, etc., paying
a fixed sum for the proceeds," *OED*.)
75. During the period Davies refers to, the mark was valued at approximately 13s.4d.
76. *control*: confirm, verify.

the duty of my place) to visit all the Pipe Rolls wherein the Accounts of Customs are contained and found those duties answered in every port for 250 years together, but did not find that at any time they did exceed £[1,000]*per annum*; and no marvel, for the subsidy of poundage[77] was not then known, and the greatest profit did arise by the cocket[78] of hides, for wool and wool-fells[79] were ever of little value in this kingdom.

But now again, let us see how the martial affairs proceeded in Ireland. Sir William Windsor continued his government till the latter end of the reign of King Edward III, keeping, but not enlarging, the English borders.

How the War Proceeded in the Time of King Richard II

In the beginning of the reign of King Richard II, the state of England began to think of the recovery of Ireland, for then was the first statute made against absentees,[80] commanding all such as had land in Ireland to return and reside thereupon, upon pain to forfeit two-third parts of the profit thereof.* Again, this king, before himself intended to pass over, committed the government of this realm to such great lords successively as he did most love and favor: first, to the earl of Oxford, his chief minion, whom he created marquess of Dublin and duke of Ireland; next, to the duke of Surrey, his half-brother; and lastly, to the Lord Mortimer, earl of March and Ulster, his cousin and heir apparent.[81]

77. *poundage*: "an impost, duty, or tax of so much per pound sterling on merchandise" (*OED*).

78. *cocket*: customs duties.

79. *wool-fells*: sheepskins still possessing the wool.

80. Actually, the Crown had begun enacting legislation against absentees as early as 1297 (see Edmund Curtis, *A History of Medieval Ireland from 1086 to 1513* [London, 1938], pp. 173–74).

81. Robert de Vere, earl of Oxford, was created duke of Ireland on 12 October 1386 and marquis of Dublin on 1 December 1386, in effect giving him the lordship of Ireland.

Davies's sequence is faulty: Oxford was viceroy during 1386–88; and

Among the Patent Rolls in the Tower (9 Richard II),* we find 500 men at arms at 12*d.* apiece, *per diem*, and [1,000] archers at 6*d.* apiece, *per diem*, appointed for the duke of Ireland, "during the conquest of that land for two years"[82] (for those are the words of that record). But for the other two lieutenants, I do not find the certain numbers whereof their armies did consist. But certain it is that they were scarce able to defend the English borders, much less to reduce the whole island. For one of them, namely, the earl of March, was himself slain upon the borders of Meath; for revenge of whose death the king himself made his second voyage into Ireland in the last year of his reign. For his first voyage in the eighteenth year of his reign (which was indeed a voyage royal) was made upon another motive and occasion, which was this: upon the vacancy of the empire, this king, having married the king of Bohemia's daughter (whereby he had great alliance in Germany), did by his ambassadors solicit the princes electors to choose him emperor;[83]* but another being elected and his ambassadors returned, he would needs know of them the cause of his repulse in that competition. They told him plainly that the princes of Germany did not think him fit to command the empire, who was neither able to hold that which his ancestors had gained in France, nor to rule his insolent subjects in England, nor to master his rebellious people of Ireland. This was enough to kindle in the heart of a young prince a desire to perform some great enterprise. And therefore, finding it no fit

---

although several Mortimer earls of March and Ulster served Richard II as viceroys, the reference in the following paragraph indicates that Davies intends here Richard's heir, Roger Mortimer, fourth earl of March and seventh earl of Ulster, who was killed at Kellistown, near Carlow (not Meath) 20 July (or 10 June) 1398; Thomas Holland, duke of Surrey, served as king's lieutenant 1398–99.

82. "Super Conquestu illius terrae per duos annos."

83. On 14 January 1382, Richard II married Anne of Luxemburg, daughter of Charles IV, king of Bohemia and Holy Roman emperor. Anne died in 1394, but beginning that year and continuing through 1397, Richard futilely maneuvered to be elected Holy Roman emperor.

time to attempt France, he resolved to finish the conquest of Ireland; and to that end he levied a mighty army consisting of 4,000 men at arms and 30,000 archers, which was a sufficient power to have reduced the whole island if he had first broken the Irish with a war and after established the English laws among them, and not have been satisfied with their light submissions only, wherewith in all ages they have mocked and abused the state of England. But the Irish lords, knowing this to be a sure policy to dissolve the forces which they were not able to resist (for their ancestors had put the same trick and imposture upon King John and King Henry II), as soon as the king was arrived with his army, which he brought over under St. Edward's banner (whose name was had in great veneration amongst the Irish), they all made offer to submit themselves. Whereupon, the Lord Thomas Mowbray, earl of Nottingham and marshal of England, was authorized by special commission to receive the homages and oaths of fidelity of all the Irishry of Leinster.[84]* And the king himself, having received humble letters from O'Neill (wherein he styleth himself "Prince of the Irishry in Ulster," and yet acknowledgeth the king to be his sovereign lord, "and lord of Ireland forever"),[85] removed to Drogheda to accept the like submissions from the Irish of Ulster. The men of Leinster, namely, MacMurrough, O'Byrne, O'More, O'Murrough, O'Nolan, and the chief of the Kinsellas, in an humble and solemn manner did their homages and made their oaths of fidelity to the earl marshal, laying aside their girdles, their skeans,[86] and their caps, and falling down at his feet upon their knees; which when they had performed, the earl gave unto each of them *osculum pacis*.[87]

84. In February 1395.

85. "et perpetuus Dominus Hiberniae."

86. *girdles*: belts worn about the waist and employed for carrying weapons. *skeans*: knives, daggers; a skean (from the Gaelic *scian*) was one of the principal weapons of the kern or light infantryman.

87. *osculum pacis*: the kiss of peace.

Besides, they were bound by several indentures upon great pains to be paid to the Apostolic Chamber,[88] not only to continue loyal subjects, but that by a certain day prefixed they and all their swordmen should clearly relinquish and give up unto the king and his successors all their lands and possessions which they held in Leinster and (taking with them only their movable goods) should serve him in his wars against his other rebels; in consideration whereof, the king should give them pay and pensions during their lives, and bestow the inheritance of all such lands upon them as they should recover from the rebels in any other part of the realm. And thereupon, a pension of 80 marks, *per annum*, was granted to Art MacMurrough, chief of the Kavanaughs, the enrollment whereof I found in the White Book of the exchequer here. And this was the effect of the service performed by the earl marshal by virtue of his commission. The king in like manner received the submissions of the lords of Ulster, namely, O'Neill, O'Hanlon, MacDonnell, MacMahon, and others, who with the like humility and ceremony did homage and fealty to the king's own person. The words of O'Neill's homage as they are recorded are not unfit to be remembered: "I, Neill O'Neill the Elder, your liegeman, come for myself just as for my son and my whole nation and kindred, and for all my subjects," etc.[89] And in the indenture between him and the king, he is not only bound to remain faithful to the Crown of England, but to restore the *bonaght*[90] of Ulster to the earl of Ulster, as of right belonging to that earldom and usurped among other things by the O'Neills.

These indentures and submissions, with many other of the

88. The Apostolic Chamber served as both treasury and exchequer of the popes as heads of the Catholic church and sovereigns of the Papal States.

89. "Ego Nelanus Oneal Senior tam pro meipso, quam pro filiis meis, et tota Natione mea et Parentelis meis, et pro omnibus subditis meis devenio' Ligeus homo vester, etc."

90. *bonaght*: from the Gaelic *buanacht* ("military service," "the billeting of soldiers"); "a tax or tribute formerly levied by Irish chiefs for the maintenance of soldiers" (*OED*).

same kind (for there was not a chieftain or head of an Irish sept but submitted himself in one form or other), the king himself caused to be enrolled and testified by a notary public, and delivered the enrollments with his own hands to the bishop of Salisbury,[91] then lord treasurer of England, so as they have been preserved and are now to be found in the Office of the King's Remembrancer there.

With these humilities they satisfied the young king, and by their bowing and bending avoided the present storm and so brake that army which was prepared to break them. For the king, having accepted their submissions, received them in *osculo pacis*, feasted them, and, given the honor of knighthood to divers of them, did break up and dissolve his army and returned into England with much honor and small profit (saith Froissart). For though he had spent a huge mass of treasure in transporting his army, by the countenance whereof he drew on their submissions, yet did he not increase his revenue thereby one sterling pound nor enlarged the English borders the breadth of one acre of land; neither did he extend the jurisdiction of his courts of justice one foot further than the English colonies, wherein it was used and exercised before. Besides, he was no sooner returned into England but those Irish lords laid aside their masks of humility and, scorning the weak forces which the king had left behind him, began to infest the borders; in defense whereof the Lord Roger Mortimer,[92] being then the king's lieutenant and heir apparent of the crown of England, was slain, as I said before. Whereupon, the king, being moved with a just appetite of revenge, came over again in person in the twenty-second year of his reign with as potent an army as he had done before, with a full purpose to make a full conquest of Ireland. He landed at

91. Richard Medford, also titular treasurer of Ireland.

92. Mortimer, wearing only the linen dress of an Irish chieftan, was slain at the battle of Kellistown, near Carlow, 20 July 1398. Reportedly, his body was dismembered.

Waterford, and passing from thence to Dublin through the waste countries of the Murroughs, Kinsellas, Kavanaghs, Byrnes, and Tooles, his great army was much distressed for want of victuals and carriages,[93] so as he performed no memorable thing in that journey: only, in the Kavanaghs' Country he cut and cleared the paces,[94] and bestowed the honor of knighthood upon the Lord Henry, the duke of Lancaster's son, who was afterwards King Henry V; and so came to Dublin, where entering into counsel how to proceed in the war, he received news out of England of the arrival of the banished duke of Lancaster at Ravenspurgh, usurping the regal authority, and arresting and putting to death his principal officers.[95]*

This advertisement suddenly brake off the king's purpose touching the prosecution of the war in Ireland and transported him into England, where shortly after he ended both his reign and his life: since whose time, until 39 Queen Elizabeth, there was never any army sent over of a competent strength or power to subdue the Irish, but the war was made by the English colonies, only to defend their borders; or if any forces were transmitted over, they were sent only to suppress the rebellions of such as were descended of English race, and not to enlarge our dominion over the Irish.

Henry IV:
The Lord Thomas of Lancaster His Service

During the reign of King Henry IV, the Lord Thomas of Lancaster,[96] the king's second son, was lieutenant of Ireland, who for the first eight years of that the king's reign made the Lord

93. *carriages*: either baggage, matériel; or transports, wagons used for carrying equipment.
94. *paces*: passes between mountains or bogs; passages.
95. Henry of Lancaster landed at Ravenspurgh in 1399.
96. King's lieutenant, 1401–13.

Scrope[97] and others his deputies, who only defended the marches
with forces levied within the land. In the eight[h] year that
prince came over in person with a small retinue; so as, wanting
a sufficient power to attempt or perform any great service, he
returned within seven months after into England. Yet during his
personal abode there, he was hurt in his own person within one
mile of Dublin upon an encounter with the Irish enemy. He
took the submissions of O'Byrne of the Mountains, MacMahon,
and O'Reilly by several indentures, wherein O'Byrne doth covenant that the king shall quietly enjoy the manor of Newcastle;
MacMahon accepteth a state in the Farney[98] for life, rendering
£10 a year; and O'Reilly doth promise to perform such duties to
the earl of March and Ulster as were contained in an indenture
dated 18 Richard II.*

Henry V:
The Lord Furnival His Service

In the time of King Henry V, there came no forces out of
England. Howbeit, the Lord Furnival,[99] being the king's lieutenant, made a martial circuit or journey roundabout the marches
and borders of the Pale,[100] and brought all the Irish to the king's
peace, beginning with the Byrnes, Tooles, and Kavanaghs on the
South; and so passing to the Mores, O'Connors, and O'Ferrals in
the West; and ending with the O'Reillys, MacMahons, O'Neills,
and O'Hanlons in the North.* He had power to make them seek
the king's peace, but not power to reduce them to the obedience
of subjects: yet this was then held so great and worthy a service

97. Sir Stephen la Scrope, lord deputy 1401–4.
98. In what is now County Monaghan.
99. John Talbot, Lord Furnival, king's lieutenant 1414–19.
100. For centuries, the Pale—Dublin and the surrounding four or five
counties—constituted the only settled English enclave in Ireland and as such
was the seat of the Irish government.

as that the lords and chief gentlemen of the Pale made certificate thereof in French unto the king, being then in France; which I have seen recorded in the White Book of the exchequer at Dublin. Howbeit, his army was so ill-paid and governed as the English suffered more damage by the cess of his soldiers (for now that monster, coyne and livery, which the Statute of Kilkenny had for a time abolished, was risen again from Hell) than they gained profit or security by abating the pride of their enemies for a time.

Henry VI

During the minority of King Henry VI[101] and for the space of seven or eight years after, the lieutenants and deputies made only a bordering war upon the Irish with small and scattered forces; howbeit, because there came no treasure out of England to pay the soldier, the poor English subject did bear the burden of the men of war in every place and were thereby so weakened and impoverished as the state of things in Ireland stood very desperate.

Richard Duke of York His Service

Whereupon the cardinal of Winchester[102] (who after the death of Humphrey duke of Gloucester did wholly sway the state of England), being desirous to place the duke of Somerset in the regency of France, took occasion to remove Richard duke of

101. The weak King Henry VI (1421–71) ruled from 1422 to 1461, when he was deposed. He was restored to the throne in 1470.

102. Henry Beaufort (ca. 1377–1447), cardinal of Winchester and one of the principal policy makers during the weak reign of Henry VI, died 10 April 1447, well before Richard duke of York's appointment to the lieutenancy of Ireland on 9 December 1447. Another of the powerful Beaufort faction, probably William de la Pole, duke of Suffolk, engineered York's "honorable exile" to Ireland. In any case, York's tenure as lieutenant ran, with occasional interruptions, from 1447 to his death in December 1460.

York from that government and to send him into Ireland, pretending that he was a most able and willing person, to perform service there because he had a great inheritance of his own in Ireland, namely, the earldom of Ulster and the lordships of Connaught and Meath, by descent from Lionel duke of Clarence.

We do not find that this great lord came over with any numbers of waged soldiers, but it appeareth upon what good terms he took that government by the covenants between the king and him, which are recorded and confirmed by Act of Parliament in Ireland, and were to this effect:*

1. that he should be the king's lieutenant of Ireland for ten years;
2. that to support the charge of that country, he should receive all the king's revenues there, both certain and casual, without account;
3. that he should be supplied also with treasure out of England in this manner: he should have 4,000 marks for the first year, whereof he should be imprested[103] £2,000 beforehand, and for the other nine years, he should receive £2,000 *per annum*;
4. that he might let to farm the king's lands, and place and displace all officers at his pleasure;
5. that he might levy and wage what numbers of men he thought fit;
6. that he might make a deputy and return at his pleasure.

We cannot presume that this prince kept any great army on foot, as well because his means out of England were so mean, and those ill-paid, as appeareth by his passionate letter written to the earl of Salisbury, his brother-in-law, the copy whereof is registered in the story[104] of this time;* as also because the whole land, except the English Pale and some [part] of the earldom of Ulster upon the seacoasts, were possessed by the Irish. So as the revenue of the kingdom which he was to receive did amount to little. He kept the borders and marches of the Pale with much ado. He held many parliaments, wherein sundry laws were made for

103. *imprested*: advanced, loaned.
104. *story*: history, chronicle (Davies refers here to Richard Neville, earl of Salisbury.)

erecting of castles in Louth, Meath, and Kildare to stop the incursions of the Irishry. And because the soldiers for want of pay were cessed and laid upon the subjects against their wills, upon the prayer and importunity of the Commons this extortion was declared to be high treason. But to the end that some means might be raised to nourish some forces for defense of the Pale, by another Act of Parliament every £20 land[105] was charged with the furnishing and maintenance of one archer on horseback.*

Besides, the native subjects of Ireland, seeing the kingdom utterly ruined, did pass in such numbers into England as one law was made in England to transmit them back again and another law made here to stop their passage in every port and creek.* Yet afterwards, the greatest parts of the nobility and gentry of Meath passed over into England and were slain with him at Wakefield in Yorkshire.[106]*

Lastly, the state of England was so far from sending an army to subdue the Irish at this time, as among the articles of grievances exhibited by the duke of York against King Henry VI, this was one: that divers lords about the king had caused His Highness to write letters unto some of his Irish enemies, whereby they were encouraged to attempt the conquest of the said land; which letters the same Irish enemies had sent unto the duke, marveling greatly that such letters should be sent unto them and speaking therein great shame of the realm of England.*

After this, when this great lord was returned into England, and making claim to the Crown, began the War betwixt the Two Houses, it cannot be conceived but that the kingdom fell into a worse and weaker estate.

105. *£20 land*: land valued (for administrative purposes) at £20.
106. The Lancastrians defeated the Yorkists at the Battle of Wakefield, 31 December 1460.

Edward IV: How the War Was
Maintained in the Time of King Edward IV

When Edward IV was settled in the kingdom of England, he made his brother George duke of Clarence lieutenant of Ireland.[107] This prince was born in the Castle of Dublin during the government of his father, the duke of York; yet did he never pass over into this kingdom to govern it in person, though he held the lieutenancy many years. But it is manifest that King Edward IV did not pay any army in Ireland during his reign, but the men of war did pay themselves by taking coyne and livery upon the country: which extortion grew so excessive and intolerable as the Lord Tiptoft,[108] being deputy to the duke of Clarence, was enforced to execute the law upon the greatest earl in the kingdom, namely, Desmond, who lost his head at Drogheda for this offense.[109]*

The Fraternity of St. George in Ireland

Howbeit, that the state might not seem utterly to neglect the defense of the Pale, there was a fraternity of men at arms called the Brotherhood of St. George erected by Parliament (14 Edward IV) consisting of thirteen the most noble and worthy persons within the four shires.* Of the first foundation were Thomas earl of Kildare, Sir Roland Eustace, lord of Portlester, and Sir Robert Eustace for the county of Kildare; Robert, lord of Howth, the mayor of Dublin, and Sir Robert Dowdall, for the county of Dublin; the viscount of Gormanston, Edward Plunket, seneschal of Meath, Alexander Plunket, and Barnabe Barnewall,

107. Clarence, who had been born in Dublin Castle in 1449, was appointed in March 1462 to the lieutenancy for seven years.
108. John Tiptoft, earl of Worcester, lord deputy from 1467 to 1470, after which he was appointed king's lieutenant.
109. On 15 February 1468.

for the county of Meath; the mayor of Drogheda, Sir Lawrence Taaffee, and Richard Bellewe, for the county of Louth.[110] These and their successors were to meet yearly upon St. George's Day and to choose one of themselves to be captain of that brotherhood for the next year to come; which captain should have at his command 120 archers on horseback, 40 horsemen, and 40 pages to suppress outlaws and rebels. The wages of every archer should be 6d., *per diem*, and every horseman, 5d., *per diem*, and 4 marks, *per annum*. And to pay these entertainments and to maintain this new fraternity, there was granted unto them by the same Act of Parliament a subsidy of poundage out of all merchandises exported or imported throughout the realm (hides and the goods of freemen of Dublin and Drogheda only excepted). These 200 men were all the standing forces that were then maintained in Ireland. And as they were natives of the kingdom, so the kingdom itself did pay their wages without expecting any treasure out of England.

Henry VII: How the War Was Prosecuted in the Time of King Henry VII

But now the wars of Lancaster and York being ended, and Henry VII being in the actual and peaceable possession of the kingdom of England, let us see if this king did send over a competent army to make a perfect conquest of Ireland. Assuredly, if those two idols or counterfeits which were set up against him in the beginning of his reign had not found footing and followers in this land, King Henry VII had sent neither horse nor foot hither, but let the Pale to the guard and defense of the Fraternity of St. George, which stood till the tenth year of his reign. And therefore, upon the erection of the first idol, which was Lambert,

110. The Fraternity of St. George was established in 1474. Among the thirteen charter members were Thomas FitzGerald (seventh earl of Kildare), Sir Roland FitzEustace (Baron Portlester, d. 1496), Robert St. Lawrence (fifteenth Baron Howth, d. 1483).

the priest's boy, he transmitted no forces, but sent over Sir Richard Edgecomb[111] with commission to take an oath of allegiance of all the nobility, gentry, and citizens of this kingdom; which service he performed fully and made an exact return of his commission to the king.* And immediately after that, the king sent for all the lords of Parliament in this realm, who repairing to his presence, were first in a kingly manner reproved by him. For among other things, he told them that if their king were still absent from them, they would at length crown apes; but at last entertained them and dismissed them graciously.*

Sir Edward Poynings' Service

This course of clemency he held at first. But after, when Perkin Warbeck,[112] who was set up and followed chiefly by the Geraldines in Leinster and the citizens of Cork in Munster, to suppress this counterfeit the king sent over Sir Edward Poynings with an army (as the histories call it) which did not consist of a thousand men by the poll; and yet it brought such terror with it as all the adherents of Perkin Warbeck were scattered and retired for succor into the Irish countries; to the marches whereof he marched with his weak forces, but eftsoons returned and held a parliament;* wherein, among many good laws, one

111. In 1487 an Oxford priest, Richard Simons, produced a young boy, Lambert Simnel, who, he asserted, was really Edward, earl of Warwick, properly Edward VI. On 27 June 1488, Sir Richard Edgecomb landed in Ireland to take new oaths of allegiance from the Irish nobility, many of whom had strongly supported Simnel's claim to Henry's title.

112. In the autumn of 1491, a great number of the Irish nobility accepted the claim of Perkin Warbeck (or Osbeck) to be Richard, younger son of Edward IV and the surviving Yorkist heir to the Crown. During this time, Perkin Warbeck was using Ireland as his base. One of Lord Deputy Sir Edward Poynings's tasks, beginning in 1494, was to stamp out this Yorkist conspiracy against Henry VII. Warbeck was finally executed at Tyburn in November 1499.

For a discussion of the Simnel and Warbeck risings, see Steven G. Ellis, *Tudor Ireland: Crown, Community and the Conflict of Cultures, 1470–1603* (London, 1985), pp. 69–86.

act was made: that no subject should make any war or peace within the land without the special license of the king's lieutenant or deputy*—a manifest argument that at that time the bordering wars in this kingdom were made altogether by voluntaries, upon their own head, without any pay or entertainment, and without any order or commission from the state. And though the lords and gentlemen of the Pale in the nineteenth year of this king's reign joined the famous battle of Knocktoe[113] in Connaught, wherein MacWilliam with 4,000 of the Irish and degenerate English were slain,* yet was not this journey made by warrant from the king or upon his charge (as it is expressed in the Book of Howth),[114] but only upon a private quarrel of the earl of Kildare, so loosely were the martial affairs of Ireland carried during the reign of King Henry VII.

Henry VIII: How the War Was
Carried During the Reign of King Henry VIII
The Earl of Surrey's Service

In the time of King Henry VIII, the earl of Surrey,[115] lord admiral, was made lieutenant, and though he were the greatest captain of the English nation then living, yet brought he with him rather an honorable guard for his person than a competent army to recover Ireland, for he had in his retinue 200 tall yeoman of the King's Guard. But because he wanted means to perform any great action, he made means to return the sooner. Yet in the meantime he was not idle, but passed the short time he

---

113. On 19 August 1504, at Knocktoe, a hill near Clare Galway, the Lord Deputy Gerald FitzGerald, eighth earl of Kildare, obtained a decisive victory over the rebels, who were led by Ulick MacWilliam Burke, lord of Clanricard.

114. *The Book of Howth* chronicles the conquest of Ulster, begun in 1177 by John de Courcy.

115. Thomas Howard, earl of Surrey, lord lieutenant 1520–21.

spent here in holding a parliament and divers journeys against the rebels of Leinster; insomuch as he was hurt in his own person upon the borders of Leix. After the revocation of this honorable personage, King Henry VIII sent no forces into Ireland till the rebellion of the Geraldines, which happened in the twenty-seventh year of his reign. Then sent he over Sir William Skeffington[116] with 500 men only to quench that fire and not to enlarge the border or to rectify the government.

The Lord Leonard Grey's Service

This deputy died in the midst of the service, so as the Lord Leonard Grey[117] was sent to finish it; who arriving with a supply of 200 men or thereabouts did so prosecute the rebels as the Lord Gerrat, their chieftain, and his five uncles[118] submitted themselves unto him and were by him transmitted into England.

But this service being ended, that active nobleman with his little army and some aids of the Pale did oftentimes repel O'Neill and O'Donnell attempting the invasion of the civil shires, and at last made that prosperous fight at Bellahoe[119] on the confines of Meath; the memory whereof is yet famous, as that he defeated (well-nigh) all the power of the North, and so quieted the border for many years.*

Hitherto, then, it is manifest that since the last transfretation[120]

116. Appointed lord deputy 22 June 1530.

117. Lord deputy, 1536–40.

118. Gerald FitzGerald, claimant to the attainted earldom of Kildare, was finally driven out of Ireland, into France, in 1540. Davies, however, seems here to be referring to the capture in 1535 and execution in 1537 (in England) of Gerald's half-brother "Silken" Thomas, tenth earl of Kildare, and his five uncles (see Ellis, *Tudor Ireland*, pp. 4–5, & 129; Art Cosgrove, *Late Medieval Ireland, 1370–1541* [Dublin, 1981], p. 120).

119. In a surprise attack, Grey defeated the Ulster confederacy at Bellahoe, on the Meath-Monaghan border, in 1539.

120. *transfretation*: "crossing or passing over a strait, channel, or narrow sea" (*OED*).

of King Richard II the Crown of England never sent over either numbers of men or quantities of treasure sufficient to defend the small territory of the Pale, much less to reduce that which was lost or to finish the conquest of the whole island.

Sir Anthony St. Leger

After this, Sir Anthony St. Leger[121] was made chief governor, who performed great service in a civil course, as shall be expressed hereafter.

Sir Edward Bellingham in the Time of King Edward VI

But Sir Edward Bellingham,[122] who succeeded him, proceeded in a martial course against the Irishry, and was the first deputy, from the time of King Edward III till the reign of King Edward VI, that extended the border beyond the limits of the English Pale by beating and breaking the Mores and Connors, and building the forts of Leix and Offaly. This service he performed with 600 horse, the monthly charge whereof did arise to £770, and 400 foot, whose pay did amount to £446, *per mensum*;[123] as appeareth upon the treasurer's account remaining in the Office of the King's Remembrancer in England.*

Thomas Earl of Sussex in the Time of Queen Mary

Yet were not these countries so fully recovered by this deputy, but that Thomas earl of Sussex[124] did put the last hand to this work, and rooting out these two rebellious septs, planted English

121. Lord deputy, 1540–47, 1550–51, and 1553–56.
122. Lord deputy, 1548–49.
123. *per mensum*: per month.
124. Thomas Radcliffe, Lord FitzWalter and later third earl of Sussex, served as lord deputy and lord lieutenant 1556–66.

colonies in their rooms, which in all the tumultuous times since have kept their habitations, their loyalty, and religion.

Queen Elizabeth

And now are we come to the time of Queen Elizabeth, who sent over more men and spent more treasure to save and reduce the land of Ireland than all her progenitors since the conquest.

How the War Was Prosecuted in the Time of Queen Elizabeth

During her reign, there arose three notorious and main rebellions, which drew several armies out of England: the first, of Shane O'Neill; the second, of Desmond; the last, of Tyrone (for the particular insurrections of the Viscount Baltinglass and Sir Edmund Butler, the Mores, the Kavanaghs, the Byrnes, and the Burkes of Connaught were all suppressed by the standing forces here).

Shane O'Neill's Rebellion

To subdue Shane O'Neill[125] in the height of his rebellion, in the year 1566 Captain Randal transported a regiment of 1,000 men into Ulster and planted a garrison at Lough Foyle; before the coming of which supply, viz., in the year 1565, the list of the standing army of horse and foot, English and Irish, did not exceed the number of 1,200 men, as appeareth by the Treasurer's Account of Ireland, now remaining in the exchequer of England.* With these forces did Sir Henry Sidney[126] (then lord

125. In 1566 the crown dispatched Colonel Edward Randolph to Lough Foyle to contain Shane O'Neill, who had gone into rebellion about 1565.

126. Lord deputy 1565–71, appointed again 5 August 1575.

deputy) march into the farthest parts of Tyrone and, joining with Captain Randal, did much distress, but not fully defeat, O'Neill, who was afterwards slain upon a mere accident by the Scots, and not by the queen's army.[127]

Desmond's Rebellion

To prosecute the wars in Munster against Desmond[128] and his adherents, there were transmitted out of England at several times three or four thousand men; which, together with the standing garrisons and some other supplies raised here, made at one time an army of 6,000 and upwards, which with the virtue and [va]lor of Arthur Lord Grey[129] and others the commanders did prove a sufficient power to extinguish that rebellion.

Tyrone's Rebellion

But that being done, it was never intended that these forces should stand till the rest of the kingdom were settled and reduced: only that army which was brought over by the earl of Essex,[130] lord lieutenant and governor general of this kingdom, in 39 Queen Elizabeth to suppress the rebellion of Tyrone,[131] which was spread universally over the whole realm; that army, I say (the command whereof, with the government of the realm, was shortly after transferred to the command of the Lord

127. After his defeat by the O'Donnells at Letterkenny, Shane O'Neill fled across Ulster to MacDonald's Country, where, at a feast given in his honor by Alexander MacDonald, Shane was killed and dismembered, his head being sent for reward to Sidney in Dublin in 1567.

128. Gerald FitzGerald, fourteenth earl of Desmond, who went into rebellion in 1579, was killed in November 1584.

129. Lord Arthur Grey de Wilton, lord deputy 1580–82.

130. Robert Devereux, second earl of Essex, lord lieutenant 1599–1600.

131. Hugh O'Neill, second earl of Tyrone, went into rebellion about 1594 and submitted in 1603.

Mountjoy,[132] afterwards earl of Devonshire, who with singular wisdom, valor, and industry did prosecute and finish the war), did consist of such good men of war and of such numbers (being well-nigh 20,000 by the poll), and was so royally supplied and paid, and continued in full strength so long a time as that it brake and absolutely subdued all the lords and chieftains of the Irishry and degenerate or rebellious English. Whereupon the multitude, who ever loved to be followers of such as could master and defend them, admiring the power of the Crown of England, being brayed,[133] as it were, in a mortar with the sword, famine, and pestilence altogether, submitted themselves to the English government, received the laws and magistrates, and most gladly embraced the king's pardon and peace in all parts of the realm with demonstration of joy and comfort; which made, indeed, an entire, perfect, and final conquest of Ireland. And though upon the finishing of the war, this great army was reduced to less numbers, yet hath His Majesty in his wisdom thought it fit still to maintain such competent forces here as the law may make her progress and circuit about the realm under the protection of the sword (as Virgo, the figure of Justice, is by Leo in the zodiac)[134] until the people have perfectly learned the lesson of obedience and the conquest be established in the hearts of all men.

Four Main Defects in the Prosecution of the War

Thus far have I endeavored to make it manifest that from the first adventure and attempt of the English to subdue and conquer Ireland until the last war with Tyrone (which, as it was roy-

132. Charles Blount, Lord Mountjoy, was lord deputy from 1600 to 1603, at which time he was appointed lord lieutenant by James I.

133. *brayed*: crushed, pulverized, pounded.

134. In the zodiacal progression, the martial figure of Leo the Lion precedes Virgo, who, as a representatiion of justice, is depicted holding a pair of balance scales and a sword.

ally undertaken, so it was really prosecuted to the end), there hath been four main defects in the carriage of the martial affairs here. First, the armies for the most part were too weak for a conquest. Secondly, when they were of a competent strength (as in both the journeys of Richard II), they were too soon broken up and dissolved. Thirdly, they were ill-paid. And fourthly, they were ill-governed, which is always a consequent of ill-payment.

Why None of the Kings of England before Queen Elizabeth Did Finish the Conquest of Ireland

But why was not this great work performed before the latter end of Queen Elizabeth's reign, considering that many of the kings her progenitors were as great captains as any in the world and had elsewhere larger dominions and territories? First, who can tell whether the Divine Wisdom, to abate the glory of those kings, did not reserve this work to be done by a queen, that it might rather appear to be His own immediate work? and yet, for her greater honor, made it the last of her great actions, as it were, to crown all the rest? and, to the end that a secure peace might settle the conquest and make it firm and perpetual to posterity, caused it to be made in that fullness of time when England and Scotland became to be united under one imperial crown, and when the monarchy of Great Britainy was in league and amity with all the world? Besides, the conquest at this time doth perhaps fulfill that prophecy wherein the four great prophets of Ireland do concur, as it is recorded by Giraldus Cambrensis, to this effect: that after the first invasion of the English, they should spend many ages in "frequent conflicts and long battles, and with much bloodshed"; and that

almost all the English will be thrown out of Ireland; nevertheless, they will always hold the east coast; but they [i.e., the Four Prophets] hardly promise the people of England a complete victory before the Day of

Judgment, or that Ireland shall be completely subjugated and castles built from sea to sea.[135]

If St. Patrick and the rest did not utter this prophecy, certainly Giraldus is a prophet who hath reported it. To this, we may add the prophecy of Merlin, spoken of also by Giraldus: "the Sixth shall overthrow the walls [or castles] of Ireland and make [all] the regions into a [single] kingdom"[136]—which is performed in the time of King James VI,[137] in that all the paces are cleared and places of fastness laid open, which are the proper walls and castles of the Irish, as they were of the British in the time of Agricola, and withal, the Irish countries' being reduced into counties make but one entire and undivided kingdom.

But to leave these high and obscure causes, the plain and manifest truth is that the kings of England in all ages had been powerful enough to make an absolute conquest of Ireland if their whole power had been employed in that enterprise, but still there arose sundry occasions which divided and diverted their power some other way.

How the Several Kings of England Were Diverted from the Conquest of Ireland

Let us therefore take a brief view of the several impediments which arose in every king's time since the first overture of the conquest, whereby they were so employed and busied as they could not intend the final conquest of Ireland.

135. "crebris conflictibus, longoque certanime et multis coedibus.... Omnes fere Anglici ab Hibernia turbabuntur: nihilominus orientalia maritima semper obtinebunt; Sed vix paulo ante diem Juditii; plenam Anglorum populo victoriam compromittunt; Insula Hibernica de mari usque ad mare de toto subacta et incastellata."

136. "Sextus moenia Hiberniae subvertet, et regiones in Regnum redigentur."

137. James I of England, who assumed the Crown simultaneously with the end of the Nine Years' War in 1603, was also James VI of Scotland.

King Henry II

King Henry II was no sooner returned out of Ireland but all his four sons[138] conspired with his enemies, rose in arms, and moved war against him, both in France and in England.

This unnatural treason of his sons did the king express in a emblem painted in his chamber at Winchester, wherein was an eagle with three eaglets tiring[139] on her breast, and the fourth pecking at one of her eyes.* And the truth is, these ungracious practices of his sons did impeach his journey to the Holy Land (which he had once vowed), vexed him all the days of his life, and brought his gray hairs with sorrow to the grave. Besides, this king, having given the lordship of Ireland to John, his youngest son, his ingratitude afterwards made the king careless to settle him in the quiet and absolute possession of that kingdom.

Richard I

Richard I, which succeeded Henry II in the kingdom of England, had less reason to bend his power towards the conquest of this land, which was given in perpetuity to the Lord John, his brother. And therefore went he in person to the holy war, by which journey and his captivity in Austria and the heavy ransom that he paid for his liberty,[140] he was hindered and utterly disabled to pursue any so great an action as the conquest of Ireland. And after his delivery and return, hardly was he able to maintain a frontier war in Normandy, where by hard fortune he lost his life.

138. Prince Henry, Richard ("the Lionhearted"), Geoffrey of Brittany, and John ("Lackland").

139. *tiring*: tearing, ripping (in order to feed).

140. Captured and held prisoner for ransom by the duke of Austria in 1192, Richard I was freed 2 March 1194, deeply in debt.

King John

King John, his brother, had greatest reason to prosecute the war of Ireland because the lordship thereof was the portion of his inheritance, given unto him when he was called John *Sansterre*. Therefore, he made two journeys thither: one when he was earl of Morton and very young, about twelve years of age; the other when he was king, in the twelfth year of his reign. In the first, his own youth and his youthful company—Roboam's councillors[141]—made him hazard the loss of all that his father had won. But in the latter, he showed a resolution to recover the entire kingdom in taking the submissions of all the Irishry, and settling the estates of the English, and giving order for the building of many castles and forts, whereof some remain until this day. But he came to the Crown of England by a defeasible[142] title, so as he was never well-settled in the hearts of the people, which drew him the sooner back out of Ireland into England; where shortly after he fell into such trouble and distress, the clergy cursing him on the one side, and the barons rebelling against him on the other, as he became so far unable to return to the conquest of Ireland, as besides the forfeiture of the territories in France, he did in a manner lose both the kingdoms. For he surrendered both to the pope and took them back again to hold in feefarm,[143] which brought him into such hatred at home and

141. II Chronicles 10 tells of King Rehoboam who, heeding the cruel advice of his younger councillors and ignoring the compassionate, experienced judgment of his elder advisers, stirred the people of Israel to revolt against him.

142. *defeasible*: "capable of being, or liable to be, undone, 'defeated' or made void; subject to forfeiture" (*OED*). (On his deathbed, Richard I compelled his barons to swear their fealty to John as their next king, even though Arthur of Brittany, son of John's older brother, Geoffrey, had a better claim to the Crown than John.)

143. *feefarm*: a form of tenure whereby land is held in perpetuity at a yearly rent, usually without homage, fealty, or other services except those specified in the feoffment.

such contempt abroad as all his lifetime after he was possessed rather with fear of losing his head than with hope of reducing the kingdom of Ireland.

Henry III

During the infancy of Henry III, the barons were troubled in expelling the French, whom they had drawn in against King John. But this price was no sooner come to his majority but the barons raised a long and cruel war against him.

Into these troubled waters the bishops of Rome did cast their nets and drew away all the wealth of the realm by their provisions and infinite exactions, whereby the kingdom was so impoverished as the king was scarce able to feed his own household and train, much less to nourish armies for the conquest of foreign kingdoms. And albeit he had given this land to the Lord Edward, his eldest son, yet could not that worthy prince ever find means or opportunity to visit this kingdom in person. For, from the time he was able to bear arms, he served continually against the barons, by whom he was taken prisoner at the battle of Lewes.[144] And when that rebellion was appeased, he made a journey to the Holy Land (an employment which in those days diverted all Christian princes from performing any great actions in Europe), from whence he was returned when the Crown of England descended upon him.

Edward I

This King Edward I, who was a prince adorned with all virtues, did in managing of his affairs show himself a right good husband,[145] who being owner of a lordship ill-husbanded, doth

144. On the royalist defeat at the Battle of Lewes, May 1264, Henry III and his son Edward, lord of Ireland, were taken prisoner.
145. *husband*: manager, governor.

first enclose and manure his demesnes near his principal house before he doth improve his wastes afar off. Therefore, he began first to establish the commonwealth of England by making many excellent laws and instituting the form of public justice, which remaineth to this day. Next, he fully subdued and reduced the dominion of Wales. Then by his power and authority he settled[146] the kingdom of Scotland. And lastly, he sent a royal army into Gascoigne to recover the duchy of Aquitaine. These four great actions did take up all the reign of this prince. And therefore we find not in any record that this king transmitted any forces into Ireland. But on the other side, we find it recorded both in the annals and in the Pipe Rolls of this kingdom that three several armies were raised of the king's subjects in Ireland and transported, one into Scotland, another into Wales, and the third into Gascoigne, and that several aids were levied here for the setting forth of those armies.*

Edward II

The son and successor of this excellent prince was Edward II, who much against his will sent one small army into Ireland, not with a purpose to finish the conquest, but to guard the person of his minion, Piers Gaveston, who being banished out of England, was made lieutenant of Ireland that so his exile might seem more honorable.

He was no sooner arrived here but he made a journey into the mountains of Dublin, brake and subdued the rebels there, built Newcastle in the Byrne's Country, and repaired Castle Kevin;[147] and after passed up into Munster and Thomond, performing everywhere great service with much virtue and valor. But the king, who could not live without him, revoked him within less

146. *settled*: resolved the problems with.
147. Castle Kevin, located in the Wicklow Mountains, had been burned in 1308.

than a year; after which time the invasion of the Scots and rebellion of the barons did not only disable this king to be a conqueror, but deprived him both of his kingdom and life.* And
when the Scottish nation had overrun all this land under the
conduct of Edward le Bruce (who styled himself "king of Ireland"),[148] England was not then able to send either men or
money to save this kingdom. Only, Roger de Mortimer,[149] then
justice of Ireland, arrived at Youghal, "with 38 soldiers,"[150] saith
Friar Clynn in his annals.[151]

But Bremingham, Verdun, Stapleton, and some other private
gentlemen rose out with the commons of Meath and Uriel, and
at Fagher, near Dundalk (a fatal place to the enemies of the
Crown of England), overthrew a potent army of them:[152] "and
thus," saith the Red Book of the exchequer, wherein the victory
was briefly recorded, "by the common hand of the people and
the right hand of God, the people of God were delivered from
treacherous and premeditated servitude."[153]

148. Following his victory over Edward II on 24 June 1314, the king of Scotland, Robert Bruce, partly to divert Edward's armies from Scotland to Ireland
and partly to extend his own rule, sent his brother Edward, commanding six
thousand soldiers, to Ireland. Landing in Antrim at Larne on 25 May 1315,
Edward made good headway against the English and was crowned king of Ireland near Dundalk on 1 May 1316. Allying himself with certain Irish rulers
such as the Lacys, and reinforced for a while by his brother, Edward Bruce
caused considerable disorder in Ireland until he was killed at Faughart, near
Dundalk, on 14 October 1318. For a discussion of the impact of the Bruce invasion on Ireland, see Robin Frame, *Colonial Ireland, 1169–1369* (Dublin, 1981),
pp. 114–18.
149. Roger Mortimer, first earl of March, justiciar 1319–21.
150. "cum 38 milit[ibus]."
151. John Clynn (fl. 1336), a Franciscan friar, chronicled the years 1315–49.
152. John de Bremingham (or Bermingham) of Tethmoy, lord of Louth,
commanded the English and Irish army which decisively defeated the Scots
under Edward Bruce at Faughart, near Dundalk, on 14 October 1318.
153. "per manus communis populi, et dextram dei deliberatur populus dei
aservitute machinata et praecogitata."

Edward III

In the time of King Edward III, the impediments of the conquest of Ireland are so notorious as I shall not need to express them; to wit, the war which the king had with the realms of Scotland and of France, but especially the wars of France, which were almost continual for the space of forty years. And, indeed, France was a fairer mark to shoot at than Ireland and could better reward the conqueror. Besides, it was an inheritance newly descended upon the king, and therefore he had great reason to bend all his power and spend all his time and treasure in the recovery thereof. And this is the true cause why Edward III sent no army into Ireland till the thirty-sixth year of his reign, when the Lord Lionel brought over a regiment of 1,500 men, as is before expressed; which that wise and warlike prince did not transmit as a competent power to make a full conquest, but as an honorable retinue for his son and, withal, to enable him to recover some part of his earldom of Ulster, which was then overrun with the Irish. But on the other part, though the English colonies were much degenerate in this king's time and had lost a great part of their possessions, yet, lying at the siege of Calais, he sent for a supply of men out of Ireland, which were transported under the conduct of the earl of Kildare and Fulco de la Freyn[154] in the year 1347.*

Richard II

And now are we come again to the time of King Richard II, who for the first ten years of his reign was a minor and much disquieted with popular commotions, and after that was more

154. By summons of Edward III, Maurice FitzGerald, earl of Kildare, and Fulk de la Frene, lord of Listerling (in Kilkenny), brought reinforcements to the siege of Calais in 1347.

troubled with the factions that arose between his minions and the princes of the blood. But at last he took a resolution to finish the conquest of this realm, and to that end he made two royal voyages hither. Upon the first, he was deluded by the feigned submissions of the Irish; but upon the later, when he was fully bent to prosecute the war with effect, he was diverted and drawn from hence by the return of the duke of Lancaster into England and the general defection of the whole realm.

Henry IV

As for Henry IV, he, being an intruder upon the Crown of England, was hindered from all foreign actions by sundry conspiracies and rebellions at home moved by the House of Northumberland in the North, by the dukes of Surrey and Exeter in the South, and by Owen Glendower in Wales; so as he spent his short reign in establishing and settling himself in the quiet possession of England and had neither leisure nor opportunity to undertake the final conquest of Ireland.

Henry V

Much less could King Henry V perform that work, for in the second year of his reign, he transported an army into France for the recovery of that kingdom and drew over to the siege of Harfleur the prior of Kilmainham[155] with 1,500 Irish; in which great action[156] this victorious prince spent the rest of his life.*

155. Davies has confused the sieges of Harfleur (1415) and Rouen (1418–19). Requiring reinforcements for the siege of Rouen in 1418, Henry V directed Thomas le Botiller (or Butler), prior of Kilmainham, to bring additional troops from Ireland (see A. J. Otway-Ruthven, *A History of Medieval Ireland*, 2d ed. [New York, 1980], pp. 354–55; and Cosgrove, *Late Medieval Ireland*, pp. 73–74).

156. The attempt to recover the kingship of France.

Henry VI

And after his death, the two noble princes his brothers, the duke[s] of Bedford and Gloucester, who during the minority of King Henry VI had the government of the kingdoms of England and France, did employ all their counsels and endeavors to perfect the conquest of France; the greater part whereof being gained by Henry V and retained by the duke of Bedford, was again lost by King Henry VI, a manifest argument of his disability to finish the conquest of this land. But when the civil War between the Two Houses[157] was kindled, the kings of England were so far from reducing all the Irish under their obedience as they drew out of Ireland, to strengthen their parties, all the nobility and gentry descended of English race, which gave opportunity to the Irishry to invade the lands of the English colonies, and did hazard the loss of the whole kingdom. For though the duke of York did, while he lived in Ireland, carry himself respectively[158] towards all the nobility to win the general love of all—bearing equal favor to the Geraldines and the Butlers (as appeared at the christening of George duke of Clarence, who was born in the Castle of Dublin, where he made both the earl of Kildare and the earl of Ormond his gossips); and having occasion divers times to pass into England, he left the Sword[159] with Kildare at one time and with Ormond at another; and when he lost his life at Wakefield,[160] there were slain with him divers of both those families*—yet afterwards, those two noble Houses of Ireland did severally follow the two royal Houses of England, the Geraldines adhering to the House of York, and the Butlers to

157. The Wars of the Roses, between the Houses of York and Lancaster (1455–85).

158. *respectively*: respectfully, courteously.

159. The Sword of State, the most important of the regalia of the Irish viceroys.

160. See note 106.

the House of Lancaster. Whereby it came to pass that not only the principal gentlemen of both those surnames, but all their friends and dependents did pass into England, leaving their lands and possessions to be overrun by the Irish.* These impediments, or rather impossibilities of finishing the conquest of Ireland, did continue till the wars of Lancaster and York were ended, which was about 12 King Edward IV.[161]

Thus hitherto the kings of England were hindered from finishing this conquest by great and apparent impediments: Henry II, by the rebellion of his sons; King John, Henry III, and Edward II, by the Barons' Wars; Edward I, by his wars in Wales and Scotland; Edward III and Henry V, by the wars of France; Richard II, Henry IV, Henry VI, and Edward IV, by domestic contention for the Crown of England itself.

Edward IV

But the fire of the civil war being utterly quenched and King Edward IV settled in the peaceable possession of the Crown of England, what did then hinder that warlike prince from reducing of Ireland also? First, the whole realm of England was miserably wasted, depopulated, and impoverished by the late civil dissensions. Yet as soon as it had recovered itself with a little peace and rest, this king raised an army and revived the title of France again: howbeit, this army was no sooner transmitted and brought into the field but the two kings also were brought to an interview.[162] Whereupon, partly by the fair and white promises of Louis XI, and partly by the corruption of some of King Edward's minions, the English forces were broken and dismissed, and King Edward returned into England, where shortly

161. Actually, the wars between Lancaster and York did not end until the end of Richard III's reign in 1485.

162. In return for Edward IV's disbanding his army and returning to England, Louis XI agreed, by the treaty of Pecquigny in 1475, to pay Edward an annual subsidy. Some years later Louis stopped the payments.

after, finding himself deluded and abused by the French, he died with melancholy and vexation of spirit.

Richard III

I omit to speak of Richard the Usurper,[163] who never got the quiet possession of England, but was cast out by Henry VII within two years and a half after his usurpation.

Henry VII

And for King Henry VII himself, though he made that happy union of the two Houses, yet for more than half the space of his reign there were walking spirits of the House of York, as well in Ireland as in England, which he could not conjure down without expense of some blood and treasure. But in his later times, he did wholly study to improve the revenues of the Crown in both kingdoms, with an intent to provide means for some great action which he intended; which doubtless, if he had lived, would rather have proved[164] a journey into France than into Ireland because in the eyes of all men it was a fairer enterprise.

Henry VIII

Therefore, King Henry VIII in the beginning of his reign made a voyage royal into France,[165] wherein he spent the greatest part of that treasure which his father had frugally reserved, perhaps for the like purpose. In the latter end of his reign, he made

163. In denigrating Richard III, Davies expresses the conventional Elizabethan and Jacobean attitude.
164. *proved*: turned out, or come to be.
165. In 1513 Henry VIII led an expedition against France. In addition, meeting Francis I of France in 1520 in France, at what came to be known as the Field of the Cloth of Gold, Henry VIII endeavored to increase his role as arbiter between Francis and the Holy Roman Emperor Charles V.

the like journey, being enriched with the revenues of the abbey lands.[166] But in the middle time between these two attempts, the great alteration which he made in the state ecclesiastical caused him to stand upon his guard at home, the pope having solicited all the princes of Christendom to revenge his quarrel in that behalf.[167] And thus was King Henry VIII detained and diverted from the absolute reducing of the kingdom of Ireland.

King Edward VI and Queen Mary

Lastly, the infancy of King Edward VI and the coverture[168] of Queen Mary (which are both *non abilities*[169] in the law) did in fact disable them to accomplish the conquest of Ireland.

Queen Elizabeth

So as now this great work did remain to be performed by Queen Elizabeth, who though she were diverted by suppressing the open rebellion in the North;[170] by preventing divers secret conspiracies against her person; by giving aids to the French and states of the Low Countries; by maintaining a naval war with Spain for many years together: yet the sundry rebellions, joined with foreign invasions upon this island, whereby it was in danger to be utterly lost and to be possessed by the enemies of the

166. The royal confiscation of monastic lands began in 1535.

167. Following his divorce from Katherine of Aragon and marriage to Ann Boleyn in 1533, Henry VIII was excommunicated, thereby opening England to a crusade to be undertaken by the Catholic powers.

168. *coverture*: "the condition or position of a woman during her married life, when she is by law under the authority and protection of her husband" (*OED*). (As Protestant attorney-general, Davies minimizes and denigrates the authority of the Catholic Queen Mary [ruled 1553–58], who was married to King Philip II of Spain.)

169. *non abilities*: without legal power (to rule in their own right).

170. Led by the earls of Westmoreland and Northumberland, the Catholic north of England rebelled in 1569.

Crown of England, did quicken Her Majesty's care for the preservation thereof; and to that end, from time to time during her reign, she sent over such supplies of men and treasure as did suppress the rebels and repel the invaders. Howbeit, before the transmitting of the last great army, the forces sent over by Queen Elizabeth were not of sufficient power to break and subdue all the Irishry, and to reduce and reform the whole kingdom. But when the general defection came, which came not without a special providence for the final good of that kingdom (though the second causes thereof were the faint prosecution of the war against Tyrone, the practices of priests and Jesuits, and the expectation of the aids from Spain), then the extreme peril of losing the kingdom, the dishonor and danger that might thereby grow to the Crown of England, together with a just disdain conceived by that great-minded queen that so wicked and ungrateful a rebel should prevail against her (who had ever been victorious against all her enemies), did move and almost enforce her to send over that might army and did, withal, inflame the hearts of the subjects of England cheerfully to contribute towards the maintaining thereof a million of sterling pounds at least, which was done with a purpose only to save, and not to gain, a kingdom; to keep and retain that sovereignty which the Crown of England had in Ireland (such as it was), and not to recover a more absolute dominion. But as it falleth out many times that when a house is on fire, the owner, to save it from burning, pulleth it down to the ground, but that pulling down doth give occasion of building it up again in a better form, so these last wars, which to save the kingdom did utterly break and destroy this people, produced a better effect than was at first expected. For every rebellion, when it is suppressed, doth make the subject weaker and the prince stronger: so this general revolt, when it was overcome, did produce a general obedience and reformation of all the Irishry, which ever before had been disobedient and unreformed. And thereupon ensued the final and full conquest of Ireland.

And thus much may suffice to be spoken touching the defects in the martial affairs and the weak and faint prosecution of the war, and of the several impediments or employments which did hinder or divert every king of England successively from reducing Ireland to their absolute subjection.

[The] Defects in the Civil Policy and Government

It now remaineth that we show the defects of the civil policy and government, which gave no less impediment to the perfection of this conquest.

[The] Laws of England Were Not Given to the Mere Irish; The Mere Irish Not Admitted to Have the Benefit of the Laws of England

The first of that kind doth consist in this: that the Crown of England did not from the beginning give laws to the Irishry; whereas to give laws to a conquered people is the principal mark and effect of a perfect conquest. For albeit King Henry II, before his return out of Ireland, held a council or parliament at Lismore, "where the laws of England were willingly received by all and confirmed by giving a sworn oath,"[171] as Matthew Paris writeth.* And though King John in the twelfth year of his reign did establish the English laws and customs here, and placed sheriffs and other ministers to rule and govern the people according to the law of England,* and to that end, "he had with him discerning men, expert in the law, by whose common council he established and prescribed the English laws to be maintained in Ireland," etc.,[172] as we find it recorded among the Patent Rolls in the Tower (11 Henry III, m.3); though likewise King Henry III

171. "Ubi Leges Angliae ab omnibus sunt gratanter receptae, et Juratoria cautione prastita confirmatae."
172. "Ipse duxit secum viros discretos et legis peritos, quorum communi consilio statuit et praecepti, leges Anglicanas teneri in Hibernia, etc."

did grant and transmit the like charter of liberties to his subjects of Ireland as himself and his father had granted to the subjects of England, as appeareth by another record in the Tower (1 Henry III, pat. m.13), and afterwards by a special writ did command the lord justice of Ireland,

so that when the archbishops, bishops, earls, barons, etc., were called together, he could in their presence make the charter of King John legally binding [?]; which he did make legally binding [?] and to be sworn to by the magnates of Ireland for the observance of the laws and ordinances of England, and that they would uphold and observe those laws; (12 Henry III, claus. m.8)[173]

and after that again, the same king by letters patents under the Great Seal of England did confirm the establishment of the English laws made by King John, in this form:

Since for the common good of the land of Ireland and the unity of the land, it was provided that all the laws and customs which are upheld in the kingdom of England should be upheld in Ireland, and that same land shall submit to those same laws and be governed through them, just as King John, when he was there, did establish and firmly command. Likewise we wish that all writs of common law which are in general use in England shall also be in general use in Ireland. Under our new seal, etc. Myself as witness at Woodstock, etc.;[174]

which confirmation is found among the Patent Rolls in the Tower (30 Henry III [pat. m.20]): notwithstanding, it is evident by all the records of this kingdom that only the English colonies

173. "Quod convocatis Archiepiscopis, Episcopis, Comitibus, Baronibus, etc. Coram eis legi faceret Chartam Regis Johannis; quam ipse legi fecit et jurari a Magnatibus Hiberniae, de legibus et Constitutionibus Angliae observandis, et quod leges illas teneant et observent."

174. "Quia pro Communi utilitate terrae Hiberniae, ac unitate terrarum, de Communi Consilio provisum sit, quod omnes leges et consuetudines quae in regno Angliae tenentur, in Hiberniae teneantur, et eadem terra eiusdem legibus subjaceat, ac per easdem regatur, sicut Johannes Rex, cum illic esset, Statuit et firmiter mandauit; ideo volumus quod omnia bevia de Communi Jure, quae currunt in Anglia, similiter currant in Hibernia, sub novo sigillo nostro, etc. Teste meipso apud Woodstocke, etc."

and some few septs of the Irishry, which were enfranchised by special charters, were admitted to the benefit and protection of the laws of England, and that the Irish generally were held and reputed aliens, or rather enemies, to the Crown of England; insomuch as they were not only disabled to bring any actions, but they were so far out of the protection of the law as it was often adjudged no felony to kill a mere Irishman in the time of peace.

The Mere Irish Reputed Aliens

That the mere Irish were reputed aliens appeareth by sundry records wherein judgment is demanded if they shall be answered in actions brought by them, and likewise by the charters of denization,[175] which in all ages were purchased by them.

In the Commonplea Rolls of 28 Edward III (which are yet preserved in Bremingham's Tower), this case is adjudged: Simon Neill brought an action of trespass against William Newlagh for breaking his close[176] in Clondalkin in the county of Dublin. The defendant doth plead that the plaintiff is "Irish and not of the five [royal] bloods,"[177] and demandeth judgment if he shall be answered. The plantiff replieth

that he is from the five [royal] bloods, that is, from the O'Neills of Ulster, who, through the concession of the ancestors of the lord king, ought to rejoice and enjoy the friendship of free Englishmen, and they are reckoned as free men.[178]

175. *denization*: naturalization.
176. *breaking his close*: entering without the owner's consent upon his land or property; trespassing.
177. "Hibernicus, et non de Quinque sanguinibus."
From very early times, the English accorded the five royal clans of Ulster, Meath, Connaught, Munster, and Leinster special privileges. See Davies below; Geoffrey Hand, *English Law in Ireland, 1290–1324* (Cambridge, Eng., 1967), pp. 205–6; and Frame, *Colonial Ireland*, p. 107.
178. "Quod ipse est de quinque sanguinibus (viz) De les Oneiles de Ulton, qui per Concessionem progenitorum Domini Regis; Libertatibus Anglicis gaudere debent et utuntur, et pro liberis hominibus reputantur."

The defendant rejoineth that the plaintiff is not of the O'Neills of Ulster, "nor of the five [royal] bloods."[179] And thereupon they are at issue: which being found for the plaintiff, he had judgment to recover his damages against the defendant. By this record it appeareth that five principal bloods, or septs, of the Irishry were by special grace enfranchised and enabled to take benefit of the laws of England and that the nation of O'Neills in Ulster was one of the five. And in the like case (3 Edward II, among the Plea Rolls in Bremingham's Tower), all the five septs or bloods "which enjoy the English law as far as the writs apply"[180] are expressed: namely, "O'Neill of Ulster, O'Melaghlin of Meath, O'Connor of Connaught, O'Brien of Thomond, and MacMurrough of Leinster."[181] And yet I find that O'Neill himself long after, viz., in 20 Edward IV, upon his marriage with a daughter of the house of Kildare (to satisfy the friends of the lady) was made denizen by a special act of Parliament (20 Edward IV, c.8).

Again, in 29 Edward I, before the justices in Eire at Drogheda, Thomas le Bottiler brought an action of *detinue*[182] against Robert de Almain for certain goods. The defendant pleadeth

that he need not answer him in this case because he [Thomas] is Irish and not of free blood. And the aforementioned Thomas says that he is English and claims this in order to be investigated concerning his country. Therefore it happened that jurors, etc. [were summoned?]. The jurors say on their honor that the aforementioned Thomas is English, and should be so considered that he might recover [his goods], etc.[183]*

179. "Nec de quinque sanguinibus."

180. "Qui gaudeant lege Anglicana quoad brevia portanda."

181. "Oneil de Ultonia; O Mulaghlin de Midia; O Connoghor de Connacia; O Brien de Thotmonia; et MacMurrough de Lagenia."

182. *action of detinue*: "an action at law to recover a personal chattell (or its value) wrongfully detained by the defendant" (*OED*).

183. "Quod non tenetur ei inde respondere, eo quod est Hibernicus, et non de libero sanguine. Et praedictus Thomas dicit, quod Anglicus est, et hoc petit quod inquiratur per patriam, Ideo fiat inde Jurat, etc. Jurat' dicunt super Sacrament' suum, quod praedict' Thomas Anglicus est, ideo consideratum est quod recuperet, etc."

These two records, among many other, do sufficiently show that the Irish were disabled to bring any actions at the common law. Touching their denizations, they were common in every king's reign since Henry II and were never out of use till His Majesty that now is came to the Crown.

Among the Pleas of the Crown (4 Edward II),* we find a confirmation made by Edward I of a charter of denization granted by Henry II to certain Ostmen, or Easterlings,[184] who were inhabitants of Waterford long before Henry II attempted the conquest of Ireland:

Edward by the Grace of God, etc. To his justiciar in Ireland, greeting. It is apparent to us by the inspection of the charters of the Lord Henry FitzEmperess the king, former lord of Ireland and our great-grandfather, that the Easterlings of Waterford ought to live under the law of the English and be judged by and submit to this same law. Thus to you we command that Gillicrist MacGilmurray, William and John MacGilmurray, and other Easterlings of the city and county of Waterford who trace their lineage from the aforementioned Easterlings of our great-grandfather the Lord Henry, shall maintain the law of England in their territories according to the contents of the aforementioned charter, and insofar as possible that you shall cause them to live according to that same law until we shall have considered another to be ordained by our council. In which affair, etc. By my own witness at Acton Burnell. 5 October, in the eleventh year of our reign.[185]

---

184. *Ostmen*: ("men of the East"), Danish and/or Norwegian Viking settlers, or their descendants.

185. "Edwardus dei gratia, etc. Justitiario suo Hiberniae Salutem: Quia per Inspectionem Chartae Dom. Hen. Reg. filii Imperatricis quondam Dom. Hiberniae proavi nostri nobis Constat, quod Ostmanni de Waterford legem Anglicorum in Hibernia habere, et secundam ipsam legem Judicari et deduci debent: vobis mandamus quod Gillicrist MacGilmurrii, Willielmum et Johannem MacGilmurrii et altos Ostmannos de civitate et Comitatu Waterford, qui de predictis Ostmannis praedict. Dom. Henr. proavi nostri originem duxerunt, legem Anglicorum in partibus illis juxta tenorem Chartae praedict. habere, et eos secundum ipsam legem (quantum in nobis est, deduci faciatis) donec aliud de Consilio nostro inde duxerimus ordinand. In Cuius rei, etc. Teste meipso apud Acton Burnell. 5 Octobris anno regni nostri undecimo."

Again, among the Patent Rolls of 1 Edward IV remaining in the chancery here,* we find a patent of denization granted 13 Edward I, in these words:

Edward by the Grace of God, king of England, lord of Ireland, duke of Aquitaine, etc. To all his bailiffs and those loyal to him in Ireland, greeting. Desiring to grant special favor to Christopher MacDonald the Irishman, we grant in behalf of ourselves and our heirs that this same Christopher shall have his freedom. Since this individual has, moreover, employed the laws of the English in Ireland, we forbid that anything against this concession vex or perturb said Christopher in any way. Witness to this, etc. With myself as witness at Westminster. 27 June in the thirteenth year of our reign[186]

In the same roll, we find another charter of denization, granted in 1 Edward IV in a more larger and beneficial form:

Edward by the Grace of God, etc. To all his bailiffs, etc., greeting. Know that we wish William O'Bolger, present chaplain of the Irish nation, to work with the attendant support of our special grace. We therefore have granted to this same William that he shall have the status of a freeman without conditions, free and quit of all servitude in Ireland, and that this man will be able to use and enjoy the laws of the English in all cases in the same manner in which Englishmen in this said land obey, enjoy, and utilize them. And this man shall make appeal and be appealed to in all of our courts. And he shall be allowed to inquire completely into the lands, holdings, incomes, and household servants for himself and his heirs forever, etc.[187]

---

186. "Edwardus Dei gratia, Rex Angliae, Dom. Hiberniae, Dux Aquitaniae, etc. Omnibus Ballivis et fidelibus suis in Hibernia, Salutem: Volentes Christophero filio Donaldi Hibernico gratiam facere specialem, concedimus pro nobis et haeredibus nostris, quod idem Christopherus hanc habeat libertatem (viz.) Quod ipse de caetero in Hibernia utatur legibus Anglicanis, et prohibemus ne quisquam contra hanc concessionem nostram dictum Christopherum vexet in aliquo vel perturbet. In cuius rei Testimonium, etc. Teste meipso apud Westm. 27 die Junii, anno regni nostri. 13."

187. "Edw. Dei gratia, etc. Omnibus Ballivis, etc., Salutem. Sciatis quod nos volentes Willielmum O Bolgir capellanum de Hibernica Natione existentem, favore prosequi gratioso, de gratia nostra speciali, etc. Concessimus eidem

If I should collect out of the records all the charters of this kind, I should make a volume thereof, but these may suffice to show that the mere Irish were not reputed free subjects nor admitted to the benefit of the laws of England until they had purchased charters of denization.

That the Mere Irish Were Reputed Enemies to the Crown

Lastly, the mere Irish were not only accounted aliens, but enemies, and altogether out of the protection of the law, so as it was no capital offense to kill them; and this is manifest by many records. At a gaol delivery at Waterford, before John Wogan,[188] lord justice of Ireland (4 Edward II), we find it recorded among the Pleas of the Crown of that year*

that Robert le Wayleys was charged in the death of John FitzIvor MacGilmurray, slain feloniously by the same, etc. He came and freely admitted that he killed the above-named John. This notwithstanding, he said that he had not committed a felony by this slaying because he said that the aforementioned John was pure Irish and not of free blood, etc. And when the master of said John, on the day of the slaying (John being his Irishman), shall have asked for payment for the same slain John, Robert will be ready to respond concerning the aforementioned payment just as justice shall recommend. And a certain John le Poer came forward concerning this affair and said on behalf of the lord king that from the time the Lord Henry FitzEmpress, formerly lord of Ireland, now great-great-great grandfather of the lord king, was in Ireland, the aforementioned John FitzIvor MacGilmurray and his predecessors of said surname ought to have kept the law of the English in

---

Willielmo, quod ipse liberi sit Status et liberae conditionis, et ab omni servitute Hibernicae liber et quietus, et quod ipse legibus Anglicanis in omnibus et per omnia uti possit et gaudere, eodem modo, quo homines Anglici infra dictam terram eas habent, et iis gaudeat et utuntur, quodque ipse respondeat, et respondeatur, in quibuscumque Curiis nostris: acomminod. terras, tenementa, redditus, et servitia per quirere possit sibi et haeredibus suis imperpetuum, etc."

188. Justiciar, October 1295–September 1308 and May 1309–August 1312.

Ireland up to the present day and be judged and led according to this same law.[189]

And so pleaded the charter of denization granted to the Ostmen recited before; all which appeareth at large in the said record, wherein we may note that the killing of an Irishman was not punished by our law as manslaughter, which is felony and capital (for our law did neither protect his life nor revenge his death), but by a fine or pecuniary punishment, which is called an *erick*[190] according to the brehon, or Irish, law.

Again, at a gaol delivery before the same lord justice at Limerick, in the roll of the same year, we find that

William FitzRoger, charged in the death of Roger de Canteton, feloniously killed by him, came and said that he had not committed a felony in the aforesaid slaying because he said that the aforementioned Roger was an Irishman and not of free blood. He also said that the said Roger was of the surname of O'Driscoll and not of the surname of Canteton; and for this he places himself under oath to his country, etc. And the jurors say on their honor that the aforesaid Roger is an Irishman and of the surname of O'Driscoll, and his whole life was spent in Ireland. Therefore, the aforementioned William is free from said felony. But because the aforesaid Roger O'Driscoll was an Irishman of the lord king, said William shall be committed to jail until such time as he shall

189. "Quod Robertus le Wayleys rectatus de morte Johannis filii Ivor MacGillemory felonice per ipsum interfecti, etc. Venit et bene cognovit quod praedictum Johannem interfecit: dicit tamen quod per eius interfectionem feloniam committere non potuit, quia dicit, quod praedictus Johannes fuit purus Hibernicus, et non de libero sanguine, etc. Et cum Dominus dicti Johannis (cuius Hibernicus idem Johannes fuit) die quo interfectus fuit, solutionem pro ipso Johanne Hibernico suo sic interfecto petere voluerit, ipse Robertus paratus erit ad respondend' de solutione praedict prout Justitia sua debit. Et super hoc venit quidam Johannes le Poer, et dicit pro Domino Rege, quod praedict. Johannes filius Ivor MacGillemory, et antecessores sui de cognonime praedict. a tempore quo Dominus Henricus filius Imperatricis, quondam Dominus Hiberniae, Tritavus Domini Regis nunc, fuit in Hibernia, legem Anglicorum in Hibernia usque ad hunc diem habere, et secundum ipsam legem Judicari et deduci debent."

190. *erick*: from the Gaelic *eiric* ("blood-fine"); a fine paid by the malefactor to the relatiives of the person he had killed.

find pledges for five marks to give the lord king in payment of the aforementioned Irishman.[191]

But on the other side, if the jury had found that the party slain had been of English race and nation, it had been adjudged felony, as appeareth by a record of 29 Edward I in the Crown Office here:*

In the presence of Walter L'Enfant and his associate itinerant justices at Drogheda in county Louth: John Lawrence, accused of the death of Galfrid Dowdall, came and does not deny the said death, but says that this Galfrid was Irish, and not of free blood, and for good or evil pledges this by his country, etc. And the jurors swear that Galfrid was English, and therefore said John is guilty of the death of said Galfrid. Therefore, he is fined goods worth 13*s.* for which Hugo Viscount of of Clinton gave surety.[192]

Hence it is that in all the Parliament Rolls which are extant from 40 Edward III, when the Statutes of Kilkenny were enacted, till the reign of King Henry VIII, we find the degenerate and disobedient English called "rebels," but the Irish which

191. "Willielmus filius Rogeri rectatus de morte Rogeri de Canteton felonice per ipsum interfecti, venit et dicit, quod feloniam per interfectionem praedictam committere non potuit, quia dicit quod praedict. Rogerus Hibernic. est, et non de libero sanguine; dicit etiam quod praedict. Rogerus fuit de Cognomine de Ohederiscal et non de cognonime de cantetons, et de hoc ponit se super patriam, etc. Et Jurati dicunt super Sacram. suum quod praedictus Rogerus Hibernicus fuit et de cognonime de Ohederiscal et pro Hibernico habebatur tota vita sua. Ideo praedict. Willielmus quoad feloniam praedict. quietus. Sed quia praedictus Rogerus Ottederiscall fuit Hibernicus Domini Regis, praedict. Willielmus recommittatur Gaolae, quousque plegios invenerit de quinque marcis solvendis Domino Regi pro solutione praedicti Hibernici."

192. "Coram Waltero Lenfant et sociis suis Justitiariis Itinerantibus apud Drogheda in Comitatu Louth. Johannes Laurens indictat. de morte Galfridi Douedal venit et non dedicit mortem praedictam: sed dicit quod preadict. Galfridus fuit Hibernicus, et non de libero sanguine, et de bono et malo ponit se super patriam, etc. Et Jurat. dicunt super Sacram. suum quod praedict. Galfridus Anglicus fuit, et ideo praedict. Johannes culpabilis est de morte Galfridi praedict. Ideo suspend. Catalla 13.s. unde Hugo de Clinton Vicecom. respondet."

were not in the king's peace are called "enemies." Statute Kilkenny, c.1.10 and 11; 11 Henry IV, c.24; 10 Henry VI, c.1.18; 18 Henry VI, c.4; 5 Edward IV, c.6; 10 Henry VII, c.17*—all these statutes speak of English "rebels" and Irish "enemies," as if the Irish had never been in condition of subjects, but always out of the protection of the law and were indeed in worse case than aliens of any foreign realm that was in amity with the Crown of England. For by divers heavy penal laws, the English were forbidden to marry, to foster, to make gossips with the Irish, or to have any trade or commerce in their markets or fairs. Nay, there was a law made no longer since than 28 Henry VIII* that the English should not marry with any person of Irish blood, though he had gotten a charter of denization, unless he had done both homage and fealty to the king in the chancery and were also bound by recognizance with sureties to continue a loyal subject. Whereby it is manifest that such as had the government of Ireland under the Crown of England did intend to make a perpetual separation and enmity between the English and the Irish, pretending, no doubt, that the English should in the end root out the Irish; which the English not being able to do did cause a perpetual war between the nations, which continued four hundred and odd years, and would have lasted to the world's end if in the end of Queen Elizabeth's reign the Irishry had not been broken and conquered by the sword, and since the beginning of His Majesty's reign had not been protected and governed by the law.

The Irish Did Desire to Be Admitted to the Benefit and Protection of the English Laws, but Could Not Obtain It

But perhaps the Irishry in former times did willfully refuse to be subject to the laws of England and would not be partakers of the benefit thereof, though the Crown of England did desire it; and therefore they were reputed aliens, outlaws, and enemies.

Assuredly, the contrary doth appear, as well by the charters of denization purchased by the Irish in all ages, as by a petition preferred by them to the king (2 Edward III [claus.17]), desiring that an act might pass in Ireland whereby all the Irishry might be enabled to use and enjoy the laws of England without purchasing of particular denizations; upon which petition, the king directed a special writ to the lord justice, which is found amongst the Close Rolls in the Tower of London, in this form:

The king to his dear and faithful John Darcy *le neveu*, his justiciar in Ireland, greeting. A petition has come before us from certain men in Ireland that we might grant by statute that all Irishmen who so wish may use the laws of the English. Since they do not have what is here requisite to demand foreign charters from us, we wish to know for certain if we may act on this without prejudice to you, and command that in your next parliament you make diligent inquiries into the desire of the great lords of that land concerning this matter and that you will communicate that which you discover there to us together with counsel and advice.[193]

Whereby I collect that the great lords of Ireland had informed the king that the Irishry might not be naturalized without damage and prejudice either to themselves or to the Crown.

But I am well assured that the Irishry did desire to be admitted to the benefit of the law, not only in this petition exhibited to King Edward III, but by all their submissions made to King Richard II and to the Lord Thomas of Lancaster before the Wars of the Two Houses, and afterwards to the Lord Leonard Grey

193. "Rex dilecto et fideli suo Johannis Darcile Nepieu Justic. suo Hiber niae, Salutem. Ex parte quorundam hominum de Hibernia nobis extitit supplicatum, ut per Statutum inde faciendum concedere velimus, quod omnes Hibernici qui voluerint, legibus utantur Anglicanis: ita quod necesse non habeant super hoc Chartas alienas a nobis impetrare: nos igitur Certiorari volentes si sine alieno praejudicio praemissis annuere valeamus, vobis mandamus quod volunt atem magnatum terr. illius in proximo Parliamento nostro ibidem tenendo super hoc cum diligentia perscrutari facias: et de eo quod inde inveneritis una cum Consilio et advisamento nobis certificetis, etc."

and Sir Anthony St. Leger,[194] when King Henry VIII began to reform this kingdom. In particular, the Byrnes of the Mountains in 34 Henry VIII desire that their country might be made shire-ground[195] and called the county of Wicklow;* and in 23 Henry VIII, O'Donnell doth covenant with Sir William Skeffington, "that if the king wishes to reform Ireland,"[196] whereof it should seem he made some doubt, that he and his people would gladly be governed by the laws of England. Only that ungrateful traitor Tyrone, though he had no color or shadow of title to that great lordship, but only by grant from the Crown and by the law of England (for by the Irish law he had been ranked with the meanest[197] of his sept), yet in one of his capitulations with the state he required that no sheriff might have jurisdiction within Tyrone and consequently that the laws of England might not be executed there: which request was never before made by O'Neill or any other lord of the Irishry when they submitted themselves; but contrariwise they were humble suitors to have the benefit and protection of the English laws.

What Mischief Did Grow by Not Communicating the English Laws to the Irish

This, then, I note as a great defect in the civil policy of this kingdom, in that for the space of 350 years at least after the conquest first attempted, the English laws were not communicated to the Irish, nor the benefit and protection thereof allowed unto them, though they earnestly desired and sought the same. For, as

194. Leonard Grey, lord deputy 1536–40; Anthony St. Leger, lord deputy 1540–47, 1550–51, and 1553–56.

195. *shire-ground*: "country divided into shires; a tract of country subject to the control of the authorities of a shire" (*OED*); hence land over which the Crown had extended its administrative authority.

196. "Quod si Dominus Rex velit reformare Hiberniam."

197. *meanest*: lowest, least important. (Davies maintains this claim because Hugh O'Neill was the second son of the younger, and illegitimate, son of Conn Baccagh, first earl of Tyrone.)

long as they were out of the protection of the law, so as every Englishman might oppress, spoil, and kill them without controlment, how was it possible they should be other than outlaws and enemies to the Crown of England? If the king would not admit them to the condition of subjects, how could they learn to acknowledge and obey him as their sovereign? When they might not converse or commerce with any civil men, nor enter into any town or city without peril of their lives, whither should they fly but into the woods and mountains, and there live in a wild and barbarous manner? If the English magistrates would not rule them by the law which doth punish treason and murder and theft with death, but leave them to be ruled by their own lords and laws, why should they not embrace their own brehon law, which punisheth no offense but with a fine or *erick*? If the Irish be not permitted to purchase estates of freeholds or inheritance which might descend to their children according to the course of our common law, must they not continue their custom of tanistry[198] which makes all their possessions uncertain and brings confusion, barbarism, and incivility? In a word, if the English would neither in peace govern them by the law, nor could in war root them out by the sword, must they not needs be pricks in their eyes and thorns in their sides till the world's end? —and so the conquest never be brought to perfection?

What Good Would Have Ensued if the Mere Irish Had Been Governed by the English Laws

But on the other side, if from the beginning the laws of England had been established, and the brehon or Irish law

198. *tanistry*: from the Gaelic *tanaiste* ("next heir to an estate," or "next chieftain of a clan"); hence "a system of life-tenure among the ancient Irish and Gaels, whereby the succession to an estate or dignity was conferred by election upon the 'eldest and worthiest' among the surviving kinsmen of the deceased lord" (*OED*). (The selection of the *tanist* usually occurred during the chieftain's lifetime to assure a peaceful succession.)

utterly abolished, as well in the Irish countries as the English colonies; if there had been no difference made between the nations in point of justice and protection, but all had been governed by one equal, just, and honorable law—as Dido speaketh in Virgil: "*Tros Tyriusque mihi nullo discrimine habetur*"[199]—; if upon the first submission made by the Irish lords to King Henry II, "whom they received as lord and king,"[200] saith Matthew Paris; or upon the second submission made to King John, when "more than twenty terrified chiefs did homage and fealty to him out of the greatest fear,"[201] as the same author writeth; or upon the third general submission made to King Richard II, when they did not only do homage and fealty, but bound themselves by indentures and oaths (as is before expressed) to become and continue loyal subjects to the Crown of England—if any of these three kings, who came each of them twice in person into this kingdom, had upon these submissions of the Irishry received them all, both lords and tenants, into their immediate protection; divided their several countries into counties; made sheriffs, coroners, and wardens-of-the-peace therein; sent justices itinerants half-yearly into every part of the kingdom, as well to punish malefactors, as to hear and determine causes between party and party, according to the course of the laws of England; taken surrenders of their lands and territories, and granted estates unto them to hold by English tenures; granted them markets, fairs, and other franchises; and erected corporate towns among them—all which hath been performed since His Majesty came to the Crown—assuredly, the Irish countries had long since been reformed and reduced to peace, plenty, and civility, which are the effects of laws and good government: they had builded houses, planted orchards and gardens, erected townships, and

199. "As far as I am concerned, there shall be no difference between a Trojan and a Tyrian" (Vergil, *Aeneid*, 1.574).
200. "Quem in Regem et Dominum receperunt."
201. "Plusquam viginti Reguli maximo timore perterriti homagium ei et fidelitatem fecerunt."

made provision for their posterities; there had been a perfect union betwixt the nations and, consequently, a perfect conquest of Ireland. For the conquest is never perfect till the war be at an end; and the war is not at an end till there be peace and unity; and there can never be unity and concord in any one kingdom but where there is but one king, one allegiance, and one law.

The English Laws Were Executed
Only in the English Colonies

True it is that King John made twelve shires in Leinster and Munster: namely, Dublin, Kildare, Meath, Uriel, Catherlough,[202] Kilkenny, Wexford, Waterford, Cork, Limerick, Kerry, and Tipperary. Yet these counties did stretch no farther than the lands of the English colonies did extend. In them only were the English laws published and put in execution, and in them only did the itinerant judges make their circuits and visitations of justice, and not in the countries possessed by the Irishry, which contained two-third parts of the kingdom at least. And therefore King Edward I, before the Court of Parliament was established in Ireland, did transmit the statutes of England in this form:

The lord king issued his charter with these words: Edward by the Grace of God, king of England, lord of Ireland, etc., to his chancellor in Ireland, greeting. To you we send under our seal certain statutes made recently by us at Lincoln with the assent of the prelates, earls, barons, and the community of our realm, and certain other statutes made at York, which we wish to be observed in our land of Ireland for the common good of our people in this same land, commanding that these statutes be kept in our chancery and enrolled in the rolls of that same chancery, and you shall have them sent to each of our places in our land of Ireland and to each county of this same land for our ministers of these places and the lords of the said counties. And we command that you shall cause these statutes to be observed in each and every article. Witnessed by me at Nottingham, etc.[203]*

202. *Uriel*: Louth; *Catherlough*: Carlow.
203. "Dominus Rex mandauit Breve suum in haec verba: Edwardus Dei

By which writ and by all the Pipe Rolls of that time, it is manifest that the laws of England were published and put in execution only in the counties which were then made and limited, and not in the Irish countries, which were neglected and left wild, and have but of late years been divided in one-and-twenty counties more.

Again, true it is that by the Statute of Kilkenny [c. 4], enacted in this kingdom in 40 King Edward III, the brehon law was condemned and abolished, and the use and practice thereof made high treason. But this law extended to the English only, and not to the Irish, for the law is penned in this form:

Item: forasmuch as the diversity of government by diverse laws in one land doth make diversity of ligeance[204] and debates between the people, it is accorded and established that hereafter no Englishman have debate with another Englishman, but according to the course of the common law; and that no Englishman be ruled in the definition of their debates by the march law[205] or the brehon law, which by reason ought not to be named a law, but an evil custom; but that they be ruled as right is by the common law of the land as the lieges of our sovereign lord the king; and if any do to the contrary and thereof be attainted, that he be taken and imprisoned and judged as a traitor: and that hereafter there be no diversity of ligeance between the English born in Ireland and the

---

gratia, Rex Angliae, Dominus Hiberniae, etc., Cancellario suo Hiberniae, Salutem. Quaedam statuta per nos de assensu Praelatorum, Comitum, Baronum et Communitat. regni nostri nuper apud Lincolne, et quaedam alia statuta postmodum apud Eborum facta, quae in dicta terra nostra Hiberniae ad Communem utilitatem populi nostri eiusdem terrae observari volumus, vobis mittimus sub sigillo nostro, mandantes quod statuta illa in dicta a Cancellaria nostra Custodiri, ac in rotulis eiusdem Cancellariae irrotulari, et ad singulas placeas nostras in terra nostra Hiberniae, et singulos Commitatus eiusdem terrae mitti faciatis ministris nostris placearum illarum, et Vicecomitibus dictorum Comitatuum: mandantes, quod statuta illa coram ipsis publicari et ea in omnibus et singulis Articulis suis observari firmiter faciatis. Teste meipso apud Nottingham, etc."

204. *ligeance*: "duty of fidelity of " subjects to their "sovereign or government" (*OED*).

205. *March law*: border, frontier, or martial law; hence law adapted to the exigencies of frontier life and border warfare.

English born in England, but that all be called and reputed English and the lieges of our sovereign lord the king, etc.

This law was made only to reform the degenerate English, but there was no care taken for the reformation of the mere Irish; no ordinance, no provision made for the abolishing of their barbarous customs and manners; insomuch as the law then made for apparel and riding in saddles, after the English fashion, is penal only to Englishmen, and not to the Irish.

The Romans Did Communicate Their Laws to the Nations Which They Conquered

But the Roman state, which conquered so many nations, both barbarous and civil, and therefore knew by experience the best and readiest way of making a perfect and absolute conquest, refused not to communicate their laws to the rude and barbarous people whom they had conquered; neither did they put them out of their protection after they had once submitted themselves. But contrariwise, it is said of Julius Caesar, *qua vicit victos protegit ille manu.*[206] And again, of another emperor:

> Fecisti patriam diversis gentibus unam,
> Profuit invitis te dominante capi;
> Dumque offers victis proprii consortia juris,
> urbem fecisti, quod prius orbis erat.[207]

And of Rome itself:

> Haec est, in gremium victos quae sola recepit,
> Humanumque genus communi nomine fovit,

206. "he protects those he conquered with the hand with which he conquered them."

207. "You have made one fatherland for diverse nations. Because you are their tyrant, it had profited even the unwilling to be conquered. While you offer the protection of the law to the conquered, you have made a city of what used to be the world."

Matris, non dominae, ritu; civesque vocavit,
Quos domuit, nexuque, pio longinqua revinxit.[208]

Therefore, as Tacitus writeth,* Julius Agricola, the Roman general in Brittany, used this policy to make a perfect conquest of our ancestors, the ancient Britons. They were, saith he, rude and dispersed, and therefore prone upon every occasion to make war; but to induce them by pleasure to quietness and rest, he exhorted them in private and gave them helps in common to build temples, houses, and places of public resort. The noblemen's sons he took and instructed in the liberal sciences, etc., preferring the wits of the Britons before the students of France, as being now curious to attain the eloquence of the Roman language, whereas they lately rejected that speech. After that, the Roman attire grew to be in account and the gown to be in use among them. And so by little and little they proceeded to curiosity and delicacies in buildings and furniture of household, in baths and exquisite banquets; and so being come to the height of civility, they were thereby brought to an absolute subjection.

William the Conqueror Governed Both the Normans and the English under One Law

Likewise, our Norman Conquerer,[209] though he oppressed the English nobility very sore and gave away to his servitors the lands and possessions of such as did oppose his first invasion; though he caused all his acts of council to be published in French, and some legal proceedings and pleadings to be framed

---

208. "This is the city that alone has taken the conquered to its bosom and favored the human race with a common name. Proceeding like a mother, not a master, it has called those it conquered citizens and bound them to itself for a long time with the tie of loyalty."

209. William duke of Normandy, who conquered and became king of England (1066–87).

and used in the same tongue, as a mark and badge of a conquest; yet he governed all, both English and Normans, by one and the same law, which was the ancient common law of England long before the Conquest. Neither did he deny any Englishman that submitted himself unto him the benefit of that law, though it were against a Norman of the best rank and in greatest favor—as appeared in the notable controversy between Warin the Norman and Sherborne of Sherborne Castle in Norfolk; for the Conquerer had given that castle to Warin, yet when the [inheritor] thereof had alleged before the king that he never bore arms against him, that he was his subject as well as the other, and that he did inherit and hold his lands by the rules of that law which the king had established among all his subjects, the king gave judgment against Warin and commanded that Sherborne should hold his land in peace.* By this mean, himself obtained a peaceable possession of the kingdom within few years; whereas, if he had cast all the English out of his protection and held them as aliens and enemies to the Crown, the Normans, perhaps, might have spent as much time in the conquest of England as the English have spent in the conquest of Ireland.

King Edward I Did Communicate
the English Laws to the Welshmen

The like prudent course hath been observed in reducing of Wales, which was performed partly by King Edward I and altogether finished by King Henry VIII. For we find by the Statute of Rutland, made 12 Edward I, when the Welshmen had submitted themselves, *de alto et baso*,[210] to that king, he did not reject and cast them off as outlaws and enemies, but caused their laws and customs to be examined, which were in many points agreeable to the Irish or brehon law. "Having diligently listened to and

210. "high and low."

fully understood these things," saith the king in that ordinance, "we removed certain of them in a council of nobles; certain others we allowed; others we corrected; and still others we ordered to be added and made law"[211]—and so established a commonwealth among them according to the form of the English government. After this, by reason of the sundry insurrections of the barons, the wars in France, and the dissension between the Houses of York and Lancaster, the state of England neglected or omitted the execution of this Statute of Rutland, so as a great part of Wales grew wild and barbarous again. And therefore King Henry VIII, by the statutes of the 27th and 32nd of his reign, did revive and recontinue that noble work begun by King Edward I and brought it indeed to full perfection. For he united the dominion of Wales to the Crown of England and divided it into shires and erected in every shire one borough, as in England, and enabled them to send knights and burgesses to the Parliament; established a Court of Presidency, and ordained that justices of assize and gaol delivery should make their half-yearly circuits there, as in England; made all the laws and statutes of England in force there; and among other Welsh customs abolished that of gavelkind,[212] whereby the heirs female were utterly excluded, and the bastards did inherit as well as the legi[ti]mate, which is the very Irish gavelkind. By means whereof, that entire country in a short time was securely settled in peace and obedience, and hath attained to that civility of manners and plenty of all things, as now we find it not inferior to the best parts of England.

I will therefore knit up this point with these conclusions.

211. "Quibus diligenter auditis et plenius intellectis, quasdam illarum . . . Consilio procerum dilevimus; quasdam permissimus; quasdam correximus; ac etiam quasdam alias adjiciendas et faciend. decrevimus."
212. *gavelkind*: "a system of tribal succession, by which land, on the decease of its occupant, was thrown into the common stock, and the whole area redivided among the members of the" clan (*OED*).

First, that the kings of England which in former ages attempted the conquest of Ireland, being ill-advised and counseled by the great men here, did not upon the submissions of the Irish communicate their laws unto them, nor admit them to the state and condition of free subjects. Secondly, that for the space of two hundred years at least after the first arrival of Henry II in Ireland, the Irish would gladly have embraced the laws of England, and did earnestly desire the benefit and protection thereof, which being denied them did of necessity cause a continual bordering war between the English and the Irish. And lastly, if, according to the examples before recited, they had reduced as well the Irish countries as the English colonies under one form of civil government (as now they are), the meres and bounds of the marches and borders had been long since worn out and forgotten (for it is not fit, as Cambrensis writeth,* that a king of an island should have any marches or borders but the four seas); both nations had been incorporated and united; Ireland had been entirely conquered, planted, and improved, and returned a rich revenue to the Crown of England.

[The] Lands Conquered from the Irish Were Not Well Distributed

The next error in the civil policy which hindered the perfection of the conquest of Ireland did consist in the distribution of the lands and possessions which were won and conquered from the Irish. For the scopes of lands which were granted to the first adventurers were too large, and the liberties and royalties which they obtained therein were too great for subjects, though it stood with reason that they should be rewarded liberally out of the fruits of their own labors, since they did *militare propriis stipendiis*[213] and received no pay from the Crown of England.

213. "military service for wages."

Notwithstanding, there ensued divers inconveniences that gave great impediment to the conquest.

The Proportions of Land Granted
to the First Adventurers Were Too Large

First, the Earl Strongbow was entitled to the whole kingdom of Leinster, partly by invasion and partly by marriage, albeit he surrendered the same entirely to King Henry II, his sovereign, for that with his license he came over and with the aid of his subjects he had gained that great inheritance. Yet did the king regrant back again to him and his heirs all that province, reserving only the city of Dublin and the cantreds[214] next adjoining, with the maritime towns and principal forts and castles.* Next, the same king granted to Robert FitzStephen and Miles Cogan[215] the whole kingdom of Cork, from Lismore to the sea.* To Philip le Braose[216] he gave the whole kingdom of Limerick, with the donation of bishoprics and abbeys (except the city and one cantred of land adjoining).* To Sir Hugh de Lacy, all Meath; to Sir John de Courcy, all Ulster; to William Burke FitzAudelm, the greatest part of Connaught.* In like manner, Sir Thomas de Clare obtained a grant of all Thomond, and Otho de Grandison, of all Tipperary, and Robert le Poer,[217] of the territory of Waterford (the city itself and the cantred of the Ostmen only excepted).*

214. *cantreds*: districts "containing a hundred townships" (*OED*).

215. Henry II awarded the kingdom of Cork to FitzStephen (d. before 1188) and de Cogan (d. 1182) in 1177, the former taking the area east of the city of Cork, the latter, the western portion.

216. Henry II granted Philip de Braose (or Bruce), a knight of Brecknock (in south Wales), the lordship of Limerick in 1177.

217. Thomas de Clare (d. 1287) received the grant of Thomond on 26 January 1276. Robert le Poer (or Power) received a grant of the royal demesne lands of Waterford in 1177. And sometime after September 1263, de Grandison was granted lands in south Tipperary, formerly held by Walter de Burgo.

All Ireland Distributed to Ten Persons
Of the English Nation

And thus was all Ireland cantonized among ten persons of the English nation; and though they had not gained the possession of one-third part of the whole kingdom, yet in title they were owners and lords of all, so as nothing was left to be granted to the natives.* And therefore we do not find in any record or story for the space of three hundred years after these adventurers first arrived in Ireland that any Irish lord obtained a grant of his country from the Crown, but only the king of Thomond, who had a grant but during King Henry III his minority,* and Roderick O'Connor, king of Connaught, to whom King Henry II, before this distribution made, did grant (as is before declared) "that he [Roderick] shall be king under him," and, moreover, "that he shall hold his land of Connaught properly and in peace, just as he held it before the lord king entered Ireland";[218]* and whose successor, in 24 Henry III, when the Burkes had made a strong plantation there and had well-nigh expelled him out his territory, he came over into England (as Matthew Paris writeth)* and made complaint to King Henry III of this invasion made by the Burkes upon his land, insisting upon the grants of King Henry II and King John,* and affirming that he had duly paid an yearly tribute of 5,000 marks for his kingdom. Whereupon, the king called unto him the Lord Maurice FitzGerald, who was then lord justice of Ireland and president in the court, and commanded him that he should root out that unjust plantation which Hubert earl of Kent[219] had in the time of his greatness planted in those parts, and wrote withal to the great men of Ireland to remove the Burkes and to establish the king of Con-

---

218. "Ut sit Rex sub eo, etc. . . . Ut teneat terram suam Conactiae ita bene et in pace, sicut tenuit antequam Dominus Rex intravet Hiberniam."

219. Hubert de Burgo (d. 1243), earl of Kent, and justiciar of England (1215–32), served a short tenure as justiciar of Ireland in 1232.

naught in the quiet possession of his kingdom. Howbeit, I do not read that the king of England's commandment or direction in this behalf was ever put in execution. For the truth is, Richard de Burgo had obtained a grant of all Connaught after the death of the king of Connaught then living, for which he gave a thousand pound, as the record in the tower reciteth (3 Henry III, claus. 2).

The Liberties Granted to the First Adventurers Were Too Great: Eight Counties Palatines in Ireland at One Time

And besides, our great English lords could not endure that any kings should reign in Ireland but themselves; nay, they could hardly endure that the Crown of England itself should have any jurisdiction or power over them. For many of these lords to whom our kings had granted these petty kingdoms did by virtue and color of these grants claim and exercise *jura regalia*[220] within their territories, insomuch as there were no less than eight counties palatines[221] in Ireland at one time.

For William Marshal,[222] earl of Pembroke, who married the daughter and heir of Strongbow, being lord of all Leinster, had royal jurisdiction throughout all that province. This great lord had five sons and five daughters; every of his sons enjoyed that seigniory successively, and yet all died without issue.* Then this great lordship was broken and divided, and partition made between the five daughters, who were married into the noblest houses of England. The county of Catherlough was allotted to the eldest; Wexford to the second; Kilkenny to the third; Kildare

---

220. *jura regalia*: "royal" or absolute right.

221. *counties palatines*: lordships wherein the lords, usually earls, possessed absolute authority. See Hand, *English Law in Ireland*, pp. 113–34, for a discussion of the Anglo-Irish liberties in medieval Ireland.

222. Earl of Pembroke (1199–1219) and regent of England during the minority of Henry III.

to the fourth; the greatest part of Leix, now called the Queen's County, to the fifth:* in every of these portions, the coparceners[223] severally exercised the same jurisdiction royal which the earl marshal and his sons had used in the whole province. Whereby it came to pass that there were five county palatines erected in Leinster. Then had the lord of Meath the same royal liberty in all that territory; the earl of Ulster in all that province; and the lord of Desmond and Kerry within that county. All these appear upon record and were all as ancient as the time of King John;* only, the liberty of Tipperary, which is the only liberty that remaineth at this day, was granted to James Butler, the first earl of Ormond, in 3 King Edward III.*

These absolute palatines[224] made barons and knights, did exercise high justice in all points within their territories, erected courts for criminal and civil causes, and for their own revenues (in the same form as the king's courts were established at Dublin), made their own judges, seneschals, sheriffs, coroners, and escheators;[225]* so as the king's writ did not run in those counties (which took up more than two parts of the English colonies), but only in the church lands lying within the same, which were called the "cross," wherein the king made a sheriff. And so in each of these counties palatines there were two sheriffs, one of the liberty and another of the cross—as in Meath we find a sheriff of the liberty and a sheriff of the cross, and so in Ulster and so in Wexford. And so at this day, the earl of Ormond maketh a sheriff of the liberty, and the king a sheriff of the cross of Tipperary. Hereby it is manifest how much the king's jurisdiction was restrained and the power of these lords enlarged by these high privileges. And it doth further appear, by one article among others preferred to King Edward III touching the refor-

223. *coparceners*: cosharers; coheirs.
224. *palatines*: counts palatine (see note 221).
225. *escheators*: officials whose duties involved taking legal notice of forfeited, escheated property.

mation of the state of Ireland, which we find in the Tower, in
these words:

> Likewise, the franchises granted in Ireland, which are royal (like
> Durham and Chester), cost you great profit, as well as a great portion
> of the obedience of the enfranchised persons; and in each of which
> franchise is a chancery, an exchequer, and a court of pleas—as well as
> of the Crown, so with the other liberties—and they have granted char-
> ters of pardon [or remission], and pursuant to law and reasonable cause
> taken possession from your hand, to your great profit; and likely [to be]
> restored by command outside England [only] to [your] detriment,
> etc.[226]

Unto which article, the king made answer: "The king wishes
that the franchises which are and shall be remanded for just
cause should not be restored before the king has been apprised
of the reason for the seizing of them"[227] (26 Edward III, claus.
m.1). Again, these great undertakers were not tied to any form
of plantation, but all was left to their discretion and pleasure.
And although they builded castles and made freeholders, yet
were there no tenures or services reserved to the Crown, but the
lords drew all the respect and dependency of the common people
unto themselves. Now let us see what inconveniences did arise by
these large and ample grants of lands and liberties to the first adventurers in the conquest.

---

226. "Item les francheses grantes in Ireland, que sont Roialles, telles come
Duresme et Cestre, vous oustont cybien de les profits, Come de graunde partie
de obeisance des persons enfrancheses, et en quescun franchese est Chan-
cellerie, Chequer et Conusans de pleas, cybien de la Coronne, come autre com-
munes, et grantont auxi Charters de pardon; et sont sovent per ley et reasonable
cause seisses envostre main, a grand profit de vous; et leigerment restitues per
maundement hors de Engleterre, a damage, etc."
227. "Le Roy voet que les francheses que sont et serront per juste cause
prises en sa main, ne soent my restitues, avant que le Roy soit certifie de la
cause de la prise de icelles. 26. Ed. 3. Claus. m. 1."

The Inconveniences Which Grew
by the Large Grants of Lands and Liberties

Assuredly, by these grants of whole provinces and petty kingdoms those few English lords pretended to be proprietors of all the land, so as there was no possibility left of settling the natives in their possessions, and by consequence the conquest became impossible without the utter extirpation of all the Irish, which these English lords were not able to do, nor perhaps willing if they had been able. Notwithstanding, because they did still hope to become lords of those lands which were possessed by the Irish, whereunto they pretended title by their large grants, and because they did fear that if the Irish were received into the king's protection and made liegemen and free subjects, the state of England would establish them in their possessions by grants from the Crown, reduce their countries into counties, ennoble some of them, and enfranchise all and make them amenable to the law, which would have abridged and cut off a great part of that greatness which they had promised unto themselves, they persuaded the king of England that it was unfit to communicate the laws of England unto them; that it was the best policy to hold them as aliens and enemies, and to prosecute them with a continual war.

The English Lords in Ireland Made War
and Peace at Their Pleasure

Hereby they obtained another royal prerogative and power, which was to make war and peace at their pleasure in every part of the kingdom; which gave them an absolute command over the bodies, lands, and goods of the English subjects here. And besides, the Irish inhabiting the lands fully conquered and reduced, being in condition of slaves and villeins, did render a greater profit and revenue than if they had been made the king's free subjects.

And for these two causes last expressed, they were not willing to root out all the Irishry. We may not therefore marvel that when King Edward III, upon the petition of the Irish (as is before remembered) was desirous to be certified "whether according to the will of his magnates in the next parliament to be held in Ireland, he can grant without prejudice to others that by statute made thereafter the Irish may use the laws of the English or royal charters they might later request,"[228] that there was never any statute made to that effect. For the truth is that those great English lords did to the uttermost of their power cross and withstand the enfranchisement of the Irish for the causes before expressed; wherein I must still clear and acquit the Crown and state of England of negligence or ill policy, and lay the fault upon the pride, covetousness, and ill-counsel of the English planted here, which in all former ages have been the chief impediments of the final conquest of Ireland.

The War and Dissension of the English Lords, One with Another

Again, those large scopes of land and great liberties, with the absolute power to make war and peace, did raise the English lords to that height of pride and ambition as that they could not endure one another, but grew to a mortal war and dissension among themselves, as appeareth by all the records and stories of this kingdom. First, in the year 1204 the Lacys of Meath made war upon Sir John Courcy; who having taken him by treachery, sent him prisoner into England. In the year 1210, King John coming over in person expelled the Lacys out of the kingdom for their tyranny and oppression of the English; howbeit, upon payment of great fines, they were afterward restored.* In the year

228. "De voluntate magnatum suorum in proximo Parliamento in Hibernia tenend. si sine alieno praejudicio concedere possit, quod per statut. inde fact. Hibernici utantur legibus Anglicanis, sive chartis Regiis inde Impetrandis."

1228, that family being risen to a greater height—for Hugh de Lacy, the younger, was created earl of Ulster after the death of Courcy without issue—there arose dissension and war between that House and William Marshal, lord of Leinster, whereby all Meath was destroyed and laid waste. In the year 1264, Sir Walter Burke, having married the daughter and heir of Lacy, whereby he was earl of Ulster in right of his wife, had mortal debate with Maurice FitzMaurice the Geraldine for certain lands in Connaught, so as all Ireland was full of wars between the Burkes and Geraldines (say our annals); wherein Maurice FitzMaurice grew so insolent as that upon a meeting at [Tristledermot] he took the lord justice himself, Sir Richard Capell, prisoner, with divers lords of Munster being then in his company.[229] In the year 1288, Richard Burke, earl of Ulster (commonly called the Red Earl), pretending title to the lordship of Meath, made war upon Sir Theobald de Verdun and besieged him in the Castle of Athlone. Again, in the year 1292, John FitzThomas the Geraldine, having by contention with the Lord Vescy gotten a goodly inheritance in Kildare, grew to that height of imagination (saith the story) as he fell into difference with divers great noblemen, and among many others, with Richard the Red Earl, whom he took prisoner, and detained him in Castle Lea;[230] and by that dissension, the English on the one side, and the Irish on the other, did waste and destroy all the country.*

229. The details of the dispute between Maurice FitzMaurice and Walter de Burgo, earl of Ulster, remain unclear, but, as Davies maintains, the conflict clearly created a situation bordering on anarchy. In the event Davies alludes to, FitzMaurice on 6 December 1264 captured the justiciar Richard Capell (or Richard de la Rochelle), signaling the outbreak of civil war (see Otway-Ruthven, *History of Medieval Ireland*, pp. 195–97). (Tristledermot, the modern Castledermot, is in southern County Kildare; Castle Lea in northeastern County Laois.)

230. The conflict between FitzThomas and his overlord William de Vescy, lord of Kildare and justiciar (1290–94), came to a head when the two contentious landowners were to submit to a wager of battle in July 1294. De Vescy won by default when FitzThomas failed to appear. In another action, in December 1294, FitzThomas took the Red Earl prisoner.

After, in the year 1311, the same Red Earl, coming to besiege Bunratty[231] in Thomond, which was then held by Sir Richard de Clare as his inheritance, was again taken prisoner and all his army (consisting for the most part of English) overthrown and cut in pieces by Sir Richard de Clare.* And after this again, in the year 1327, most of the great houses were banded one against another, viz., the Geraldines, Butlers, and Breminghams on the one side, and the Burkes and Poers on the other, the ground of the quarrel being none other but that the Lord Arnold Poer had called the earl of Kildare "rhymer." [232] But this quarrel was prosecuted with such malice and violence as the counties of Waterford and Kilkenny were destroyed with fire and sword, till a parliament was called of purpose to quiet this dissension.

Shortly after, the Lord John Bremingham, who was not long before made earl of Louth for that notable service which he performed upon the Scots between Dundalk and the Faughart,[233] was so extremely envied by the Gernons, Verduns, and others of the ancient colony planted in the county of Louth, as that in the year 1329 they did most wickedly betray and murder that earl, with divers principal gentlemen of his name and family, using the same speech that the rebellious Jews are said to use in the Gospel: *nolumus hunc regnare super nos.*[234] After this, the Geraldines and the Butlers, being become the most potent families in the kingdom (for the great lordship of Leinster was divided among coparceners whose heirs for the most part lived

231. Bunratty Castle stands in southern county Clare, near the Shannon.

232. At an assembly, sometime after Michelmas 1327, Arnold le Poer (or Power) called Maurice FitzThomas (who became the fourth earl of Kildare in 1331) a "rhymer," thereby insultingly associating him with a kind of enteriner or player condemned and later outlawed by the Crown because it felt such entertainers assisted and guided the rebellious Irish. (See James Grace, *Annales Hiberniae*, ed. Richard Butler [Dublin, 1842], pp. 104–5.)

233. See note 152.

234. "we do not want him to rule over us." (Davies probably alludes to the parable in Luke 19:14 [King James Version]: "we will not have man to reign over us.")

in England; and the earldom of Ulster, with the lordship of Meath, by the match of Lionel duke of Clarence, at last descended upon the crown), had almost a continual war one with another. In the time of King Henry VI (saith Baron Finglas[235] in his *Discourse of the Decay of Ireland*), in a fight between the earls of Ormond and Desmond, almost all the townsmen of Kilkenny were slain. And as they followed contrary parties during the Wars of York and Lancaster, so after that civil dissension ended in England, these Houses in Ireland continued their opposition and feud still, even till the time of King Henry VIII, when by the marriage of Margaret FitzGerald to the earl of Ossory,[236] the Houses of Kildare and Ormond were reconciled and have continued in amity ever since.

Thus, these great estates and royalties granted to the English lords in Ireland begat pride, and pride begat contention among themselves, which brought forth divers mischiefs that did not only disable the English to finish the conquest of all Ireland, but did endanger the loss of what was already gained, and of conquerers made them slaves to that nation which they did intend to conquer. For whensoever one English lord had vanquished another, the Irish waited and took the opportunity and fell upon that country which had received the blow, and so daily recovered some part of the lands which were possessed by the English colonies.

Besides, the English lords to strengthen their parties did ally themselves with the Irish and drew them in to dwell among them, gave their children to be fostered by them, and, having no other means to pay or reward them, suffered them to take coyne and livery[237] upon the English freeholders; which oppression was

235. See note 58.
236. Margaret FitzGerald, daughter of Gerald FitzGerald, eighth earl of Kildare, married Piers Butler (d. 1539), first earl of Ossory and eighth earl of Ormond.
237. For the Irish practice of fostering, see pp. 169–70.

so intolerable as that the better sort were enforced to quit their freeholds and fly into England and never returned, though many laws were made in both realms to remand them back again.* And the rest which remained became degenerate and mere Irish, as is before declared. And the English lords, finding the Irish exactions to be more profitable than the English rents and services, and loving the Irish tyranny (which was tied to no rules of law or honor) better than a just and lawful seigniory, did reject and cast off the English law and government; received the Irish laws and customs;* took Irish surnames (as MacWilliam, MacPheris, MacYoris); refused to come to the parliaments which were summoned by the king of England's authority; and scorned to obey those English knights which were sent to command and govern this kingdom; namely, Sir Richard Capel, Sir John Morice, Sir John Darcy, and Sir Ralph Ufford.[238] And when Sir Anthony Lucy,[239] a man of great authority in the time of King Edward III, was sent over to reform the notorious abuses of this kingdom, the king, doubting that he should not be obeyed, directed a special writ or mandate to the earl of Ulster and the rest of the nobility to assist him.* And afterwards, the same king (upon good advice and counsel) resumed[240] those excessive grants of lands and liberties in Ireland by a special ordinance made in England, which remaineth of record in the Tower in this form:

Because many excessive donations of land and liberties have been made in Ireland through the sly contrivance of the claimants, etc. After a council of competent men lent him assistance, the king, wishing to destroy utterly crafty contrivances of this kind, caused the recall of all the aforementioned donations of land and liberties until he was better informed concerning the merits of the donors and the motives for

238. Richard Capell (or de la Rochelle), justiciar 1261–65; John Darcy, justiciar 1329–31, 1332–37, and other times after; Sir John Morice, lord deputy 1341–44 and justiciar 1346; and Ralph de Ufford, justiciar 1344–46.

239. Justiciar 1331–32.

240. *resumed*: recalled; took back; canceled.

granting these gifts and their value. And therefore it was commanded of the lord justice of Ireland that he proceed accordingly, etc.[241]*

Howbeit, there followed upon this resumption such a division and faction between the English of birth and the English of blood and race as they summoned and held several parliaments apart, one from the other. Whereupon, there had risen a general war betwixt them, to the utter extinguishing of the English name and nation in Ireland, if the earl of Desmond, who was head of the faction against the English of birth, had not been sent into England and detained there for a time.[242]* Yet afterwards, these liberties being restored by direction out of England (26 Edward III), complaint was made to the king of the easy restitution, whereunto the king made answer, as is before expressed. So as we may conclude this point with that which we find in the annals published by Master Camden:[243] "The Irish would have been conquered and destroyed if the sedition of the English had not prevented it."[244] Whereunto I may add this note, that though some are of opinion that grants of extraordinary honors and liberties made by a king to his subjects do no more diminish his greatness than when one torch lighteth another—for it hath no less light than it had before: *quis vetat apposito lumen de lumine*

241. "Quia plures excessivae donationes terrarum et libertatum in Hibernia ad subdolam machinationem petentium factae sunt, etc. Rex delusorias huiusmodo machinationes volens elidere, de consilio peritorum sibi assistentium omnes donationes Terrarum et libertatum praedict. duxit revocandas, quousque de meritis donatariorum et causis ac qualitatibus donationum melius fuerit informat et ideo mandatum est Justiciario Hiberniae quod seisiri faciat, etc."

242. Maurice FitzThomas, first earl of Desmond, attainted in 1345, was allowed in 1347 to go to England to answer the charges against him; he returned to Ireland in 1350.

243. William Camden (1551–1623), antiquary and author of the influential *Britannia sive Florentissimorum Regnorum Angliae, Scotiae, Hiberniae* .... (1586).

244. "Hibernici debellati et consumpti fuissent, nisi seditio Anglicorum impedivisset."

sumi?[245]—yet many times inconveniences do arise thereupon, and those princes have held up their sovereignty best which have been sparing in those grants.

The First Adventurers Obtained These Liberal Grants Because the Kings of England Did Not Prosecute the War at Their Own Charge

And truly, as these grants of little kingdoms and great royalties to a few private persons did produce the mischiefs spoken of before, so the true cause of the making of these grants did proceed from this: that the kings of England, being otherwise employed and diverted, did not make the conquest of Ireland their own work and undertake it not royally at their own charge; but as it was first begun by particular adventurers, so they left the prosecution thereof to them and other voluntaries who came to seek their fortunes in Ireland; wherein if they could prevail, they thought that in reason and honor they could do no less than make them proprietors of such scopes of land as they could conquer, people, and plant at their own charge, reserving only the sovereign lordship to the Crown of England. But if the lion had gone to hunt himself, the shares of the inferior beasts had not been so great: if the invasion had been made by an army transmitted, furnished, and supplied only at the king's charges and wholly paid with the king's treasure (as the armies of Queen Elizabeth and King James have been), as the conquest had been sooner achieved, so the servitors had been contented with lesser proportions.

How the State of Rome Rewarded Their Men of War

For when Scipio, Pompey, Caesar, and other generals of Roman armies, as subjects and servants of that state, and with

245. "who forbids the light to spring from the light nearby?"

the public charge, had conquered many kingdoms and commonweals, we find them rewarded with honorable offices and triumphs at their return, and not made lords and proprietors of whole provinces and kingdoms which they had subdued to the empire of Rome.

William the Conqueror

Likewise, when the duke of Normandy had conquered England, which he made his own work and performed it in his own person, he distributed sundry lordships and manors unto his followers, but gave not away whole shires and countries in demesne to any of his servitors whom he most desired to advance. Only, he made Hugh Lupus[246] county palatine of Chester and gave that earldom to him and his heirs to hold the same, "for his independent jurisdiction, just as the king holds England for the Crown."[247]* Whereby that earldom indeed had a royal jurisdiction and seigniory, though the lands of that county in demesne were possessed for the most part by the ancient inheritors.

Wales Distributed to the Lords Marchers

Again, from the time of the Norman Conquest till the reign of King Edward I, many of our English lords made war upon the Welshmen at their own charge (the lands which they gained they held to their own use); were called "lords marchers"; and had royal liberties within their lordships. Howbeit, these particular adventurers could never make a perfect conquest of Wales.

But when King Edward I came in person with his army

---

246. Hugh Lupus of Avranches was made earl of Chester before 1071. (Chester continued as a palatinate until 1536.)

247. "Ita libere ad gladium, sicut Rex tenebat Angliam ad Coronam."

thither; kept his residence and court there; made the reducing of Wales an enterprise of his own, he finished that work in a year or two, whereof the lords marchers had not performed a third part with their continual bordering war for two hundred years before. And withal, we may observe that though this king had now the dominion of Wales in *jure proprietatis*[248] (as the Statute of Rutland affirmeth)—which before was subject unto him, but in *jure feodali*[249]—; and though he had lost divers principal knights and noblemen in that war, yet did he not reward his servitors with whole countries or counties, but with particular manors and lordships: as to Henry Lacy, earl of Lincoln, he gave the lordship of Denbeigh; and to Reginold Grey, the lordship of Ruthin;[250] and so to others. And if the like course had been used in the winning and distributing of the lands of Ireland, that island had been fully conquered before the continent[251] of Wales had been reduced. But the truth is, when private men attempt the conquest of countries at their own charge, commonly their enterprises do perish without success: as when in the time of Queen Elizabeth, Sir Thomas Smith[252] undertook to recover the Ards, and Chatterton[253] to reconquer [the] Fews and Orier, the one lost his son, and the other himself, and both their adventures came to nothing. And as for the crown of England, it hath had the like fortune in the conquest of this land as some purchasers

248. *jure proprietatis*: proprietary right.

249. *jure feodali*: feudal right.

250. Henry Lacy (1249?–1311), third earl of Lincoln, and Reginold Grey, second baron Ruthin, were favorites of Edward I.

251. *continent*: whole area or region.

252. In 1571 Sir Thomas Smith and his son Thomas (d. 1573) privately undertook to colonize an area south of Belfast. The scheme collapsed in 1574. (Ellis, *Tudor Ireland*, pp. 266–67, describes the Smith attempt at plantation. See also David B. Quinn, "Sir Thomas Smith (1513–77) and the Beginnings of English Colonial Theory," *American Philosophical Society Preceedings* 89 (1945):543–60.

253. In 1572, with even less backing and expertise than the Smiths possessed, Thomas Chatterton and his brother futilely tried to colonize an area in the south part of Armagh.

have who desire to buy land at too easy a rate: they find those cheap purchases so full of trouble, as they spend twice as much as the land is worth before they get the quiet possession thereof.

And as the best policy was not observed in the distribution of the conquered lands, so as I conceive that the first adventurers intending to make a full conquest of the Irish were deceived in the choice of the fittest places for their plantation. For they sat down and erected their castles and habitations in the plains and open countries where they found most fruitful and profitable lands, and turned the Irish into woods and mountains; which, as they were proper places for outlaws and thieves, so were they their natural castles and fortifications—thither they drave their preys and stealths; there they lurked and lay in wait to do mischief. These fast[254] places they kept unknown by making the ways and entries thereunto impassable—there they kept their *creaghts*,[255] or herds of cattle, living by the milk of the cow, without husbandry or tillage; there they increased and multiplied unto infinite numbers by promiscuous generation among themselves; there they made their assemblies and conspiracies without discovery. But they discovered the weakness of the English dwelling in the open plains, and thereupon made their sallies and retreats with great advantage. Whereas, on the other side, if the English had builded their castles and towns in those places of fastness, and had driven the Irish into the plains and open countries where they might have had an eye and observation upon them, the Irish had been easily kept in order and in short time reclaimed from their wildness—there they would have used tillage, dwelt together in townships, learned mechanical arts and sciences. The woods had been wasted with the English habita-

254. *fast*: strong, secure against attack; fortified.
255. *creaghts*: from the Gaelic *craoidhecht* ("sheep," "cattle"); herds of cattle moved from pasture to pasture for better grazing.

tions, as they are about the forts of Maryborough and Phillipston,[256] which were built in the fastest places in Leinster, and the ways and passages throughout Ireland would have been as clear and open as they are in England at this day.

The English Lords Did Not Reduce the Woods and Wastes in Forests and Parks

Again, if King Henry II, who is said to be the king that conquered this land, had made forests in Ireland as he did enlarge the forests in England (for it appeareth by *Charta de Foresta* [c. 2 and 3][257] that he aforested many woods and wastes, to the grievance of the subject, which by that law were disaforested); or if those English lords amongst whom the whole kingdom was divided had been good hunters and had reduced the mountains, bogs, and woods within the limits of forests, chases, and parks, assuredly, the very Forest Law and the law *De Malefactoribus in Parcis*[258] would in time have driven them into the plains and countries inhabited and manured, and have made them yield up their fast places to those wild beasts which were indeed less hurtful and wild than they. But it seemeth strange to me that in all the records of this kingdom, I seldom find any mention made of a forest and never of any park or freewarren, considering the great plenty both of vert[259] and venison within this land, and that the chief of the nobility and gentry are descended of English race. And yet at this day there is but one park stored with deer in all this kingdom, which is a park of the earl of Ormond's near Kilkenny. It is then manifest by that which is before expressed that the not communicating of the English laws to the Irish; the

256. The modern Port Laoise and Daingean, respectively.
257. "the Forest Law."
258. "Concerning Wrongdoers [or Trespassers] in Parks."
259. *vert*: "green vegetation growing in a wood or forest and capable of serving as cover for a deer"(*OED*).

overlarge grants of lands and liberties to the English; the plantation made by the English in the plains and open countries, leaving the woods and mountains to the Irish, were great defects in the civil policy and hindered the perfection of the conquest very much. Howbeit, notwithstanding these defects and errors, the English colonies stood and maintained themselves in a reasonable good estate as long as they retained their own ancient laws and customs, according to that of Ennius: *moribus antiquis res stat. Romana virisque.*[260]

The English Colonies Rejected the English Laws and Customs and Embraced the Irish

But when the civil government grew so weak and so loose as that the English lords would not suffer the English laws to be put in execution within their territories and seigniories, but in place thereof both they and their people embraced the Irish customs, then the estate of things, like a game at Irish,[261] was so turned about as the English, which hoped to make a perfect conquest of the Irish, were by them perfectly and absolutely conquered, because *victi victoribus leges dedere*[262]—a just punishment to our nation that would not give laws to the Irish when they might, and therefore now the Irish gave laws to them. Therefore, this defect and failing of the English justice in the English colonies, and the inducing of the Irish customs in lieu thereof, was the main inpediment that did arrest and stop the course of the conquest and was the only mean that enabled the Irishry to recover their strength again.

260. "Rome stands firm on her ancient customs and men."
261. *game at Irish*: a game resembling backgammon or tables in which the possibilities for winning and losing change unexpectedly and frequently.
262. "the vanquished gave laws to the victors."

The Nature of the Irish Customs
The Irish Laws and Customs, Differing from the Laws and Customs of All Civil Nations

For if we consider the nature of the Irish customs, we shall find that the people which doth use them must of necessity be rebels to all good government, destroy the commonwealth wherein they live, and bring barbarism and desolation upon the richest and most fruitful land of the world. For whereas by the just and honorable law of England, and by the laws of all other well-governed kingdoms and commonweals, murder, manslaughter, rape, robbery, and theft are punished with death, by the Irish custom, or brehon law, the highest of these offenses was punished only by fine, which they called an *erick*.

The Irish Law in Criminal Causes

Therefore, when Sir William FitzWilliams, being lord deputy,[263] told Maguire that he was to send a sheriff into Fermanagh, being lately before made a county, "your sheriff," said Maguire, "shall be welcome to me, but let me know his *erick*, or the price of his head aforehand, that if my people cut it off, I may cut the *erick* upon the country." As for oppression, extortion, and other trespasses, the weaker had never any remedy against the stronger: whereby it came to pass that no man could enjoy his life, his wife, his lands or goods in safety if a mightier man than himself had an appetite to take the same from him. Wherein they were little better than cannibals, who do hunt one another, and he that hath most strength and swiftness doth eat and devour all his fellows.

263. FitzWilliams served twice as lord deputy: 1571–75 and 1588–94. The event recalled occurred during his second tenure; see Ellis, *Tudor Ireland*, p. 298.

The Irish Custom of Tanistry

Again, in England and all well-ordered commonweals men have certain estates in their lands and possessions, and their inheritances descend from father to son, which doth give them encouragement to build and to plant and to improve their lands, and to make them better for their posterities. But by the Irish custom of tanistry, the chieftains of every country and the chief of every sept had no longer estate than for life in their chieferies, the inheritance whereof did rest in no man. And these chieferies, though they had some portions of land allotted unto them, did consist chiefly in cuttings and cosheries, and other Irish exactions, whereby they did spoil and impoverish the people at their pleasure. And when their chieftains were dead, their sons or next heirs did not succeed them, but their tanists, who were elective and purchased their elections by strong hand.

The Irish Custom of Gavelkind

And by the Irish custom of gavelkind, the inferior [tenancies] were partible amongst all the males of the sept, both bastards and legitimate. And after partition made, if any one of the sept had died, his portion was not divided among his sons, but the chief of the sept made a new partition of all the lands belonging to that sept and gave everyone his part according to his antiquity.

The Mischiefs That [Did] Arise by These Two Customs

These two Irish customs made all their possessions uncertain, being shuffled and changed and removed so often from one to another by new elections and partitions; which uncertainty of estates hath been the true cause of such desolation and barbarism in this land, as the like was never seen in any country that professed the name of Christ. For though the Irishry be a nation of great antiquity and wanted neither wit nor valor; and though they had received the Christian faith above 1,200 years since, and were lovers of music, poetry, and all kind of learning, and possessed a land abounding with all things necessary for the civil life of man, yet (which is strange to be related) they did never build any houses of brick or stone (some few poor religious houses excepted) before the reign of King Henry II, though they were lords of this island for many hundred years before and since the conquest attempted by the English. Albeit, when they saw us build castles upon their borders, they have only in imitation of us erected some few piles for the captains of the country. Yet I dare boldly say that never any particular person, either before or since, did build any stone or brick house for his private habitation, but such as have lately obtained estates according to the course of the law of England. Neither did any of them in all this time plant any gardens or orchards, enclose or improve their lands, live together in settled villages or towns, nor made any provision for posterity; which being against all common sense and reason, must needs be imputed to those unreasonable customs which made their estates so uncertain and transitory in their possessions. For who would plant or improve or build upon that land which a stranger whom he knew not should possess after his death? For that (as Solomon noteth)[264] is one of the strangest vanities under the sun. And this is the true reason why Ulster and all the Irish countries are found so waste and desolate at this day, and so would they continue till the world's end if these customs were not abolished by the law of England.

Again, that Irish custom of gavelkind did breed another mischief, for thereby, every man being born to land, as well bastard as legitimate, they all held themselves to be gentlemen. And though their portions were never so small and themselves never so poor (for gavelkind must needs in the end make a poor gentility), yet did they scorn to descend to husbandry or merchandise,

264. The theme recurs throughout Ecclesiastes; see particularly chapter 2.

or to learn any mechanical art or science. And this is the true
cause why there were never any corporate towns erected in the
Irish countries. As for the maritime cities and towns, most certain it is that they were built and peopled by the Ostmen or
Easterlings, for the natives of Ireland never performed so good
a work as to build a city. Besides, these poor gentlemen were so
affected unto their small portions of land as they rather chose to
live at home by theft, extortion, and coshering than to seek any
better fortunes abroad, which increased their septs or surnames
into such numbers as there are not to be found in any kingdom
of Europe so many gentlemen of one blood, family, and surname
as there are of the O'Neills in Ulster, of the Burkes in Connaught, of the Geraldines and Butlers in Munster and Leinster.
And the like may be said of the inferior bloods and families.
Whereby it came to pass in times of trouble and dissension that
they made great parties and factions, adhering one to another
with much constancy because they were tied together, *vinculo
sanguinis*;[265] whereas rebels and malefactors which are tied to
their leaders by no band, either of duty or blood, do more easily
break and fall off one from another. And besides, their cohabita-
tion in one country or territory gave them opportunity suddenly
to assemble and conspire and rise in multitudes against the
Crown. And even now, in the time of peace, we find this inconvenience, that there can hardly be an indifferent trial had between the king and the subject, or between party and party, by
reason of this general kindred and consanguinity.

The Wicked Customs of Coyne and Livery

But the most wicked and mischievous custom of all others was
that of coyne and livery, often before mentioned, which consisted
in taking of mansmeat, horsemeat, and money of all the inhabitants of the country at the will and pleasure of the soldier, who,

265. "by a/the bond of blood."

as the phrase of Scripture is, "did eat up the people as it were bread,"[266] for that he had no other entertainment.

The Mischiefs That Did Arise by Coyne and Livery

This extortion was originally Irish, for they used to lay *bonaght* upon their people and never gave their soldier any other pay. But when the English had learned it, they used it with more insolency and made it more intolerable, for this oppression was not temporary or limited either to place or time: but because there was everywhere a continual war, either offensive or defensive, and every lord of a country and every marcher made war and peace at his pleasure, it became universal and perpetual, and was indeed the most heavy oppression that ever was used in any Christian or heathen kingdom. And therefore—*vox oppressorum*[267]—this crying sin did draw down as great, or greater, plagues upon Ireland than the oppression of the Israelites did draw upon the land of Egypt. For the plagues of Egypt, though they were grievous, were but of a short continuance; but the plagues of Ireland lasted 400 years together.

The Cause of Idleness in the Irish; Why the Irish Are Beggars in Foreign Countries

This extortion of coyne and livery did produce two notorious effects: first, it made the land waste; next, it made the people idle. For when the husbandman had labored all the year, the soldier in one night did consume the fruits of all his labor, *longique perit labor irritus anni*.[268] Had he reason then to manure the land

266. Davies seems to be alluding to Psalms 14:4 (King James Version): "Have all the workers of iniquity no knowledge? who eat up my people as they eat bread, and call not upon the Lord."
267. "the voice of oppression."
268. "and the useless labor of a long year has perished."

for the next year? Or rather, might he not complain as the shepherd in Virgil?:

> Impius haec tam culta novalia miles habebit,
> Barbarus has segetes? En quo discordia civis
> Perduxit miseros: en quis consevimus agros![269]

And hereupon of necessity came depopulation, banishment, and extirpation of the better sort of subjects; and such as remained became idle and lookers on, expecting the event[270] of those miseries and evil times. So as this extreme extortion and oppression hath been the true cause of the idleness of this Irish nation, and that rather the vulgar sort have chosen to be beggars in foreign countries than to manure their own fruitful land at home.

Why the Irish Are Reputed a Crafty People

Lastly, this oppression did of force and necessity make the Irish a crafty people, for such as are oppressed and live in slavery are ever put to their shifts: *ingenium mala saepe movent.*[271] And therefore, in the old comedies of Plautus and Terence, the bondslave doth always act the cunning and crafty part. Besides, all the common people have a whining tune or accent in their speech, as if they did still smart or suffer some oppression.

Why the Irish Are Inquisitive After News

And this idleness, together with fear of imminent mischiefs which did continually hang over their heads, have been the cause

---

269. "Shall an irreligious soldier take possession of these fallow lands, so well cultivated? Shall a foreigner get hold of these cornfields? Is this the degree of misery to which strife has brought us citizens? For whom have we sown our fields?" (Vergil, *Eclogues*, 1.70–73).

270. *event*: consequence; inevitable result.

271. "misfortunes after set the mind going."

that the Irish were ever the most inquisitive people after news, of any nation in the world—as St. Paul himself made observation upon the people of Athens, that they were an idle people and did nothing but learn and tell news.[272] And because these news-carriers did by their false intelligence many times raise troubles and rebellions in this realm, the Statute of Kilkenny doth punish news-tellers (by the name of *skelaghs*)[273] with fine and ransom.

Cosherings, Cessings, Cuttings

This extortion of coyne and livery was taken for the maintenance of their men of war, but their Irish exactions extorted by the chieftains and tanists, by color of their barbarous seigniory, were almost as grievous a burden as the other: namely, cosherings, which were visitations and progresses made by the lord and his followers among his tenants, wherein he did eat them (as the English proverb is) "out of house and home"; cessings of the kern, of his family (called *kernety*), of his horses and horseboys, of his dogs and dogboys, and the like; and lastly, cuttings, tallages, or spendings,[274] high or low, at his pleasure— all which made the lord an absolute tyrant, and the tenant a very slave and villein, and in one respect more miserable than bondslaves, for commonly the bondslave is fed by his lord, but here the lord was fed by his bondslave.

Lastly, there were two other customs proper and peculiar to the Irishry, which being the cause of many strong combinations and factions do tend to the utter ruin of a commonwealth: the one was fostering, the other, gossipred;[275] both which have ever been of greater estimation among this people than with any other nation in the Christian world.

272. See Acts 17:21.

273. *skelaghs*: from the Gaelic *sgeulaiche* ("news-monger," "storyteller"); wandering news- and storytellers.

274. *Cessings, cuttings, tallages,* and *spendings* were all forms of taxation.

275. *gossipred*: spiritual affinity achieved through some ceremony such as sponsoring a baptism.

[Fostering]

For fostering, I did never hear or read that it was in that use or reputation in any other country, barbarous or civil, as it hath been, and yet is, in Ireland, where they put away all their children to fosterers, the potent and rich men selling, the meaner sort buying, the alterage[276] of their children. And the reason is because in the opinion of this people fostering hath always been a stronger alliance than blood, and the foster children do love and are beloved of their foster fathers and their sept more than of their own natural parents and kindred, and do participate of their means more frankly and do adhere unto them in all fortunes with more affection and constancy. And though Tully in his book *Of Friendship*[277] doth observe that children of princes, being sometimes in cases of necessity for saving of their lives delivered to shepherds to be nourished and bred up, when they have been restored to their great fortunes have still retained their love and affection to their fosterers, whom for many years they took to be their parents: yet this was a rare case, and few examples are to be found thereof.

But such a general custom in a kingdom, in giving and taking children to foster, making such a firm alliance as it doth in Ireland, was never seen or heard of in any other country of the world besides.

Gossipred

The like may be said of gossipred or compaternity,[278] which though by the canon law it be a spiritual affinity, and a juror that was gossip to either of the parties might in former times have

276. *alterage*: fostering.
277. Marcus Tullius Cicero (106–43 B.C.), Roman rhetorician, moralist, and politician.
278. *compaternity*: relationship existing between the actual parents of a child and the child's godparents.

been challenged as not indifferent by our law, yet there was no nation under the sun that ever made so religious account thereof as the Irish.

Now these two customs, which of themselves are indifferent in other kingdoms, became exceeding evil and full of mischief in this realm by reason of the inconveniences which followed thereupon. For they made (as I said before) strong parties and factions, whereby the great men were enabled to oppress their inferiors and to oppose their equals, and their followers were borne out and countenanced in all their lewd and wicked actions. For fosterers and gossips by the common custom of Ireland were to maintain one another in all causes lawful and unlawful, which as it is a combination and confederacy punishable in all well-governed commonweals, so was it not one of the least causes of the common misery of this kingdom.

I omit their common repudiation of their wives; their promiscuous generation of children; their neglect of lawful matrimony; their uncleanness in apparel, diet, and lodging; and their contempt and scorn of all things necessary for the civil life of man.

How the English Colonies Became Degenerate

These were the Irish customs which the English colonies did embrace and use after they had rejected the civil and honorable laws and customs of England, whereby they became degenerate and metamorphosed like Nebuchadnezzar,[279] who, although he had the face of a man, had the heart of a beast; or like those who had drunk of Circe's cup and were turned into very beasts, and yet took such pleasure in their beastly manner of life as they would not return to their shape of men again:[280] insomuch as

279. King of Babylonia (605–562 B.C.), renowned for his cruelty.
280. In one interpretation of the myth, Odysseus's men, having drunk from the cup of the witch Circe, been transformed into swine, and easily fallen into their new identities, represent the human love of the bestial life.

within less time than the age of a man, they had no marks or differences left amongst them of that noble nation from which they were descended. For as they did not only forget the English language and scorn the use thereof, but grew to be ashamed of their very English names (though they were noble and of great antiquity) and took Irish surnames and nicknames: namely, the two most potent families of the Burkes in Connaught (after the House of the Red Earl failed of heirs males) called their chiefs "MacWilliam Eighter" and "MacWilliam Oughter." In the same province, Bremingham, Baron of Athenry, called himself "MacYoris." [DeExeter], or De'Exon, was called "MacJordan." Nangle, or de Angulo, took the name of "MacCostello." Of the inferior families of the Burkes, one was called "MacHubbard," another "MacDavid." In Munster, of the great families of the Geraldines planted there, one was called "MacMorris" [or "MacMaurice"], chief of the House of Lixnaw, and another "MacGibbon," who was also called the "White Knight." The chief of the Baron of Dunboyne's House, who is a branch of the House of Ormond, took the [surname] of "MacPheris." Condon of the county of Waterford was called "MacMaighe," and Archdeacon of the county of Kilkenny, "MacOdo."[281] And this they did in contempt and hatred of the English name and nation, whereof these degenerate families became more mortal enemies than the mere Irish. And whereas the state and government, being grown weak by their defection, did, to reduce them to obedience, grant them many protections and pardons (the cheapness whereof in all ages hath brought great dishonor and damage to this commonweal), they grew so ungrateful and unnatural as in the end they scorned that grace and favor because the acceptance thereof did argue them to be subjects, and they desired rather to be accounted enemies than rebels to the Crown of England.

281. In 1401 a definite separation occurred in the de Burgos who descended from William "Liath" (d. ca. 1322) when Edmund founded the MacWilliam

Hereupon was that old verse made which I find written in the White Book of the exchequer in a hand as ancient as the time of King Edward III:

> By granting charters of peace
> To false Englishmen withouten lease,
>   This land shall be mich undo.[282]
> But gossipred and alterage,
> And leesing[283] of our language,
>   Have mickly[284] holp thereto.

And therefore, in a Close Roll in the Tower, bearing this title, *Articuli in Hibernia Observandi*,[285] we find these two articles among others:

(1). The lord justice of Ireland shall not grant pardons for murder, nor for robbery or arson, and he shall notify the lord king of those requesting them.

Ichtarach clan (or "Lower Burkes") of Mayo, and William (or Ulick) established the MacWilliam Uachtarach clan (or "Upper Burkes") of Galway.

In detailing the Hibernization of the Anglo-Norman dynastic names, Davies rehearses what had become a commonplace in the tradition of the Irish tract. The Berminghams of Connaught assumed the patronymic MacHorish, MacYorish, or MacOrish. The descendants of Jordan d'Exeter took the surname MacJordan. The family of Costello derived its name from Oistealb, son of Gilbert de Nangle. The FitzGeralds of Lixnaw in Kerry assumed the patronymic MacMorris (from *Maurice*), while another of the Geraldine families in County Limerick, with the surname Mac- or FitzGibbon, called its head the White Knight, a hereditary title. The patronymic MacPheris derived from Feoras (or Piers). The Condon family of County Waterford and east Cork, which took the surname MacMaighe or MacMaugh (from *May*), is sometimes known in English as MacMawe-Condon. And finally, Odo le Ercedekne gave his name to the Archdeacon family, which had settled in County Kilkenny— MacOda, MacOdo, MacOde, MacAdoo, MacCody, etc. See Edward Mac-Lysaght, *Irish Families: Their Names, Arms and Origins* (Dublin, 1957); MacLysaght, *More Irish Families* (Galway, 1960); MacLysaght, *Supplement to Irish Families* (Dublin, 1969).

282. *mich undo*: much undone.

283. *leesing*: failing to preserve, maintain; losing.

284. *mickly*: greatly.

285. "Articles Observed in Ireland."

(2). Also, that neither the lord justice nor any other official of Ireland shall offer protection to anyone acting against the king's peace.[286]*

When and How the English Colonies Became Degenerate

But now it is fit to look back and consider when the Old English colonies became so degenerate, and in what age they fell away into that Irish barbarism, rejecting the English laws and customs. Assuredly, by comparing the ancient annals of Ireland with the records remaining here and in the Tower of London, I do find that this general defection fell out in the latter end of the reign of King Edward II and in the beginning of the reign of King Edward III. And all this great innovation grew within the space of thirty years, within the compass of which time there fell out divers mischievous accidents whereby the whole kingdom was in a manner lost.

The Scots Overrun [Ireland]

For first, Edward [le] Bruce invaded Ireland with the Scottish army and prevailed so far as that he possessed the maritime parts of Ulster, marched up to the walls of Dublin, spoiled the English Pale, passed through Leinster and Munster as far as Limerick, and was master of the field in every part of the kingdom.

This happened in 10 Edward II, at what time the Crown of England was weaker and suffered more dishonor in both kingdoms than it did at any time since the Norman Conquest. Then did the state of England send over John de Hotham[287] to be

286. "1. Justiciarius Hiberniae non concedat perdonationes de morte hominis, nec de Robertiis, seu incendiis, et quod de caetero certificet dominum regem de nominibus petentium. 2. Item, Quod nec Justiciarius nec aliquis Magnas Hiberniae concedat protectiones alicui contra pacem Regis existent, etc."

287. John de Hotham, lord treasurer (1317–18), had the great lords of Ireland swear an oath of loyalty to Edward II on 4 February 1316 at Dublin.

treasurer here with commission to call the great lords of Ireland together and to take of them an oath of association that they should loyally join together in life and death to preserve the right of the king of England and to expel the common enemy.* But this treasurer brought neither men nor money to perform this service.

Desmond, Chief Commander in the War against the Scots

At that time, though Richard Burke, earl of Ulster (commonly called the Red Earl) were of greater power than any other subject in Ireland, yet was he so far stricken in years as that he was unable to manage the martial affairs as he had done during all the reign of King Edward I, having been general of the Irish forces, not only in this kingdom, but in the wars of Scotland, Wales, and Gascoigne. And therefore, Maurice FitzThomas of Desmond, being then the most active nobleman in this realm, took upon him the chief command in this war; for the support whereof the revenue of this land was far too short, and yet no supply of treasure was sent out of England.

When and How the Extortion of Coyne and Livery Began among the English

Then was there no mean to maintain the army but by cessing the soldiers upon the subject, as the Irish were wont to impose their *bonaght*. Whereupon grew that wicked extortion of coyne and livery spoken of before, which in short time banished the greatest part of the freeholders out of the [counties] of Kerry, Limerick, Cork, and Waterford; into whose possessions Desmond and his kinsmen, allies, and followers, which were then more Irish than English, did enter and appropriate these lands unto themselves, Desmond himself taking what scopes he best liked for his demesnes in every country, and reserving an Irish seigniory out of the rest. And here, that I may verify and maintain by matter of record that which is before delivered touching the nature of this wicked extortion called coyne and livery, and the manifold mischiefs it did produce, I think it fit and pertinent to insert the preamble of the statute of 10 Henry VII, c.4, not printed, but recorded in Parliament Rolls of Dublin, in these words:

At the request and supplication of the Commons of this land of Ireland, that whereof long time there hath been used and exacted by the lords and gentlemen of this land many and diverse damnable customs and usages which been called coyne and livery, and pay; that is, horsemeat and mansmeat, for the finding of their horsemen and footmen; and over that, 4d. or 6d. daily to every of them to be had and paid of the poor earth-tillers and tenants, inhabitants of the said land, without anything doing or paying therefor. Besides, many murders, robberies, rapes, and other manifold extortions and oppressions by the said horsemen and footmen daily and nightly committed and done, which been the principal causes of the desolation and destruction of the said land, and hath brought the same into ruin and decay, so as the most part of the English freeholders and tenants of this land been departed out thereof, some into the realm of England, and other some to other strange lands; whereupon the foresaid lords and gentlemen of this land have intruded into the said freeholders' and tenants' inheritances, and the same keepeth and occupieth as their own inheritances, and setten under them in the same land the king's Irish enemies, to the diminishing of holy church's rites, the disherison[288] of the king and his obedient subjects, and the utter ruin and desolation of the land. For reformation whereof, be it enacted that the king shall receive a subsidy of 26s.8d. out of every 120 acres of arable land manured, etc.

But to return to [Maurice FitzThomas] of Desmond: by this extortion of coyne and livery he suddenly grew from a mean to a mighty estate, insomuch as the Baron Finglas in his *Discourse of the Decay of Ireland* affirmeth that, his ancient inheritance being not 1,000 marks yearly, he became able to dispend every way £10,000 *per annum*.

These possessions being thus unlawfully gotten could not be

---

288. *disherison*: disinheritance.

maintained by the just and honorable law of England, which would have restored the true owners to their land again. And therefore, this great man found no means to continue and uphold his ill-purchased greatness but by rejecting the English law and government, and assuming in lieu thereof the barbarous customs of the Irish. And hereupon followed the defection of those four shires containing the greatest part of Munster from the obedience of the law.

In like manner (saith Baron Finglas), the lord of Tipperary,[289] perceiving how well the House of Desmond had thrived by coyne and livery and other Irish exactions, began to hold the like course in the counties of Tipperary and Kilkenny, whereby he got great scopes of land, specially in Ormond, and raised many Irish exactions upon the English freeholders there; which made him so potent and absolute among them as at that time they knew no other law than the will of their lord. Besides, finding that the earl of Desmond excluded the ordinary ministers of justice under color of a royal liberty, which he claimed in the counties of Kerry, Cork, and Waterford by a grant of King Edward I (as appeareth in a *quo warranto*[290] brought against him, 12 Edward I, the record whereof remaineth in Bremingham's Tower among the Common Plea Rolls there).

This lord also, in 3 Edward III, obtained a grant of the like liberty in the county of Tipperary, whereby he got the law into his own hands and shut out the common law and justice of the realm.

And thus we see that all Munster fell away from the English law and government in the end of King Edward II his reign and in the beginning of the reign of King Edward III.

289. In 1328 James Butler, first earl of Ormond (1328–38), was granted the liberty of Tipperary. The Crown, however, as was customary in such grants, still reserved the right of four pleas of rape, arson, forestalling, and treasure-trove.

290. *quo warranto*: a writ of right issued on behalf of the Crown requiring a person to demonstrate by what authorization or right he exercised his authority.

The Rising of MacMurrough and O'More in Leinster; The Defect[291] and Loss of a Great Part of Leinster

Again, about the same time, viz., in 20 Edward II, when the state of England was well-nigh ruined by the rebellion of the barons and the government of Ireland utterly neglected, there arose in Leinster one of the Kavanaughs, named Donald Mac-Art,[292] who named himself MacMurrough, king of Leinster, and possessed himself of the county of Catherlough and of the greatest part of the county of Wexford.* And shortly after, Lisagh O'More called himself O'More, took eight castles in one evening, destroyed Dunamase, the principal house of the Lord Mortimer in Leix, recovered that whole country[293]—"from the servant is made the master; from the subject, the prince,"[294] saith Friar Clynn in his annals.

Besides, the earl of Kildare,[295] imitating his cousin of Desmond, did not omit to make the like use of coyne and livery in Kildare and the west part of Meath, which brought the like barbarism into those parts. And thus a great part of Leinster was lost and fell away from the obedience of the Crown near about the time before expressed.

The Earl of Ulster Murdered

Again, in 7 King Edward III, the Lord William Burke, earl of Ulster and lord of Connaught, was treacherously murdered by his own squires at Knockfergus, leaving behind him "an only

291. *defect*: defection.
292. Chosen as king by the Irish of Leinster, Donal MacArt MacMurrough (Kavanagh) led a revolt early in 1328 but was soon captured. He escaped in January 1330.
293. O'More made himself lord of Leix (or Laois) in 1342.
294. "De servo Dominus, de subjecto princeps effectus."
295. Probably Maurice FitzThomas FitzGerald, fourth earl of Kildare (1331–90).

daughter who was one year old"[296] (saith Friar Clynn). Immediately upon the murder committed, the countess, with her young daughter, fled into England, so as the government of that country was wholly neglected until, that young lady being married to Lionel duke of Clarence, that prince came over with an army to recover his wife's inheritance and to reform this kingdom (36 Edward III).

The Earldom of Ulster Recovered by the Irish

But in the meantime, what became of that great inheritance both in Ulster and Connaught? Assuredly, in Ulster the sept of Hugh Boy O'Neill, then possessing Glenconkeyne and Killeightragh in Tyrone, took the opportunity, and passing over the Bann did first expel the English out of the barony of Tuscard, which is now called the Route, and likewise out of the Glens and other lands up as far as Knockfergus, which country or extent of land is at this day called the Lower Clan Hugh-Boy.[297] And shortly after that, they came up into the Great Ards, which the Latin writers call *altitudines Ultoniae*,[298] and was then the inheritance of the Savages, by whom they were valiantly resisted for divers years.* But at last, for want of castles and fortifications—for the saying of Henry Savage mentioned in

---

296. "Unicam et unius anni filiam."

297. Describing the breakup of the great O'Neill kingship of Ulster, Curtis says, "The second branch, which took its rise from Aedh Bui, king from 1260 to 1283, being expelled by the senior line, now sought their fortunes in the vacant earldom east of the Bann, where in the next fifty years they founded the principality of Clandeboy ('Clann Aedha Buidhe') a state which by 1550 covered most of the country between the Glens of Antrim, Strangford Lough, and Lough Neagh. But along the coasts of Antrim and Down many powerful families of the Englishry survived, such as Byset or MacEoin of the Glens, and the Savages and Russells whom De Courcy planted in Down; and these families, though they became mainly Irish in speech and habit, clung to their feudal titles and English tenures" (*History of Medieval Ireland*, p. 221).

298. "high Ulster."

every story is very memorable: that a castle of bones was better than a castle of stones—the English were overrun by the multitude of the Irishry. So as, about 30 King Edward III, some few years before the arrival of the duke of Clarence, the Savages were utterly driven out of the Great Ards into a little nook of land near the river of Stangford, where they now possess a little territory called the Little Ards; and their greater patrimony took the name of the Upper Clan Hugh-Boy, from the sept of Hugh Boy O'Neill, who became invaders thereof.*

The Defection of Connaught

For Connaught, some younger branches of the family of the Burkes being planted there by the Red Earl and his ancestors, seeing their chief to be cut off and dead without heir male and no man left to govern or protect that province, intruded presently into all the earl's lands, which ought to have been seized into the king's hands by reason of the minority of the heir. And within a short space, two of the most potent among them divided that great seigniory betwixt them, the one taking the name of MacWilliam Oughter and the other of MacWilliam Eighter, as if the Lord William Burke, the last earl of Ulster, had left two sons of one name behind him to inherit that lordship in course of gavelkind.* But they well knew that they were but intruders upon the king's possession during the minority of the heir; they knew those lands were the rightful inheritance of that young lady and, consequently, that the law of England would speedily evict them out of their possession. And therefore they held it the best policy to cast off the yoke of English law and to become mere Irish, and according to their example drew all the rest of the English in that province to do the like, so as from thenceforth they suffered their possessions to run in course of tanistry and gavelkind. They changed their names, language, and apparel, and all their civil manners and customs of living.

Lastly, about 25 King Edward III, Sir Richard de Clare[299] was slain in Thomond and all the English colonies there utterly supplanted.*

Thus in that space of time, which was between 10 King Edward II and 30 King Edward III (I speak within compass), by the concurrence of the mischiefs before recited, all the Old English colonies in Munster, Connaught, and Ulster, and more than a third part of Leinster, became degenerate and fell away from the Crown of England. So as only the four shires of the English Pale remained under the obedience of the law, and yet the borders and marches thereof were grown unruly and out of order too, being subject to black rents[300] and tribute of the Irish; which was a greater defection than when ten of twelve tribes departed and fell away from the kings of Judah.

What Courses Have Been Taken to Reform This Kingdom since the English Colonies Became Degenerate

But was not the state of England sensible of this loss and dishonor? Did they not endeavor to recover the land that was lost and to reduce the subjects to their obedience?

Edward II

Truly, King Edward II, by the incursions of the Scottish nation and by the insurrection of his barons, who raised his wife and his son against him and in the end deposed him, was diverted and utterly disabled to reform the disorders of Ireland.

299. Sir Richard de Clare was slain in the Battle of Dysert O'Dea, 10 May 1318.

300. *black rents*: blackmail; tribute exacted from small landowners in return for immunity or protection from raiding.

King Edward III Did First Endeavor a Reformation

But as soon as the Crown of England was transferred to King Edward III, though he were yet in his minority, the state there began to look into the desperate estate of things here. And finding such a general defection, letters were sent from the king to the great men and prelates, requiring them particularly to swear fealty to the Crown of England.*

Sir Anthony Lucy

Shortly after, Sir Anthony Lucy, a person of great authority in England in those days, was sent over to work a reformation in this kingdom by a severe course; and to that end, the king wrote expressly to the earl of Ulster and others of the nobility to assist him, as is before remembered. Presently upon his arrival, he arrested Maurice FitzThomas, earl of Desmond, and Sir William Bremingham, and committed them prisoners to the Castle of Dublin, where Sir William Bremingham was executed for treason, though the earl of Desmond were left to mainprize[301] upon condition he should appear before the king by a certain day and in the meantime to continue loyal.*

Resumption of Liberties

After this, the king, being advertised that the overlarge grants of lands and liberties made to the lords of English blood in Ireland made them so insolent as they scorned to obey the law and the magistrate, did absolutely resume all such grants, as is before declared. But the earl of Desmond, above all men, found himself grieved with this resumption or repeal of liberties and declared his dislike and discontentment, insomuch as he did not only

---

301. *left to mainprize*: released after providing or securing guarantors or mainpernors for his appearance in court later.

refuse to come to a parliament at Dublin summoned by Sir William Morice,[302] deputy to the Lord John Darcy, the king's lieutenant, but (as we have said before) he raised such dissension between the English of blood and the English of birth as the like was never seen from the time of the first planting of our nation in Ireland. And in this factious and seditious humor, he drew the earl of Kildare and the rest of the nobility, with the citizens and burgesses of the principal towns, to hold a several[303] parliament by themselves at Kilkenny, where they framed certain articles against the deputy and transmitted the same into England to the king.*

Sir Ralph Ufford

Hereupon, Sir Ralph Ufford, who had lately before married the countess of Ulster, a man of courage and severity, was made lord justice, who forthwith calling a parliament sent a special commandment to the earl of Desmond to appear in that great council; but the earl willfully refused to come.[304]* Whereupon, the lord justice raised the king's standard and, marching with an army into Munster, seized into the king's hands all the possessions of the earl; took and executed his principal followers, Sir Eustace le Poer, Sir William Grant, and Sir John Cotterell; enforced the earl himself to fly and lurk till twenty-six noblemen and knights became mainpernors[305] for his appearance at a certain day prefixed.* But he making default the second time, the uttermost advantage was taken against his sureties. Besides, at

302. For Darcy's and Morice's tenures as lieutenant and deputy, see note 238. The parliament which Maurice FitzThomas, first earl of Desmond, refused to attend was held at Dublin in October 1341. The parliament held by Desmond at Kilkenny in November 1341 was boycotted by Morice.

303. *several*: separate, distinct.

304. Ralph de Ufford (justiciar 1344–46) held this parliament at Dublin in June 1345.

305. *mainpernors*: sureties or guarantors for a person's appearance in court on a certain day.

the same time this lord justice caused the earl of Kildare[306] to be arrested and committed to the Castle of Dublin; indicted and imprisoned many other disobedient subjects; called in and canceled such charters as were lately before resumed; and proceeded everyway so roundly and severely as the nobility which were wont to suffer no controlment did much distaste him. And the commons, who in this land have ever been more devoted to their immediate lords here, whom they saw every day, than unto their sovereign lord and king, whom they never saw, spake ill of this governor as of a rigorous and cruel man, though in troth he were a singular good justicer, and, if he had not died in the second year of his government, was the likeliest person of that age to have reformed and reduced the degenerate English colonies to their natural obedience of the Crown of England.

Maurice FitzThomas, the First Earl of Desmond: The Author of the Great Oppressions and Dissensions Which Destroyed the English Colonies

Thus much, then, we may observe by the way: that Maurice FitzThomas, the first earl of Desmond, was the first English lord that imposed coyne and livery upon the king's subjects and the first that raised his estate to immoderate greatness by the wicked extortion and oppression; that he was the first that rejected the English laws and government and drew others by his example to do the like; that he was the first peer of Ireland that refused to come to the parliament summoned by the king's authority; that he was the first that made a division and distinction between the English of blood and the English of birth.

306. Maurice FitzThomas, fourth earl of Kildare, was arrested and imprisoned in 1345.

The Fortune of the House of Desmond

And as this earl was the only author and first actor of these mischiefs which gave the greatest impediment to the full conquest of Ireland, so it is to be noted that albeit others of his rank afterwards offended in the same kind, whereby their houses were many times in danger of ruin, yet was there not ever any noble house of English race in Ireland utterly destroyed and finally rooted out by the hand of justice, but the House of Desmond only; nor any peer of this realm ever put to death (though divers have been attainted) but Thomas FitzJames, the earl of Desmond[307] only, and only for those wicked customs brought in by the first earl and practiced by his posterity, though by several laws they were made high treason. And therefore, though in 7 Edward IV, during the government of the Lord Tiptoft, earl of Worcester, both the earls of Desmond and Kildare were attainted by Parliament at Drogheda for alliance and fostering with the Irish, and for taking coyne and livery of the king's subjects, yet was Desmond only put to death, for the earl of Kildare received his pardon.[308] And albeit the son of this earl of Desmond, who lost his head at Drogheda, were restored to the earldom, yet could not the king's grace regenerate obedience in that degenerate House, but it grew rather more wild and barbarous than before. For from thenceforth they reclaimed a strange privilege: that the earls of Desmond should never come to any parliament or grand council or within any walled town but at their will and pleasure—which pretended privilege James earl of Desmond,[309] the father of Gerald, the last earl, renounced and surrendered by his deed (in the Chancery of Ireland, 32

307. Thomas FitzJames FitzGerald, seventh earl of Desmond, was executed 15 February 1468.

308. Thomas FitzMaurice, seventh earl of Kildare, was attainted and imprisoned in February 1468 and later received a pardon.

309. The "privilege" was renounced in 1540. James FitzJohn, thirteenth earl of Desmond (d. 1558), was father of the last legitimate earl, Gerald.

Henry VIII),* at what time, among the mere Irishry, he submitted himself to Sir Anthony St. Leger, then lord deputy; took an oath of allegiance; covenanted that he would suffer the law of England to be executed in his country and assist the king's judges in their circuits; and if any subsidies should be granted by Parliament, he would permit the same to be levied upon his tenants and followers—which covenants are as strange as the privilege itself spoken of before. But that which I conceive most worthy of observation upon the fortunes of the House of Desmond is this: that as Maurice FitzThomas, the first earl, did first raise the greatness of that House by Irish exactions and oppressions, so Gerald, the last earl, did at last ruin and reduce it to nothing by using the like extortions. For certain it is that the first occasion of his rebellion grew from hence, that when he attempted to charge the Decies[310] in the county of Waterford with coyne and livery, black rents, and cosheries[311] after the Irish manner, he was resisted by the earl of Ormond,[312] and upon an encounter overthrown and taken prisoner; which made his heart so unquiet as it easily conceived treason against the Crown and brought forth actual and open rebellion, wherein he perished himself and made a final extinguishment of his House and honor. Oppression and extortion did maintain the greatness, and oppression and extortion did extinguish the greatness of that House: which may well be expressed by the old emblem of a torch turned downwards, with this word, *quod me alit, extinguit.*[313]

310. The Decies, the territory roughly in western Waterford and including the port towns of Dungarvan and Youghal, was usually included within the earldom of Desmond.

311. *cosheries*: cosherings; various forms of support "for themselves and their followers exacted by Irish chiefs from their dependents" (*OED*).

312. In 1565, at the ford of Affane, near Dungarvan, Thomas ("Black Tom") Butler, tenth earl of Ormond, defeated and captured Gerald FitzGerald, fourteenth earl of Desmond.

313. "that which nourishes me has killed me."

The Course of Reformation Pursued
by Lionel Duke of Clarence

Now let us return to the course of reformation held and pursued here after the death of Sir Ralph Ufford,[314] which happened in 20 King Edward III, after which time, albeit all the power and counsel of England was converted towards the conquest of France, yet was not the work of reformation altogether discontinued. For in 25 King Edward III, Sir Thomas Rokeby, another worthy governor (whom I have once before named), held a parliament at Kilkenny, wherein many excellent laws were propounded and enacted for the reducing of the English colonies to their obedience; which laws we find enrolled in the Remembrancer's Office here, and differ not much in substance from those other Statutes of Kilkenny, which not long after (during the government of Lionel duke of Clarence) were not only enacted but put in execution. This noble prince having married the daughter and heir of Ulster, and being likewise a coparcener of the county of Kilkenny, in 36 King Edward III came over the king's lieutenant, attended with a good retinue of martial men (as is before remembered) and a grave and honorable council, as well for peace as for war. But because this army was not of a competent strength to break and subdue all the Irishry, although he quieted the borders of the English Pale and held all Ireland in awe with his name and presence, the principal service that he intended was to reform the degenerate English colonies and to reduce them to obedience of the English law and magistrate.

Statutes of Kilkenny

To that end, in 40 King Edward III, he held that famous Parliament at Kilkenny,[315] wherein many notable laws were enacted,

314. 9 April 1346.
315. In 1366.

which do show and lay open (for the law doth best discover enormities) how much the English colonies were corrupted at that time and do infallibly prove that which is laid down before: that they were wholly degenerate and fallen away from their obedience. For first, it appeareth by the preamble of these laws that the English of this realm, before the coming over of Lionel duke of Clarence, were at that time become mere Irish in their language, names, apparel, and all their manner of living, and had rejected the English laws and submitted themselves to the Irish, with whom they had many marriages and alliances, which tended to the utter ruin and destruction of the commonwealth. Therefore, alliance by marriage, nurture of infants, and gossipred with the Irish are by this statute made high treason. Again, if any man of English race should use an Irish name, Irish language, or Irish apparel, or any other guise or fashion of the Irish, if he had lands or tenements,³¹⁶ the same should be seized till he had given security to the chancery to conform himself in all points to the English manner of living. And if he had no lands, his body was to be taken and imprisoned till he found sureties, as aforesaid.*

Again, it was established and commanded that the English in all their controversies should be ruled and governed by the common law of England; and if any did submit himself to the brehon law or march law, he should be adjudged a traitor [c. 4].

Again, because the English at that time made war and peace with the bordering enemy at their pleasure, they were expressly prohibited to levy war upon the Irish, without special warrant and direction from the state [c. 10].

Again, it was made penal to the English to permit the Irish to *creaght* or graze upon their lands; to present them to ecclesiastical benefices; to receive them into any monasteries or religious

---

316. *tenements*: "the technical expression for freehold interests in things immovable considered as subjects of property" but distinct from land (Kenelm E. Digby, *An Introduction to the History of the Law of Real Property* [1875], cited in *OED*).

houses; or to entertain any of their minstrels, rhymers, or news-tellers. To impose or cess any horse or foot upon the English subjects against their wills was made felony. And because the great liberties or franchises[317] spoken of before were become sanctuaries for all malefactors, express power was given to the king's sheriffs to enter into all franchises and there to apprehend all felons and traitors. And lastly, because the great lords, when they levied forces for the public service, did lay unequal burdens upon the gentlemen and freeholders, it was ordained that four wardens of the peace in every county should set down and appoint what men and armor every man should bear, according to his freehold or other ability of estate [c. 12, 13, 15, 17, 22, 24].

The Statutes of Kilkenny Did Much Reform the Degenerate English

These and other laws tending to a general reformation were enacted in that Parliament. And the execution of these laws, together with the presence of the king's son, made a notable alteration in the state and manners of this people within the space of seven years, which was the term of this prince's lieutenancy.

For all the discourses that I have seen of the decay of Ireland do agree in this: that the presence of the Lord Lionel and these Statutes of Kilkenny did restore the English government in the degenerate colonies for divers years. And the statute of 10 Henry VII [c. 8], which reviveth and confirmeth the Statutes of Kilkenny, doth confirm as much. For it declareth that as long as these laws were put in ure[318] and execution, this land continued in prosperity and honor. And since they were not executed, the subjects rebelled and digressed from their allegiance, and the

317. *franchises*: districts or territories which were immune or exempt from the law.
318. *ure*: effect, operation, use.

land fell to ruin and desolation. And withal, we find the effect of these laws in the Pipe Rolls and Plea Rolls of this kingdom. For from 36 Edward III, when this prince entered into his government, till the beginning of Richard II his reign, we find the revenue of the Crown, both certain and casual, in Ulster, Munster, and Connaught accounted for, and that the king's writ did run and the common law was executed in every of these provinces.

The Presence of the King's Son
Did Much Advance the Reformation

I join with these laws the personal presence of the king's son as a concurrent cause of this reformation, because the people of this land, both English and Irish, out of a natural pride did ever love and desire to be governed by great persons.

[The] Absence of Our Kings and Great English Lords,
a Chief Cause Why the Kingdom Was Not Reduced

And therefore, I may here justly take occasion to note that, first, the absence of the kings of England, and, next, the absence of those great lords who were inheritors of those mighty seigniories of Leinster, Ulster, Connaught, and Meath have been main causes why this kingdom was not reduced in so many ages.

[The] Absence of Our Kings

Touching the absence of our kings, three of them only since the Norman Conquest have made royal journeys into this land, namely, King Henry II, King John, and King Richard II. And yet they no sooner arrived here but that all the Irishry (as if they had been but one man) submitted themselves, took oaths of fidelity, and gave pledges and hostages to continue loyal. And if any of those kings had continued here in person a competent time, till they had settled both English and Irish in their several possessions and had set the law in a due course throughout the kingdom, these times wherein we live had not gained the honor of the final conquest and reducing of Ireland. For the king, saith Solomon, *dissipat omne malum intuitu suo.*[319] But when Moses was absent in the Mount, the people committed idolatry;[320] and when there was no king in Israel, every man did what seemed best in his own eyes.

And therefore, when Alexander had conquered the east part of the world and demanded of one what was the fittest place for the seat of his empire, he brought and laid a dry hide before him, and desired him to set his foot on the one side thereof, which being done, all the other parts of the hide did rise up; but when he did set his foot in the middle of the hide, all the other parts lay flat and even: which was a lively demonstration that if a prince keep his residence in the border of his dominions, the remote parts will easily rise and rebel against him, but if he make the center thereof his seat, he shall easily keep them in peace and obedience.

The Absence of the Great English Lords

Touching the absence of the great lords, all writers do impute the decay and loss of Leinster to the absence of these English lords who married the five daughters of William Marshal, earl of Pembroke (to whom that great seigniory descended), when his five sons, who inherited the same successively, and during their times held the same in peace and obedience to the law of England, were all dead without issue (which happened about 40 King Henry III).* For the eldest being married to Hugh Bigod, earl of Norfolk, who in right of his wife had the marshalship of

319. "scatters all evil with his look" (King James Version, Prov. 20:8: "A king that sitteth in the throne of judgment scattereth away all evil with his eyes").
320. See Exod. 32:1–6.

England; the second, to Warin de Mountchensey, whose sole daughter and heir was matched to William de Valentia, half-brother to King Henry III, who by that match was made earl of Pembroke; the third, to Gilbert de Clare, earl of Gloucester; the fourth, to William Ferrers, earl of Derby; the fifth, to William de Broise, lord of Brecknocke[321]—these great lords, having greater inheritances in their own right in England than they had in Ireland in right of their wives (and yet each of the coparceners had an entire county allotted for her purparty,[322] as is before declared), could not be drawn to make their personal residence in this kingdom, but managed their estates here by their seneschals and servants. And to defend their territories against the bordering Irish, they entertained [323] some of the natives who pretended a perpetual title to those great lordships. For the Irish, after a thousand conquests and attainders by our law, would in those days pretend title still because by the Irish law no man could forfeit his land. These natives, taking the opportunity in weak and desperate times, usurped those seigniories. And so Donald MacArt Kavanagh, being entertained by the earl of Norfolk, made himself lord of the county of Catherlough; and Lisagh O'More, being trusted by the Lord Mortimer, who married the daughter and heir of the Lord Broise, made himself lord of the lands in Leix in the latter end of King Edward II's reign,* as is before declared.

Again, the decay and loss of Ulster and Connaught is attributed to this: that the Lord William Burke, the last earl of that name, died without issue male; whose ancestors, namely, the Red Earl and Sir Hugh de Lacy before him, being personally resi-

---

321. Matilda married Hugh Bigod (d. 1225), third earl of Norfolk; Joan (or Johanna) married Warin de Munchensey (d. 1255); Isabella married Gilbert de Clare, seventh earl of Clare (d. 1230); Sibyl married William Ferrers, earl of Derby (d. 1247); and Eva married William de Braose (or Bruce; d. 1230), lord of Abergavenny and Brecknocke (or Brecon).

322. *purparty*: "a proportion, a share, especially in an inheritance" (*OED*).

323. *entertained*: supported, assisted.

dent, held up their greatness there and kept the English in peace
and the Irish in awe. But when those provinces descended upon
an heir female and an infant, the Irish overran Ulster, and the
younger branches of the Burkes usurped Connaught. And therefore, the ordinance made in England, 3 Richard II,* against such
as were absent from their lands in Ireland and gave two-third
parts of the profits thereof unto the king until they returned or
placed a sufficient number of men to defend the same, was
grounded upon good reason of state; which ordinance was put
in execution for many years after, as appeareth by sundry sei-
zures made thereupon in the time of King Richard II, Henry IV,
Henry V, and Henry VI, whereof there remain records in the
Remembrancer's Office here. Among the rest, the duke of Norfolk himself was not spared, but was impleaded[324] upon this
ordinance for two parts of the profits of Dorburry's Island[325] and
other lands in the county of Wexford in the time of King Henry
VI. And afterwards, upon the same reason of state, all the lands
of the House of Norfolk, of the earl of Shrewsbury, the Lord
Berkeley, and others (who having lands in Ireland kept their
continual residence in England) were entirely resumed by the
Act of Absentees made in 28 King Henry VIII.

But now again, let us look back and see how long the effect
of that reformation did continue which was begun by Lionel
duke of Clarence in 40 King Edward III and what courses have
been held to reduce and reform this people by other lieutenants
and governors since that time.

The English colonies being in some good measure reformed
by the Statutes of Kilkenny did not utterly fall away into barbarism again till the Wars of the Two Houses had almost destroyed
both these kingdoms, for in that miserable time the Irish found
opportunity, without opposition, to banish the English law and

324. *impleaded*: impeached; sued.
325. Also known as Durbale's, Darbart's, Dunbarry, and Great Island;
probably the Great Saltee.

government out of all the provinces and to confine it only to the English Pale. Howbeit, in the meantime between the government of the duke of Clarence and the beginning of those civil wars of York and Lancaster, we find that the state of England did sundry times resolve to proceed in this work of reformation.

The Reformation Intended By King Richard II

For first, King Richard II sent over Sir Nicholas Dagworth[326] to survey the possessions of the Crown and to call to account the officers of the revenue.* Next, to draw his English subjects to manure and defend their lands in Ireland, he made that ordinance against absentees, spoken of before.* Again, he showed an excellent example of justice upon Sir Philip Courtney,[327] being his lieutenant of that kingdom, when he caused him to be arrested by special commissioners upon complaint made of sundry grievous oppressions and wrongs, which during his government he had done unto that people.*

After this, the Parliament of England did resolve that Thomas duke of Gloucester,[328] the king's uncle, should be employed in the reformation and reducing of that kingdom: the fame whereof was no sooner bruited in Ireland but all the Irishry were ready to submit themselves before his coming,* so much the very name of a great personage, specially of a prince of the blood, did ever prevail with this people. But the king and his minions, who were ever jealous of this duke of Gloucester, would not suffer him to have the honor of that service. But the king himself thought it a work worthy of his own presence and pains, and thereupon him-

326. During the troubled administration of William of Windsor, Sir Nicholas Dagworth was sent by Richard II in July 1375 on a special commission to expound the king's policy and find a way of obtaining additional moneys from the already impoverished island. He returned on another mission in January 1377.

327. King's lieutenant, 1 July 1383–85.

328. Commissioned in May 1392, Gloucester's patent was canceled 22 July 1392.

self in person made those two royal journeys mentioned before; at what time he received the submissions of all the Irish lords and captains, who bound themselves both by indenture and oath to become and continue his loyal subjects, and withal, laid a particular project for a civil plantation of the mountains and maritime counties between Dublin and Wexford by removing all the Irish septs from thence, as appeareth by the covenants between the earl marshal of England and those Irish septs, which are before remembered, and are yet preserved and remain of record in the King's Remembrancer's Office at Westminster. Lastly, this king, being present in Ireland, took special care to supply and furnish the courts of justice with able and sufficient judges. And to that end, he made that grave and learned judge Sir William Hankeford[329] chief justice of the King's Bench here (who afterwards for his service in this realm was made chief justice of the King's Bench in England by King Henry IV), and did withal associate unto him William Sturmy, a well-learned man in the law, who likewise came out of England with the king, that the legal proceedings (which were out of order, too, as all other things in that realm were) might be amended and made formal, according to the course and precedents of England.* But all the good purposes and projects of this king were interrupted and utterly defeated by his sudden departure out of Ireland and unhappy deposition from the Crown of England.

The Reformation Intended by Henry IV

Howbeit, King Henry IV, intending likewise to prosecute this noble work, in the third year of his reign made the Lord Thomas of Lancaster, his second son, lieutenant of Ireland; who came over in person and accepted again the submissions of divers Irish lords and captains (as is before remembered), and held also

329. Until his appointment in 1413 as chief justice of the King's Bench, Sir William Hankeford (d. 1422) served as king's serjeant and justice of the common pleas.

a parliament, wherein he gave new life to the Statutes of Kilkenny and made other good laws tending to the reformation of the kingdom. But the troubles raised against the king his father in England drew him home again so soon as that seed of reformation took no root at all; neither had his service in that kind any good effect or success.

After this, the state of England had no leisure to think of a general reformation in this realm till the civil dissensions of England were appeased and the peace of that kingdom settled by King Henry VII.

For, albeit in the time of King Henry VI, Richard duke of York, a prince of the blood, of great wisdom and valor, and heir to the third part of the kingdom at least (being earl of Ulster and lord of Connaught and Meath), was sent the king's lieutenant into Ireland to recover and reform that realm where he was resident in person for the greatest part of ten years. Yet the truth is, he aimed at another mark, which was the Crown of England. And therefore, he thought it no policy to distaste[330] either the English or Irish by a course of reformation, but sought by all means to please them and by popular courses to steal away their hearts, to the end he might strengthen his party when he should set on foot his title (as is before declared); which policy of his took such effect as that he drew over with him into England the flower of all the English colonies, specially of Ulster and Meath, whereof many noblemen and gentlemen were slain with him at Wakefield (as is likewise before remembered). And after his death, when the Wars between the Houses were in their heat, almost all the good English blood which was left in Ireland was spent in those civil dissensions, so as the Irish became victorious over all without blood or sweat. Only, that little canton of land called the English Pale, containing four small shires,[331] did main-

330. *distaste*: displease, offend.
331. The four counties or shires of the Pale were Louth, Meath, Kildare, and Dublin.

tain a bordering war with the Irish and retain the form of English government.

But out of that little precinct there were no lords, knights, or burgesses summoned to the parliament; neither did the king's writ run in any other part of the kingdom. And yet upon the marches and borders, which at that time were grown so large as they took up half Dublin, half Meath, and a third part of Kildare and Louth, there was no law in use but the march law, which in the Statutes of Kilkenny is said to be no law, but a lewd custom.

So as, upon the end of these civil wars in England, the English law and government was well-nigh banished out of Ireland, so as no footstep or print was left of any former reformation.

The Course of Reformation Held by Sir Edward Poynings in the Time of King Henry VII

Then did King Henry VII send over Sir Edward Poynings[332] to be his deputy, a right worthy servitor both in war and peace. The principal end of his employment was to expel Perkin Warbeck[333] out of this kingdom. But that service being performed, that worthy deputy finding nothing but a common misery took the best course he possibly could to establish a commonwealth in Ireland, and to that end he held a parliament no less famous than that of Kilkenny, and more available for the reformation of the whole kingdom. For whereas all wise men did ever concur in opinion that the readiest way to reform Ireland is to settle a form of civil government there, conformable to that of England, to bring this to pass Sir Edward Poynings did pass an act whereby all the statutes made in England before that time were enacted, established, and made of force in Ireland.

332. Poynings (lord deputy 1494–95) held a parliament at Drogheda in 1494 which passed the two acts Davies describes, legislation intended to make the Irish administration more directly dependent upon the Crown.
333. See note 112.

Poynings' Act

Neither did he only respect the time past, but provided also for the time to come, for he caused another law to be made, that no act should be propounded in any parliament of Ireland, but such as should be first transmitted into England and approved by the king and council there as good and expedient for that land, and so returned back again under the Great Seal of England. This act, though it seem *prima facie* to restrain the liberty of the subjects of Ireland, yet was it made at the prayer of the commons, upon just and important cause.

For the governors of that realm, specially such as were of that country birth, had laid many oppressions upon the commons, and amongst the rest they had imposed laws upon them, not tending to the general good, but to serve private turns and to strengthen their particular factions. This moved them to refer all laws that were to be passed in Ireland to be considered, corrected, and allowed, first by the state of England, which had always been tender and careful of the good of this people and had long since made them a civil, rich, and happy nation, if their own lords and governors there had not sent bad intelligence into England. Besides this, he took special order that the summons of Parliament should go into all the shires of Ireland, and not to the four shires only; and for that cause specially, he caused all the acts of a parliament lately before holden by the viscount of Gormanston to be repealed and made void.[334] Moreover, that the parliaments of Ireland might want no decent or honorable form that was used in England, he caused a particular act to pass, that the lords of Ireland should appear in the like parliament robes as the English lords are wont to wear in the parliaments of England. Having thus established all the statutes of England in Ireland, and set in order the Great Council of that realm, he did not

334. Gormanston's parliament was held shortly before Poynings landed at Howth on 13 October 1494.

omit to pass other laws, as well for the increase of the king's revenue, as the preservation of the public peace.

To advance the profits of the Crown, first he obtained a subsidy of 26s.8d. out of every six-score acres manured, payable
yearly for five years. Next, he resumed all the Crown land which
had been aliened (for the most part) by Richard duke of York.
And lastly, he procured a subsidy of poundage out of all merchandises imported and exported, to be granted to the Crown in
perpetuity.

To preserve the public peace, he revived the Statues of Kilkenny; he made willful murder high treason; he caused the
Marchers[335] to book[336] their men for whom they should answer,
and restrained the making [of] war or peace without special
commission from the state.

These laws, and others as important as these, for the making
of a commonwealth in Ireland were made in the government of
Sir Edward Poynings. But these laws did not spread their virtue
beyond the English Pale, though they were made generally for
the whole kingdom. For the provinces without the Pale, which
during the War of York and Lancaster had wholly cast off the
English government, were not apt to receive this seed of reformation because they were not first broken and mastered again
with the sword. Besides, the Irish countries, which contained
two-third parts of the kingdom, were not reduced to shire-
ground, so as in them the laws of England could not possibly be
put in execution. Therefore, these good laws and provisions
made by Sir Edward Poynings were like good lessons set for a
lute that is broken and out of tune, of which lessons little use can
be made till the lute be made fit to be played upon.

And that the execution of all these laws had no greater lati-
tude than the Pale is manifest by the statute of 13 Henry VIII,

335. *Marchers*: the English nobility living along the borders of the English-
Irish territories and accustomed to the expediency of march (or martial), not
common, law.
336. *to book*: to record, register.

c.3, which reciteth that at that time the king's laws were obeyed and executed in the four shires only—and yet then was the earl of Surrey lieutenant of Ireland, a governor much feared of the king's enemies, and exceedingly honored and beloved of the king's subjects. And the instructions given by the state of Ireland to John Allen, master of the rolls, employed into England near about the same time, do declare as much; wherein among other things he is required to advertise the king that his land of Ireland was so much decayed as that the king's laws were not obeyed twenty miles in compass.* Whereupon grew that byword used by the Irish, viz., that they dwelt "by-west the law," which dwelt beyond the River of the Barrow, which is within thirty miles of Dublin. The same is testified by Baron Finglas in his *Discourse of the Decay of Ireland*, which he wrote about 20 King Henry VIII.[337] And thus we see the effect of the reformation which was intended by Sir Edward Poynings.

The Reformation Intended by the Lord Leonard Grey (28 Henry VIII)

The next attempt of reformation was made in 28 King Henry VIII by the Lord Leonard Grey, who was created viscount of Grane in this kingdom and held a parliament wherein many excellent laws were made. But to prepare the minds of the people to obey these laws, he began first with a martial course: for being sent over to suppress the rebellion of the Geraldines (which he performed in few months), he afterwards made a victorious circuit roundabout the kingdom, beginning in Offaly against O'Connor, who had aided the Geraldines in their rebellion, and from thence passing along through all the Irish countries in Leinster, and so into Munster, where he took pledges of the degenerate earl of Desmond, and thence into Connaught, and thence into Ulster; and then concluded this warlike progress

337. See note 58.

with the battle of Bellahoe[338] in the borders of Meath,* as is before remembered.

The principal septs of the Irishry being all terrified and most of them broken in this journey, many of their chief lords upon this deputy's return came to Dublin and made their submissions to the Crown of England: namely, the O'Neills and O'Reillys of Ulster; MacMurrough, O'Bryne, and O'Carrol of Leinster; and the Burkes of Connaught.*

This preparation being made, he first propounded and passed in Parliament[339] these laws, which made the great alteration in the state ecclesiastical: namely, the act which declared King Henry VIII to be supreme head of the Church of Ireland; the act prohibiting appeals to the Church of Rome; the act for first fruits and twentieth part to be paid to the king; the act for faculties and dispensations; and lastly, the act that did utterly abolish the usurped authority of the pope. Next, for the increase of the king's revenue, by one act he suppressed sundry abbeys and religious houses and by another act resumed the lands of the absentees (as is before remembered).

And for the civil government, a special statute was made to abolish the black rents and tributes exacted by the Irish upon the English colonies; and another law enacted, that the English apparel, language, and manner of living should be used by all such as would acknowledge themselves the king's subjects.

The Course of Reformation Pursued by Sir Anthony St. Leger
Four General Submissions of the Irish

This Parliament being ended, the Lord Leonard Grey was suddenly revoked and put to death in England:[340] so as he lived

338. See note 119.

339. Davies errs in his chronology: Grey's victory over the Ulster confederacy occurred in 1539; the famous reformation parliament Davies refers to was held at Dublin in 1536.

340. As lord deputy, Grey succeeded in antagonizing friends as well as foes

not to finish the work of reformation which he had begun; which notwithstanding was well pursued by his [successor], Sir Anthony St. Leger, unto whom all the lords and chieftains of the Irishry, and of the degenerate English throughout the kingdom, made their several submissions by indenture (which was the fourth general submission of the Irish made since the first attempt of the conquest of Ireland; whereof the first was made to King Henry II, the second to King John, the third to King Richard II, and [the] last to Sir Anthony St. Leger in 33 Henry VIII).

The Irish and Degenerate English Renounce the Pope

In these indentures of submission, all the Irish lords do acknowledge King Henry VIII to be their sovereign lord and king, and desire to be accepted of him as subjects.* They confess the king's supremacy in all causes and do utterly renounce the pope's jurisdiction, which I conceive to be worth the noting because when the Irish had once resolved to obey the king, they made no scruple to renounce the pope. And this was not only done by the mere Irish, but the chief of the degenerate English families did perform the same: as Desmond, Barry, and Roche in Munster; and the Burkes, which bore the title of MacWilliam, in Connaught.

These submissions being thus taken, the lord deputy and council for the present government of those Irish countries made certain ordinances of state, not agreeable altogether with the rules of the law of England; the reason whereof is expressed in the preamble of those ordinances: "Because they do not yet know the observances and laws well enough to be able immedi-

---

of the Crown. Accused of what Bagwell has called "an enormous number of charges" (*Ireland under the Stuarts*, 1:244), Grey was recalled, tried for treason, and finally executed on 28 July 1541.

ately to live and be ruled by them."[341]* The chief points or articles of which orders registered in the Council Book are these: that King Henry VIII should be accepted, reputed, and named king of Ireland by all the inhabitants of the kingdom; that all archbishops and bishops should be permitted to exercise their jurisdiction in every diocese throughout the land; that tithes should be duly set out and paid; that children should not be admitted to benefices; that for every manslaughter and theft above 14d. committed in the Irish countries the offender should pay a fine of £40 (£20 to the king and £20 to the captain of the country); and for every theft under 14d., a fine of 5 marks should be paid (46s.8d. to the captain, and 20s. to the tanister);[342] that horsemen and kern should not be imposed upon the common people, to be fed and maintained by them; that the master should answer for his servants and the father for his children; that cuttings[343] should not be made by the lord upon his tenants to maintain war with his neighbors, but only to bear his necessary expenses, etc.

These ordinances of state being made and published, there were nominated and appointed in every province certain orderers or arbitrators who, instead of these Irish brehons, should hear and determine all their controversies: in Connaught, the archbishop of Tuam, the bishop of Clonfert, Captain Wakely, and Captain Ovington; in Munster, the bishop of Waterford, the bishop of Cork and Ross, the mayor of Cork, and mayor of Youghal; in Ulster, the archbishop of Armagh and the lord of Louth. And if any difference did arise which they could not end, either for the difficulty of the cause or for the obstinacy of the parties, they were to certify[344] the lord deputy and council, who would decide the matter by their authority.

341. "Quia nondum sic sapiunt leges et Jura, ut secundum ea iam immediate vivere et regni possint."

342. The tanister; see note 18.

343. cuttings: exactions, levies of taxes.

344. certify: inform; give a legal attestation to.

Hereupon, the Irish captains of lesser territories, which had ever been oppressed by the greater and mightier, some with risings out, others with *bonaght*, and others with cuttings and spendings at pleasure, did appeal for justice to the lord deputy, who upon hearing their complaints did always order that they should all immediately depend upon the king, and that the weaker should have no dependency upon the stronger.

Lastly, he prevailed so much with the greatest of them, namely, O'Neill, O'Brien, and MacWilliam, as that they willingly did pass into England and presented themselves to the king, who thereupon was pleased to advance them to the degree and honor of earls and to grant unto them their several countries by letters patents.[345] Besides, that they might learn obedience and civility of manners by often repairing unto the state, the king, upon the motion of the same deputy, gave each of them a house and lands near Dublin for the entertainment of their several trains.

This course did this governor take to reform the Irishry, but withal he did not omit to advance both the honor and profit of the king. For in the Parliament which he held 33 Henry VIII, he caused an act to pass which gave unto King Henry VIII, his heirs and successors, the name, style, and title of "king of Ireland"; whereas before that time the kings of England were styled but "lords of Ireland," albeit, indeed, they were absolute monarchs thereof and had in right all royal and imperial jurisdiction and power there as they had in the realm of England. And yet because in the vulgar conceit the name of *king* is higher than the name of *lord*, assuredly, the assuming of this title hath not a little raised the sovereignty of the king of England in the minds of this people. Lastly, this deputy brought a great augmentation to the king's revenue by dissolving of all the monas-

345. Conn Bacagh ("the Lame") O'Neill was granted the earldom of Tyrone in 1542; Murrough O'Brien, the earldom of Thomond in 1543; William (or Ulick) MacWilliam Burke, the earldom of Clanricard in 1543.

teries and religious houses in Ireland, which was done in the
same Parliament, and afterward by procuring Min and Cavendish,[346] two skillful auditors, to be sent over out of England; who
took an exact survey of all the possessions of the Crown and
brought many things into charge which had been concealed and
subtracted for many years before. And thus far did Sir Anthony
St. Leger proceed in the course of reformation, which though it
were a good beginning, yet was it far from reducing Ireland to
the perfect obedience of the Crown of England. For all this
while, the provinces of Connaught and Ulster, and a good part
of Leinster, were not reduced to shire-ground. And though
Munster were anciently divided into counties, the people were so
degenerate as no justice of assize durst execute his commission
amongst them. None of the Irish lords or tenants were settled in
their possessions by any grant or confirmation from the Crown,
except the three great earls before named; who, notwithstanding,
did govern their tenants and followers by the Irish or brehon
law, so as no treason, murder, rape, or theft committed in those
countries was inquired of or punished by the law of England,
and consequently, no escheat, forfeiture, or fine, no revenue (certain or casual) did accrue to the Crown out of those provinces.

The Course of Reformation Prosecuted
by Thomas Earl of Sussex in the Time of Queen Mary
Leix and Offaly Made Two Counties
(3 and 4 Philip and Mary)

The next worthy governor that endeavored to advance this
reformation was Thomas earl of Sussex, who having thoroughly
broken and subdued the two most rebellious and powerful Irish

346. Sir William Cavendish (1505?–57), treasurer of the Court of Augmentation, and John Min (or Mynne), revenue commissioner, were sent to Ireland
in 1541.

septs in Leinster (namely, the Mores and O'Connors possessing the territories of Leix and Offaly), did by Act of Parliament, 3 and 4 Philip and Mary, reduce those countries into two several counties, naming the one, the King's, and the other, the Queen's County; which were the first two counties that had been made in this kingdom since 12 King John, at what time the territories then possessed by the English colonies were reduced into twelve shires, as is before expressed.

This noble earl, having thus extended the jurisdiction of the English law into two counties more, was not satisfied with that addition, but took a resolution to divide all the rest of the Irish countries unreduced into several shires; and to that end, he caused an act to pass in the same Parliament authorizing the lord chancellor from time to time to award commissions to such persons as the lord deputy should nominate and appoint, to view and perambulate those Irish territories, and thereupon to divide and limit the same into such and so many several counties as they should think meet; which being certified to the lord deputy and approved by him, should be returned and enrolled in the chancery, and from thenceforth be of like force and effect as if it were done by Act of Parliament.

Thus did the Earl of Sussex lay open a passage for the civil government into the unreformed parts of this kingdom, but himself proceeded no further than is before declared.

The Course of Reformation Followed by Sir Henry Sidney in the Time of Queen Elizabeth

Howbeit, afterwards, during the reign of Queen Elizabeth, Sir Henry Sidney (who hath left behind him many monuments of a good governor in this land) did not only pursue that course which the earl of Sussex began in reducing the Irish countries into shires and placing therein sheriffs and other ministers of the law—for first he made the Annaly, a territory in Leinster possessed by the sept of O'Ferrals, one entire shire by itself, and called it the county of Longford; and after that he divided the whole province of Connaught into six counties more, namely, Clare (which containeth all Thomond), Gallaway,[347] Sligo, Mayo, Roscommon, and Leitrim—but he also had caused divers good laws to be made and performed sundry other services tending greatly to the reformation of this kingdom. For first, to diminish the greatness of the Irish lords and to take from them the dependency of the common people, in the Parliament which he held (11 Elizabeth), he did abolish their pretended and usurped captainships, and all exactions and extortions incident thereunto. Next, to settle their seigniories and possessions in a course of inheritance according to the course of the common law, he caused an act to pass whereby the lord deputy was authorized to accept their surrenders and to regrant estates unto them, to hold of the Crown by English tenures and services. Again, because the inferior sort were loose and poor, and not amenable to the law, he provided by another act that five of the best and eldest persons of every sept should bring in all the idle persons of their surname to be justified by the law. Moreover, to give a civil education to the youth of this land in the time to come, provision was made by another law that there should be one free school at least erected in every diocese of the kingdom. And lastly, to inure and acquaint the people of Munster and Connaught with the English government again (which had not been in use among them for the space of 200 years before), he instituted two presidency courts in those two provinces, placing Sir Edward Fitton in Connaught and Sir John Perrot[348] in Munster.

To augment the [queen's] revenue in the same Parliament, upon the attainder of Shane O'Neill[349] he resumed and vested in the Crown more than half the province of Ulster; he raised the

347. Galway.

348. Fitton served as lord president of Connaught 1569–79; Perrot as lord president of Munster 1570–76.

349. Shane O'Neill, who went into rebellion about 1565, was attainted in 11 Elizabeth (1569).

customs[350] upon the principal commodities of the kingdom; he
reformed the abuses of the Exchequer by many good orders and
instructions sent out of England; and lastly, he established the
composition[351] of the Pale in lieu of purveyance[352] and cess of soldiers.

These were good proceedings in the work of reformation, but
there were many defects and omissions withal; for though he
reduced all Connaught into counties, he never sent any justices
of assize to visit that province, but placed commissioners there
who governed it only in a course of discretion, part martial and
part civil. Again, in the law that doth abolish the Irish captainships, he gave way for the reviving thereof again by excepting
such as should be granted by letters patents from the Crown;
which exception did indeed take away the force of that law, for
no governor during Queen Elizabeth's reign did refuse to grant
any of those captainships to any pretended Irish lord who would
desire and, with his thankfulness, deserve the same. And again,
though the greatest part of Ulster were vested by Act of Parliament in the actual and real possession of the Crown, yet was
there never any seizure made thereof, nor any part thereof
brought into charge, but the Irish were permitted to take all the
profits without rendering any duty or acknowledgment for the
same. And though the name of O'Neill were damned by that act
and the assuming thereof[353] made high treason, yet after that was
Turlough Luineach[354] suffered to bear that title and to intrude

350. *customs*: taxes, duties.

351. *composition*: "agreement for the payment . . . of a sum of money, in lieu
of the discharge of some other obligation, or in a different way from that
required by the original contract" (*OED*).

352. *purveyance*: commandeering or exacting horses and vehicles for the
Crown.

353. That is, the assuming of the title "O'Neill" or "The O'Neill," which
designated the chieftainship of the O'Neills and hence revealed adherence to
the brehon law and defiance of common law.

354. Following the murder of Shane O'Neill, Shane's tanist, Turlough, succeeded to the O'Neillship, which he held until he abdicated in 1593 to Hugh
O'Neill, second earl of Tyrone.

upon the possessions of the Crown, and yet was often entertained by the state with favor. Neither were these lands resumed
by the act of 11 Elizabeth neglected only, for the abbeys and religious houses in Tyrone, Tyrconnell, and Fermanagh, though
they were dissolved in 33 Henry VIII, were never surveyed nor
reduced into charge, but were continually possessed by the religious persons until His Majesty that now is came to the Crown;
and that which is more strange, [neither were the] donations of
bishoprics, being a flower of the Crown (which the kings of England did ever retain in all their dominions, when the popes'
usurped authority was at the highest). There were three bishoprics in Ulster, namely, Derry, Rapho, and Clogher, which neither
Queen Elizabeth nor any of her progenitors did ever bestow,
though they were the undoubted patrons thereof. So as King
James was the first king of England that did ever supply those
sees with bishops, which is an argument either of great negligence or of great weakness in the state and governors of those
times. And thus far proceeded Sir Henry Sidney.

The Reformation Advanced by Sir John Perrot

After him, Sir John Perrot,[355] who held the last Parliament in
this kingdom, did advance the reformation in three principal
points: first, in establishing the great Composition of Connaught, in which service the wisdom and industry of Sir Richard
Bingham[356] did concur with him; next, in reducing the unreformed parts of Ulster into seven shires, namely, Armagh, Monaghan, Tyrone, Coleraine, Donegal, Fermanagh, and Cavan,
though in his time the law was never executed in these new

355. Lord deputy 1584–88. Perrot summoned Parliament on 26 April 1585
and dissolved it on 14 May 1586. Apparently Queen Elizabeth was so dis-
pleased with this parliament that she never summoned another in Ireland for
the duration of her reign. See Ellis, *Tudor Ireland*, pp. 286–88.
356. Almost universally condemned by his contemporaries for his cruelty,
Bingham was governor of Connaught, with some interruption, 1584–96.

counties by any sheriffs or justices of assize, but the people left to be ruled still by their own barbarous lords and laws; and lastly, by vesting in the Crown the lands of Desmond and his adherents in Munster, and planting the same with English, though that plantation were imperfect in many points[357]

The Service of William FitzWilliams, Tending to Reformation

After Sir John Perrot, Sir William FitzWilliams did good service in two other points: first, in raising a composition in Munster; and then, in settling the possessions both of the lords and tenants in Monaghan, which was one of the last acts of state tending to the reformation of the civil government that was performed in the reign of Queen Elizabeth.

Thus we see by what degrees and what policy and success the governors of this land from time to time since the beginning of the reign of King Edward III have endeavored to reform and reduce this people to the perfect obedience of the Crown of England. And we find that before the civil wars of York and Lancaster they did chiefly endeavor to bring back the degenerate English colonies to their duty and allegiance, not respecting the mere Irish, whom they reputed as aliens or enemies of the Crown. But after King Henry VII had united the Roses, they labored to reduce both English and Irish together; which work, to what pass and perfection it was brought in the latter end of Queen Elizabeth's reign, hath been before declared.

Whereof sometimes when I do consider, I do in mine own conceit compare these later governors who went about to reform the civil affairs in Ireland unto some of the kings of Israel, of whom it is said that they were good kings, but they did not cut down the groves and high places, but suffered the people still to

357. Following the suppressing of Desmond's rebellion and the confiscation of his lands, Munster was opened to colonization in the 1580s.

burn incense and commit idolatry in them: so Sir Anthony St.
Leger, the earl of Sussex, Sir Henry Sidney, and Sir John Perrot
were good governors, but they did not abolish the Irish customs
nor execute the law in the Irish countries, but suffered the people
to worship their barbarous lords and to remain utterly ignorant
of their duties to God and the king.

How the Defects and Errors in the Government of Ireland Have Been Supplied and Amended since the Beginning of His Majesty's Reign

And now am I come to the happy reign of my most Gracious
Lord and Master, King James, in whose time, as there hath been
a concurrence of many great felicities, so this among others may
be numbered in the first rank: that all the defects in the government of Ireland spoken of before have been fully supplied in the
first nine years of his reign; in which time, there hath been more
done in the work and reformation of this kingdom than in the
440 years which are passed since the conquest was first attempted.

Howbeit, I have no purpose in this discourse to set forth at
large all the proceedings of the state here in reforming of this
kingdom since His Majesty came to the Crown, for the parts and
passages thereof are so many, as to express them fully would
require a several treatise.[358] Besides, I for my part, since I have
not flattered the former times, but have plainly laid open the
negligence and errors of every age that is past, would not willingly seem to flatter the present by amplifying the diligence and
true judgment of those servitors that have labored in this vine-
yard since the beginning of His Majesty's happy reign.

I shall therefore summarily, without any amplification at all,
show in what manner and by what degrees all the defects which
I have noted before in the government of this kingdom have

358. *several treatise*: discourse having many distinct parts.

been supplied since His Majesty's happy reign began, and so conclude these observations concerning the state of Ireland.

Errors in the Carriage of the Martial Affairs Amended

First then, touching the martial affairs, I shall need to say little, in regard that the war which finished the conquest of Ireland was ended almost in the instant when the Crown descended upon His Majesty, and so there remained no occasion to amend the former errors committed in the prosecution of the war. Howbeit, sithence[359] His Majesty hath still maintained an army here, as well for a seminary of martial men as to give strength and countenance to the civil magistrate, I may justly observe that this army hath not been fed with coyne and livery or cess (with which extortions the soldier hath been nourished in the times of former princes), but hath been as justly and royally paid as ever prince in the world did pay his men of war. Besides, when there did arise an occasion of employment for this army against the rebel O'Dougherty,[360] neither did His Majesty delay the reinforcing thereof, but instantly sent supplies out of England and Scotland. Neither did the martial men dally or prosecute the service faintly, but did forthwith quench that fire, whereby themselves would have been the warmer the longer it had continued, as well by the increase of their entertainment, as by booties and spoil of the country. And thus much I thought fit to note touching the amendment of the errors in the martial affairs.

How the Defects in the Civil
Government Have Been Supplied

Secondly, for the supply of the defects in the civil government, these courses have been pursued since His Majesty's prosperous reign began.

359. *sithence*: because.
360. Sir Cahir O'Dougherty, lord of Inishowen, went into rebellion in 1608.

[By] Establishing the Public Peace

First, albeit upon the end of the war, whereby Tyrone's universal rebellion was suppressed, the minds of the people were broken and prepared to obedience of the law, yet the state upon good reason did conceive that the public peace could not be settled till the hearts of the people were also quieted by securing them from the danger of the law, which the most part of them had incurred one way or other in that great and general confusion.

Therefore, first by a general act of the state, called the Act of Oblivion, published by proclamation under the Great Seal, all offenses against the Crown and all particular trespasses between subject and subject, done at any time before His Majesty's reign, were (to all such as would come in to the justices of assize by a certain day and claim the benefit of this act) pardoned, remitted, and utterly extinguished, never to be revived or called in question. And by the same proclamation, all the Irishry (who for the most part in former times were left under the tyranny of their lords and [chieftains], and had no defense or justice from the Crown) were received into His Majesty's immediate protection. This bred such comfort and security in the hearts of all men as thereupon ensued the calmest and most universal peace that ever was seen in Ireland.

[By] Establishing the Public Justice in Every Part of the Kingdom

The public peace being thus established, the state proceeded next to establish the public justice in every part of the realm. And to that end, Sir George Carey[361] (who was a prudent governor, and a just, and made a fair entry into the right way of

361. Lord deputy 1603–5; not to be confused with Sir George Carew, the lord president of Munster during the Nine Years' War (*Carey* and *Carew* were often spelled and pronounced the same: *Carey*).

reforming this kingdom) did in the first year of His Majesty's reign make the first sheriffs that ever were made in Tyrone and Tyrconnell, and shortly after sent Sir Edmund Pelham,[362] chief baron, and myself thither, the first justices of assize that ever sat in those countries. And in that circuit we visited all the shires of that province's besides[;] which visitation, though it were somewhat distasteful to the Irish lords, was sweet and most welcome to the common people, who, albeit they were rude and barbarous, yet did they quickly apprehend the difference between the tyranny and oppression under which they lived before, and the just government and protection which we promised unto them for the time to come.

The law having made her progress into Ulster with so good success, Sir Arthur Chichester[363] (who with singular industry, wisdom, and courage hath now for the space of seven years and more prosecuted the great work of reformation and brought it well-near to an absolute perfection) did in the first year of his government establish two other new circuits for justices of assize, the one in Connaught and the other in Munster. I call them "new circuits," for that, although it be manifest by many records that justices itinerant have in former times been sent into all the shires of Munster and some part of Connaught, yet certain it is that in 200 years before (I speak much within compass) no such commission had been executed in either of these two provinces. But now, the whole realm being divided into shires, and every bordering territory whereof any doubt was made in what county the same should lie, being added or reduced to a county certain—among the rest, the mountains and glens on the south side of Dublin were lately made a shire by itself and called the county of Wicklow, whereby the inhabitants which were wont to be thorns in the side of the Pale are become civil and quiet neigh-

362. Chief baron of the exchequer, 1602–6.
363. Sir Arthur Chichester, governor of Carrickfergus Castle during the Nine Years' War, was lord deputy from 1605 to 1616.

bors thereof—the streams of the public justice were derived[364] into every part of the kingdom, and the benefit and protection of the law of England communicated to all, as well Irish as English, without distinction or respect of persons. By reason whereof, the work of deriving the public justice grew so great as that there was *magna messis, sed operarii pauci.*[365] And therefore, the number of judges in every bench was increased, which do now every half-year (like good planets in their several spheres or circles) carry the light and influence of justice roundabout the kingdom; whereas the circuits in former times went but roundabout the Pale, like the circuit of the *cynosura* about the Pole:[366] *quae cursu interiore, brevi convertitur orbe.*[367]

The Good Effects Which Followed the Execution of the Law throughout the Kingdom

Upon these visitations of justice whereby the just and honorable law of England was imparted and communicated to all the Irishry, there followed these excellent good effects.

First, the common people were taught by the justices of assize that they were free subjects to the kings of England, and not slaves and vassals to their pretended lords; that the cuttings, cosheries, cessings, and other extortions of their lords were unlawful, and that they should not any more submit themselves thereunto, since they were now under the protection of so just and mighty a prince as both would and could protect them from all wrongs and oppressions. They gave a willing ear unto these lessons, and thereupon the greatness and power of those Irish

364. *derived*: caused to flow; directed.
365. "The harvest truly is plenteous, but the laborers are few" (Matt. 9:37).
366. *cynosura*: the constellation Ursa Minor or the Little Dipper, having Polaris, the "fixed" North Star, as its outermost star.
367. "Whatever is moved on an internal course, is moved in a short circle."

lords over the people suddenly fell and vanished when their oppressions and extortions were taken away which did maintain their greatness. Insomuch, as divers of them who formerly made themselves owners of all, by force, were now by the law reduced to this point: that wanting means to defray their ordinary charges, they resorted ordinarily to the lord deputy and made petition that by license and warrant of the state they might take some aid and contribution from their people, as well to discharge their former debts as for competent maintenance in time to come. But some of them being impatient of this diminution fled out of the realm to foreign countries.[368] Whereupon, we may well observe that, as extortion did banish the Old English freeholder who could not live but under the law, so the law did banish the Irish lord who could not live but by extortion.

Again, these circuits of justice did, upon the end of the war, more terrify the loose and idle persons than the execution of the martial law, though it were more quick and sudden, and in a short time after did so clear the kingdom of thieves and other capital offenders, as I dare affirm that for the space of five years last past there have not been found so many malefactors worthy of death in all the six circuits of this realm (which is now divided into thirty-two shires at large) as in one circuit of six shires, namely, the Western Circuit in England. For the truth is that in time of peace the Irish are more fearful to offend the law than the English or any other nation whatsoever.

Again, whereas the greatest advantage that the Irish had of us in all their rebellions was our ignorance of their countries, their persons, and their actions, since the law and her ministers have had a passage among them, all their places of fastness have been

368. Although such chieftains as Donal O'Sullivan Beare fled Ireland shortly after the conclusion of the Nine Years' War in 1603, Davies probably refers here to the Flight of the Earls in 1607, when the great Ulster chieftains Coconaught Maguire, Rory O'Donnell, and Hugh O'Neill went into permanent exile.

discovered and laid open, all their paces[369] cleared, and notice taken of every person that is able to do either good or hurt. It is known, not only how they live and what they do, but it is foreseen what they purpose or intend to do: insomuch as Tyrone hath been heard to complain that he had so many eyes watching over him as he could not drink a full carouse of sack, but the state was advertised thereof within few hours after. And therefore, those allowances which I find in the ancient Pipe Rolls *pro guidagio* and *spiagio*[370] may be well spared at this day. For the undersheriffs and bailiffs errant are better guides and spies in the time of peace than any were found in the time of war.

Moreover, these civil assemblies at assizes and sessions have reclaimed the Irish from their wildness; caused them to cut off their glibs[371] and long hair, to convert their mantles into cloaks, to conform themselves to the manner of England in all their behavior and outward forms. And because they find a great inconvenience in moving their suits by an interpreter, they do for the most part send their children to schools, especially to learn the English language: so as, we may conceive an hope that the next generation will in tongue and heart, and every way else, become English, so as there will be no difference or distinction but the Irish Sea betwixt us. And thus we see a good conversion, and the Irish game[372] turned again.

For heretofore, the neglect of the law made the English degenerate and become Irish; and now, on the other side, the execution of the law doth make the Irish grow civil and become English.

Lastly, these general sessions now do teach the people more

369. *paces*: passes.
370. "for guidance" and "[for] spying."
371. *glibs*: from the Gaelic *glib* ("a bang"), bangs; matted hair cut immediately above the eyes. (The wearing of a glib distinguished a male as native Irish or one seeking identification with Irish culture.)
372. See note 261.

obedience and keep them more in awe than did the general host-
ing in former times. These progresses of the law renew and confirm the conquest of Ireland every half-year and supply the
defect of the king's absence in every part of the realm, in that
every judge sitting in the seat of justice doth represent the person
of the king himself.

These effects hath the establishment of the public peace and
justice produced since His Majesty's happy reign began.

[The] Settling of the States and Possessions
of the Irishry as Well as of the English

Howbeit, it was impossible to make a commonweal in Ireland
without performing another service, which was the settling of all
the estates and possessions, as well of Irish as English, throughout the kingdom.

For, although that in 12 Queen Elizabeth a special law was
made which did enable the lord deputy to take surrenders and
regrant estates unto the Irishry (upon signification of Her Majesty's pleasure in that behalf), yet were there but few of the Irish
lords that made offer to surrender during her reign; and they
which made surrenders of entire countries obtained grants of the
whole again to themselves only and to no other, and all in
demesne; in passing of which grants there was no care taken of
the inferior septs of people inhabiting and possessing these countries under them, but they held their several portions in course
of tanistry and gavelkind and yielded the same Irish duties or
exactions as they did before. So that upon every such surrender
and grant, there was but one freeholder made in a whole country, which was the lord himself; all the rest were but tenants at
will, or rather tenants in villeinage, and were neither fit to be
sworn in juries, nor to perform any public service; and by reason
of the uncertainty of their estates did utterly neglect to build or
to plant or to improve the land. And therefore, although the
lord were become the king's tenant, his country was no whit

reformed thereby, but remained in the former barbarism and desolation.

Again, in the same queen's time there were many Irish lords which did not surrender, yet obtained letters patents of the captainships of their countries and of all lands and duties belonging to those captainships. For the statute which doth condemn and abolish these captainries usurped by the Irish doth give power to the lord deputy to grant the same by letters patents. Howbeit, these Irish captains, and likewise the English which were made seneschals of the Irish countries, did by color of these grants and under pretense of government claim an Irish seigniory and exercise plain tyranny over the common people. And this was the fruit that did arise of the letters patents granted of the Irish countries in the time of Queen Elizabeth: where before they did extort and oppress the people only by color of a lewd and barbarous custom, they did afterwards use the same extortions and oppressions by warrant under the Great Seal of the realm.

How the Commissions for Surrenders and Defective Titles Have Been Put in Execution

But now, since His Majesty came to the Crown, two special commissions have been sent out of England for the settling and quieting of all the possessions in Ireland: the one for accepting surrenders of the Irish and degenerate English, and for regranting estates unto them according to the course of the common law; the other for strengthening of defective titles—in the execution of which commissions, there hath ever been had a special care to settle and secure the undertenants, to the end there might be a repose and establishment of every subject's estate, lord and tenant, freeholder and farmer, throughout the kingdom.

Upon surrenders, this course hath been held from the beginning: when a Irish lord doth offer to surrender his country, his surrender is not immediately accepted, but a commission is first awarded to inquire of three special points: first, of the quantity and limits of the land whereof he is reputed owner; next, how much himself doth hold in demesne, and how much is possessed by his tenants and followers; and thirdly, what customs, duties, and services he doth yearly receive out of those lands. This inquisition being made and returned, the lands which are found to be the lord's proper possessions in demesne are drawn into a particular,[373] and his Irish duties, as cosherings, cessings, rents of butter and oatmeal, and the like, are reasonably valued and reduced into certain sums of money to be paid yearly in lieu thereof. This being done, the surrender is accepted and thereupon a grant passed, not of the whole country, as was used in former times, but of those lands only which are found in the lord's possession, and of those certain sums of money, as rents issuing out of the rest. But the lands which are found to be possessed by the tenants are left unto them, respectively charged with these certain rents only, in lieu of all uncertain Irish exactions.

In like manner, upon all grants which have passed by virtue of the commission for defective titles, the commissioners have taken special caution for preservation of the estates of all particular tenants.

No Grant of Irish Captainships or Seneschalships since His Majesty's Reign

And as for grants of captainships or seneschalships in the Irish countries: albeit this deputy [i.e., Chichester] had as much power and authority to grant the same as any other governors had before him, and might have raised as much profit by bestowing the same if he had respected his private, more than the public, good, yet hath he been so far from passing any such in all his time, as he hath endeavored to resume all the grants of that kind that have been made by his predecessors; to the end, the inferior

373. *particular*: "statement setting forth the several points or details of a matter" (*OED*).

subjects of the realm should make their only and immediate dependency upon the Crown. And thus we see how the greatest part of the possessions (as well of the Irish as of the English) in Leinster, Connaught, and Munster are settled and secured since His Majesty came to the Crown; whereby the hearts of the people are also settled, not only to live in peace, but raised and encouraged to build, to plant, to give better education to their children, and to improve the commodities of their lands, whereby the yearly value thereof is already increased double of that it was within these few years, and is like daily to rise higher, till it amount to the price of our land in England.

The Plantation of Ulster

Lastly, the possessions of the Irishry in the province of Ulster, though it were the most rude and unreformed part of Ireland, and the seat and nest of the last great rebellion, are now better disposed and established than any the lands in the other provinces which have been passed and settled upon surrenders. For as the occasion of the disposing of those lands did not happen without the special providence and finger of God, which did cast out those wicked and ungrateful traitors who were the only enemies of the reformation of Ireland, so the distribution and plantation thereof hath been projected and prosecuted by the special direction and care of the king himself; wherein His Majesty hath corrected the errors before spoken of committed by King Henry II and King John in distributing and planting the first conquered lands. For, although there were six whole shires to be disposed, His Majesty gave not an entire country or county to any particular person; much less did he grant *jura regalia* or any extraordinary liberties. For the best British undertaker had but a proportion of 3,000 acres for himself, with power to create a manor and hold a court-baron,[374] albeit many of these undertak-

---

374. *court-baron*: judicial "assembly of the freehold tenants of a manor under the presidency of the lord or his steward" (*OED*).

ers were of as great birth and quality as the best adventurers in the first conquest. Again, His Majesty did not utterly exclude the natives out of this plantation, with a purpose to root them out, as the Irish were excluded out of the first English colonies, but made a mixed plantation of British and Irish, that they might grow up together in one nation: only, the Irish were in some places transplanted from the woods and mountains into the plains and open countries, that being removed (like wild fruit trees) they might grow the milder, and bear the better and sweeter fruit. And this truly is the masterpiece and most excellent part of the work of reformation and is worthy indeed of His Majesty's royal pains. For when this plantation hath taken root, and been fixed and settled but a few years, with the favor and blessing of God—for the Son of God himself hath said in the Gospel, *omnis plantio, quam non plantauit pater meus, eradicabitur*[375]—it will secure the peace of Ireland, assure it to the Crown of England forever, and finally make it a civil and a rich, a mighty and a flourishing kingdom.

I omit to speak of the increase of the revenue of the Crown, both certain and casual, which is raised to a double proportion, at least, above that it was by deriving the public justice into all parts of the realm; by settling all the possessions, both of the Irish and English; by reestablishing the compositions; by restoring and resuming the customs; by reviving the tenures *in capite* and knight's-service,[376] and reducing many other things into charge, which by the confusion and negligence of former times became concealed and subtracted from the Crown. I forbear likewise to speak of the due and ready bringing in of the revenue, which is brought to pass by the well ordering of the court

375. Matt. 15:13: "Every plant, which my heavenly Father hath not planted, shall be rooted up."
376. *tenures "in capite"*: lands "held immediately of the King, or of the crown" (*OED*); *knight's-service*: "the tenure of land under the condition of performing military service" (*OED*).

of exchequer and the authority and pains of the commissioners for accounts.

I might also add hereunto the encouragement that hath been given to the maritime towns and cities, as well to increase their trade of merchandise as to cherish mechanical arts and sciences, in that all their charters have been renewed and their liberties more enlarged by His Majesty than by any of his progenitors since the conquest; as likewise, the care and course that hath been taken to make civil commerce and intercourse between the subjects newly reformed and brought under obedience, by granting markets and fairs to be holden in their countries and by erecting of corporate towns among them.

Briefly, the clock of the civil government is now well set, and all the wheels thereof do move in order. The strings of this Irish harp, which the civil magistrate doth finger, are all in tune (for I omit to speak of the state ecclesiastical) and make a good harmony in this commonweal. So as we may well conceive a hope that Ireland (which heretofore might properly be called the "land of ire" because the irascible power was predominant there for the space of 400 years together) will from henceforth prove a land of peace and concord. And though heretofore it hath been like the lean cow of Egypt in Pharaoh's dream,[377] devouring the fat of England and yet remaining as lean as it was before, it will hereafter be as fruitful as the land of Canaan, the description whereof in 8 Deuteronomy doth in every part agree with Ireland, being,

terra rivorum, aquarumque; et fontium; in cuius campis, et montibus, erumpunt fluviorum abyssi; terra frumenti, et hordei; terra lactis et mellis; ubi absque ulla penuria comedes panem tuum, et rerum abundantia perfrueris.[378]

377. See Gen. 41:15–27.
378. The freely rendered King James Version of this passage is as follows: "For the Lord thy God bringeth thee into a good land, a land of brooks of water, of fountains and depths that spring out of valleys and hills; a land of

And thus I have discovered and expressed the defects and errors, as well in the managing of the martial affairs as of the civil, which in former ages gave impediment to the reducing of all Ireland to the obedience and subjection of the Crown of England. I have likewise observed what courses have been taken to reform the defects and errors in government and to reduce the people of this land to obedience since the beginning of the reign of King Edward III till the latter end of the reign of Queen Elizabeth.

And lastly, I have declared and set forth how all the said errors have been corrected and the defects supplied under the prosperous government of His Majesty; so as I may positively conclude in the same words which I have used in the title of this discourse: that until the beginning of His Majesty's reign, Ireland was never entirely subdued and brought under the obedience of the Crown of England. But since the Crown of this kingdom, with the undoubted right and title thereof, descended upon His Majesty, the whole island from sea to sea hath been brought into His Highness's peaceable possession, and all the inhabitants, in every corner thereof, have been absolutely reduced under his immediate subjection; in which condition of subjects they will gladly continue, without defection or adhering to any other lord or king as long as they may be protected and justly governed, without oppression on the one side or impunity on the other. For there is no nation of people under the sun that doth love equal and indifferent justice better than the Irish, or will rest better satisfied with the execution thereof, although it be against themselves, so as they may have the protection and benefit of the law when upon just cause they do desire it.

FINIS

---

wheat, and barley, and vines, and fig trees, and pomegranates; a land of oil olive and honey; a land wherein thou shalt eat bread without scarceness, thou shalt not lack any thing in it" (Deut. 8:7–9).

Appendix I
Davies's Marginal Notes

73 Giraldus Cambrenis.
Archiu. Remem. Regis apud
Westm.
76 Bodin de Repub.
77 Houeden in Henrico secundo.
fol. 312.
6. Iohannis Claus. membrana.
18. 17. Iohannis Chart.
m.3.
6. Hen. 3. chart. m.2.
78 Archiu. in Castro Dublin. 42
Hen. 3. Compotus Will. de
la Zouch.
36. Hen. 3. compotus Huberti
de Rouly.
79 Giraldus Cambrensis.
Giraldus Cambrensis.
80 Giraldus Cambrensis.
Matth. Paris in Richardo
primo fo. 1519.
81 Matth. Paris.
82 This Charter yet remaineth
perfect, with an entire Seale
in the Treasury at
Westminster.
Archiu. in Castro Dublin. &
Archiu. Turr. 52. Hen. 3.
patent m.9.
83 Archiu. in Castro Dublin.
84 Statu. 10 H. 7. cap. 4. Rot.
Parliam. in Castro Dublin.
Annales Hiberniae in Camden.
Baron Finglas. Manus. Stat. 10.
H. 7. cap. 4. Rot. Parliam.
in Castro Dublin.
85 Statu. 11. H. 4. cap. 6

Baron Finglas. M.S.
Archiu. Remem. regis apud.
Westm.
88 Archiu. Turr. 36. Edw. 3.
Claus. m.21. in dorso. &
m.30.
47. Edw. 3. Claus. m.1.
Stow. in Rich. 2.
89 Archiu. Turr. 11. H. 3 patent
m.3.
47. Ed. 3. claus. pers. 2. m.24
& 26.
90 Hollingshead in R. 2.
Archiu. in Castro Dublin. 5.
Edw. 3.
91 Rich. 2. Archiu. Turr. Rot.
Parliam. 42.
92 Pat. 2. pars. 9. Rich. 2. m.24.
Walsingham in Richard the 2.
Annales. Tho. Otterbourne
Manuscript.
93 Stow in Rich. 2.
Archiu. in officio Rememorat.
regis apud Westmin.
96 Hollingshead in Richard the 2.
97 Archiu. Rememort. regis apud
Westm.
Alb. libr. Scacc. Dublin.
99 Archiu. in Castro Dublin.
Hollingshead in Henry the
sixt.
100 Rot. Parliam. in Castro
Dublin.
Archiu. Tur. 17. Hen. 6. Claus.
m.20.
Manuscript of Baron Finglas.

Hollingshead in Hen. 6
101   Hollingshead in Edward the 4.
      Booke of Howth. Manus.
      14. of Edw. 4. Rot. Parliam.
      Dublin.
103   Archiu. Remem. Regis apud
      Westm.
      The Booke of Howth. Manus.
      Hollingshead in Henry the 7.
104   Rot. Parliam. in Castro
      Dublin.
      The Booke of Howth.
105   Booke of Howth. Manus.
106   Archiu. Remem. Regis apud
      Westm.
107   Archiu. Remem. Regis apud
      Westm.
112   The Booke of Howth. Manus.
115   Archiu. in Castro Dublin.
      Annales Hiberniae in Camden.
116   Annales Hiberniae in Camden.
      Archiu. in Castro Dublin.
117   Annales Hiberniae in Camden.
118   Annales Hiberniae in Camden.
119   Hollingshead in Hen. 6.
120   Manuscript of Baron Finglas.
124   Matth. Paris Histor. maior.
      fol. 121.
      Matth. Paris Histor. maior
      220.b.
127   Archiu. in Castro Dublin.
128   Archiu. in Castro Dublin.
129   Archiu. in Castro Dublin.
130   Archiu. in Castro Dublin.
132   Archiu. in Castro Dublin.
133   Archiu. in Castro Dublin.
      Stat. de Kilkenny C.2 & 3. 10.
      Hen. 6. c. r. 28. H. 8. C.13.
135   The Counsell Booke of
      Ireland. 34. Hen. 8.
138   Archiu. in Castro Dublin.
141   Tacitus in vita Agricolae.
142   Camden in Northfolke.
144   Giraldus Cambrensis. lib. 2.
      de Hiberniae expugnata.

145   Giraldus Cambrensis. lib. 2.
      de Hiberniae expugnata.
      In Archiu. Tur. 5. Edw. 3.
      Escheat nunc. ro 104.
      2 Iohannis Chart. m. 15 &
      m.38.
      6 Iohan. Chart. m.1. 7. Iohan.
      Chart. m.12 & m.109.
      6. Ed. I. Chart. m. 19.
      18. Ed. 1. m. 29.
146   Girald. Cambr. lib. 2. de
      Hiberniae expug.
      6. H. 3. Chart. m.2.
      Houeden in H. 2. fol. 302.
      Archiu. turr. 17. Iohannis
      Chart. m.3.
      Matth. Paris in Henry the
      third.
      6. Iohannis Claus. m.18.
147   Annales Hiberniae in Camden.
148   In Archiu. Tur. 11. Edw. 3.
      Escheat. m.28.
      Archiu. in Castro Dublin.
      Archiu. Turr. pat. 3. E. 3.
      m.28.
      Archiu. in Castro Dublin.
151   Annales Hiberniae in Camden.
152   Annales Hiberniae in Camden.
153   Annales Iohannis Clynne.
      Manuscript.
155   Sta. 10. H. 7. C4. Rot. Parliam.
      in Castro Dublin.
      Baron Finglas, Manuscript.
      Archiu. Turr. 5. Ed. 3. claus.
      m.4.
156   Archiu. Tur. 15. Ed. 3. claus.
      m.4.
      Annales Hiberniae in Camden.
158   Camden in Chester.
174   5. Ed. 3. m.25.
175   Annales Hiberniae in Camden.
178   Annales Hiberniae in Camden.
179   Abridgement of Salus populi.
      Manuscript.
      Baron Finglas, Manuscript.

180   Annales Hiberniae in Camden.
      Baron Finglas, Manuscript.
181   Annales Hiberniae in Camden.
182   Archiu. Turr. 2. E. 3. claus.
      pers. 1. m. 16.
      Annales Hiberniae in Camden.
183   Annales Hiberniae in Camden.
      Annales Iohan. Clynne.
      Manus.
      Annales Hiberniae in Camden.
186   The Counsell Booke of
      Ireland. 32. H. 8.
188   Archiu. in Castro Dublin.
      Statutes of Kilkenny. C.2.
      C.3.
191   Baron Finglas, Manuscript.
192   Baron Finglas, Manuscript.
193   Archiu. Turr. Rot. parliam. 42.

194   Archiu. Turr. 3. Rich. 2. cl.
      m.3.
      3. Rich. 2. Rot. Parliam. 11.42.
      9 Rich. 2. claus. m.1.
      Walsingham in Rich. 2.349.a.
195   Plac. coram Rege in Hibernia.
      Hillar. 18 Ric. 2.
200   The Counsell Booke of
      Ireland. 16. H. 8.
201   Annales Hiberniae Manus.
      The Counsell Booke of
      Ireland. 28. H. 8.
202   The Counsell Booke of
      Ireland. 32. 33. and 34.
      of H. 8.
203   The Counsell Booke of
      Ireland. 33. H. 8.

Appendix II
Textual Emendations

The Title. Modern practice has preserved the wording found on the title page of the edition of 1612: A DISCOVERIE OF THE TRVE CAV-//SES why Ireland was neuer entire-//ly Subdued, nor brought vnder Obedience of// the Crowne of England, vntill the//Beginning of his Maiesties hap-//pie Raigne. The title on page 1 introducing Davies's text, however, substitutes an *and* for the title page's *nor*: A Discouery of the true// *causes, why* Ireland *was ne-// uer entirely subdued, and brought//vnder Obedience*.... (Here hyphens indicate a word broken across two lines and a double slash indicates a line break.) In the last paragraph of the *Discovery*, moreover, Davies, referring to his own title, cites this latter wording: "So as I may positively conclude in the same words, which I haue vsed in the Title of this Discourse; *That vntill the beginning of his Maiesties Raigne, Ireland was neuer entirely subdued, and brought vnder the Obedience of the Crown of England"* (Davies's italics). Following the author's expressed intent in the text, I have, therefore, chosen to follow the wording of page 1 of the *Discovery*.

77	Bremingham's [Bremighams		surname [surnames
84	Rokeby [Rookesby	174	IRELAND [*Iceland*
87	entertainments [entertainment		le [de
90	eighth [eight	175	counties [County
91	1,000 [a thousand	176	Maurice FitzThomas
92	1,000 [a 1000		[Tho:Fitz-Maurice
97	eighth [eight	190	THE ABSENCE [Absence
99	part [patt		THE ABSENCE [Absence
108	valor [lour	199	making of [making
119	dukes [Duke	202	successor [successors
124	THE [2. The		the [his
	THE [1. The	207	queen's [kings
142	inheritor [inheritors	209	neither were the donations
143	legitimate [Legimate		[donations
144	THE [2. The	213	BY [1. By chieftains
152	Tristledermot [*Thistledermot*		[chieftainies
159	the [then		BY [2. By
164	tenancies [Tennanties	214	province's besides; which
	THAT DID [that		[Prouince: Besides which
170	FOSTERING [[*no title in Davies*]		[from the *errata* page: "... Read Prouinces besides ..."]
172	DeExeter [Dexecester	218	THE [3. The

Bibliography

Editions of Sir John Davies's *A Discovery of the True Causes Why Ireland Was Never Entirely Subdued* . . . (listed chronologically)

A Discouerie of the true causes, why Ireland was never entirely subdued, and brought under Obedience of the Crowne of England, untill the beginning of his Maiesties happy raigne. London, 1612. [Title as found on p. 1].

A Discoverie of the State of Ireland: with the true Causes why that Kingdom was neuer entirely Subdued, nor brought under Obedience of the Crowne of England, untill the Beginning of his Maiesties most happie Raigne. London, 1613. [A reissue of the 1612 printing.]

Historical Relations: or, A Discovery of the True Causes Why Ireland was never Entirely Subdued . . . Dublin, 1664, 1704, 1733, 1751.

A Discoverie of the True Causes . . . *Printed exactly from the edition in 1612.* Edited by A. Millar. London, 1747; Dublin, 1761. [Contains index and biographical essay.]

Historical Tracts: consisting of I: A Discovery of the True Causes . . . *to which Is prefixed a new Life of the Author.* . . . Edited by George Chalmers. London, 1786.

A Collection of Tracts and Treatises Illustrative of the Natural History, Antiquities, and the Political and Social State of Ireland. 2 vols. Dublin, 1860–61. [In vol. 1: 594–714.]

The Works in Verse and Prose . . . *of Sir John Davies.* Edited by Alexander B. Grosart. Blackburn, Eng., 1869–76. [Also privately printed, Blackburn, Eng., 1876.]

Ireland under Elizabeth and James I. Edited by Henry Morley, pp. 213–342. London, 1890.

Discovery of the True Causes why Ireland was never entirely subdued. Introduction by John Barry. Shannon, 1969. [A facsimile of the 1612 ed.]

Printed Calendars and Contemporary Sources

Advertisements for Ireland . . . [1623]. Edited by George O'Brien. Dublin, 1923.

Arber, Edward, ed. *A Transcript of the Registers of the Company of Stationers, 1554–1640.* 5 vols. London, 1874–94.

Calendar of Patent and Close Rolls of Chancery in Ireland, Elizabeth. Edited by James Morrin. 3 vols. Dublin, 1861–63.

Calendar of Patent Rolls, Elizabeth I. London, 1966.

Calendar of State Papers, Domestic Series, 1547–1695. 81 vols. London, 1856–1972.

Calendar of State Papers, Relating to Ireland, 1509–1670. 24 vols. London, 1860–1912.

Calendar of the Carew Manuscripts, Preserved . . . at Lambeth, 1515–1624. 6 vols. London, 1867–73.

Calendar of the Manuscripts of the . . . Marquess of Salisbury . . . Preserved at Hatfield House. 23 vols. Historical Manuscripts Commission, London, 1883–1973.

Camden, William. *Britannia sive . . . Angliae, Scotiae, Hiberniae chorographica descriptio.* London, 1586.

Campion, Edmund. *A Historie of Ireland.* London, 1571.

Chamberlain, John. *The Letters of John Chamberlain.* Edited by Norman E. McClure. 2 vols. Philadelphia, 1939.

Collier, John Payne, ed., *The Egerton Papers.* London, 1840.

Falkiner, C. Litton, ed. *Illustrations of Irish History and Topography, Mainly of the Seventeenth Century.* London, 1904.

Finglas, Patrick. *A Breviat of the Getting of Ireland and of the Decaie of the Same* [ca. 1515]. [Copies in various states of completeness appear in the *Carew MSS.* It is also reprinted in Walter Harris, ed., *Hibernica: or Some Ancient Pieces Referring to Ireland.* 2 vols. Dublin, 1747–50, 1:39–52.]

Gernon, Luke. *A Discourse of Ireland* [ca. 1620]. In C. Litton Falkiner, ed., *Illustrations of Irish History and Topography, Mainly of the Seventeenth Century* London, 1904, pp. 345–64; and James P. Myers, Jr. *Elizabethan Ireland: A Selection of Writings by Elizabethan Writers on Ireland* (Hamden, Conn., 1983), pp. 241–57.

Grace, James. *Annales Hiberniae* [ca. 1538]. Edited by Richard Butler. Dublin, 1842.

Harris, Walter, ed., *Hibernica: or Some Ancient Pieces Referring to Ireland.* 2 vols. Dublin, 1747–50.

Holinshed, Raphael. *The . . . Chronicles of England, Scotlande and Irelande . . . .* London, 1577. Edited by John Hooker, alias Vowell, et al. 3 vols. London, 1587.

Maxwell, Constantia, ed. *Irish History from Contemporary Sources, 1509–1610.* London, 1923.

Morley, Henry, ed. *Ireland under Elizabeth and James I.* London, 1890.

Moryson, Fynes. *An Itinerary. . . .* 3 pts. London, 1617.

Myers, James P., Jr., ed. *Elizabethan Ireland: A Selection of Writings by Elizabethan Writers on Ireland.* Hamden, Conn., 1983.

Report on the Manuscripts of the Late Reginald Rawdon Hastings. . . . Edited by Francis Bickley. 4 vols. Historical Manuscripts Commission, London, 1928–47.

Report on the Manuscripts of the Marquess of Downshire. 4 vols. Historical Manuscripts Commission, London, 1924–40.

Spenser, Edmund. *A View of the Present State of Ireland* [1596]. In James Ware, ed., *The Historie of Ireland, Collected by Three Learned Authors. . . .* Dublin, 1633.

Wood, Anthony. *Athenae Oxoniensis. . . .* Edited by Philip Bliss. 5 vols. London, 1813–20.

Secondary Sources

Aylmer, G. E. *The King's Servants*. London, 1961.

Bagwell, Richard. *Ireland under the Stuarts and during the Interregnum*. 3 vols. London, 1909–16.

Bradshaw, Brendan. *The Irish Constitutional Revolution of the Sixteenth Century*. Cambridge, Eng., 1979.

———. "Sword, Word and Strategy in the Reformation in Ireland," *Historical Journal* 21 (1978): 475–502.

Brady, Ciaran, and Raymond Gillespie, eds. *Natives and Newcomers: Essays on the Making of Irish Colonial Society, 1534–1641*. Dublin, 1986.

Canny, Nicholas P. "Edmund Spenser and the Development of an Anglo-Irish Identity." *Yearbook of English Studies* 13 (1983): 1–19.

———. *The Elizabethan Conquest of Ireland: A Pattern Established, 1565–76*. New York, 1976.

———. "The Flight of the Earls, 1607." *Irish Historical Studies* 17 (1971): 380–99.

———. "Hugh O'Neill, Earl of Tyrone, and the Changing Face of Gaelic Ulster." *Studia Hibernica* 10 (1970): 7–35.

Casway, Jerrold. "Henry O'Neill and the Formation of the Irish Regiment in the Netherlands, 1605." *Irish Historical Studies* 18 (1973): 481–88.

Cosgrove, Art. *Late Medieval Ireland, 1370–1541*. Dublin, 1981.

Curtis, Edmund. *A History of Medieval Ireland from 1086 to 1513*. London, 1938.

Ellis, Steven G. *Tudor Ireland: Crown, Community and the Conflict of Cultures, 1470–1603*. London, 1985.

Falkiner, C. Litton. *Essays Relating to Ireland: Biographical, Historical, and Topographical*. London, 1909.

Falls, Cyril. *Mountjoy: Elizabethan General*. London, 1955.

Farrell, Brian, ed. *The Irish Parliamentary Tradition*. Dublin, 1973.

Frame, Robin. *Colonial Ireland, 1169–1369*. Dublin, 1981.

———. *English Lordship in Ireland, 1318–1361*. Oxford, 1982.

Grennan, Eamon. "Language and Politics: A Note on Some Metaphors in Spenser's *A View of the Present State of Ireland*." *Spenser Studies* 3 (1982): 99–110.

Grosart, Alexander B. "Memorial-Introduction." In Grosart, ed., *The Complete Works of Sir John Davies*. 3 vols. Blackburn, Eng., 1869–76.

Hand, Geoffrey. *English Law in Ireland, 1290–1324*. Cambridge, Eng., 1967.

Harris, F. W. "The Commission of 1609: Legal Aspects." *Studia Hibernica* 20 (1980): 32–55.

———. "Matters Relating to the Indictments of 'The Fugitive Earls and Their Principal Adherents.'" *Irish Jurist* 18 (1983): 344–59.

———. "The Rebellion of Sir Cahir O'Doherty and Its Legal Aftermath." *Irish Jurist* 15 (1980): 298–325.

———. "The State of the Realm: English Military, Political and Diplomatic Responses to the Flight of the Earls, Autumn 1607 to Spring 1608." *Irish Sword* 14 (1980): 47–65.

Hayes-McCoy, G. A. "Sir John Davies in Cavan in 1606 and 1610." *Breifne* 1 (1960): 177–91.

————, ed. *Ulster and Other Irish Maps, c. 1600*. Dublin, 1964.

Hindle, C. J. "A Bibliography of the Printed Pamphlets and Broadsides of Lady Eleanor Douglas, the Seventeenth-Century Prophetess." *Edinburgh Bibliographical Society Transactions* 1 (1935–38): 68–75.

Jones, Frederick M. *Mountjoy, 1563–1606: The Last Elizabethan Deputy*. London, 1958.

Krueger, Robert. "General Introduction." In Krueger, ed., *The Poems of Sir John Davies*. Oxford, 1975.

MacCaffrey, Wallace. "Place and Patronage in Elizabethan Politics." In S. T. Bindoff, J. Hurtsfield, and C. H. Williams, eds., *Elizabethan Government and Society: Essays Presented to Sir John Neale*. pp. 95–126. London, 1961.

MacCurtain, Margaret. "The Roots of Irish Nationalism." In Robert O'Driscoll, ed., *The Celtic Consciousness*, pp. 371–82. New York, 1981.

————. *Tudor and Stuart Ireland*. Dublin, 1972.

MacLysaght, Edward. *Irish Families: Their Names, Arms and Origins*. Dublin, 1957.

————. *More Irish Families*. Galway, 1960.

————. *Supplement to Irish Families*. Dublin, 1969.

McNeill, T. E. *Anglo-Normal Ulster, 1177–1400*. Edinburgh, 1980.

Meehan, C. P. *The Fate and Fortunes of Hugh O'Neill, Earl of Tyrone, and Rory O'Donnel, Earl of Tyrconnel. . . .* New York, 1868.

Moody, T. W. "The Irish Parliament under Elizabeth and James I." *Royal Irish Academy Proceedings* 45 (1939): 41–81.

Moody, T.W., F. X. Martin, and F. J. Byrne, eds. *A New History of Ireland*. Vol. 3, *Early Modern Ireland, 1534–1691*. Oxford, 1976.

Neale, J. E. "The Elizabethan Political Scene." In *Essays in English History*, pp. 59–84. London, 1958.

Nicholls, Kenneth, *Gaelic and Gaelicised Ireland in the Middle Ages*. Dublin, 1972.

Otway-Ruthven, A. J. *A History of Medieval Ireland*. 2d ed. New York, 1980.

Pawlisch, Hans S. *Sir John Davies and the Conquest of Ireland: A Study in Legal Imperialism*. Cambridge, Eng., 1985.

Peck, Linda Levy. *Northampton: Patronage and Policy at the Court of James I*. London, 1982.

Pocock, J. G. A. *The Ancient Constitution and the Feudal Law*. New York, 1967.

Powicke, Sir F. Maurice, ed. *Handbook of British Chronology*. 2d ed. London, 1961.

Quinn, David Beers. "The Irish Parliamentary Subsidy in the Fifteenth and Sixteenth Centuries." *Royal Irish Academy Proceedings* 42 (1936): 219–46.

————. "Sir Thomas Smith (1513–77) and the Beginnings of English Colonial Theory." *American Philosophical Society Proceedings* 89 (1945): 543–60.

Sanderson, James L. "Recent Studies in Sir John Davies." *English Literary Renaissance* 4 (1974): 411–17.

————. *Sir John Davies*. Boston, 1975.

Waterman, D. M. "Sir John Davies and His Ulster Buildings: Castlederg and Castle Curlews, Co. Tyrone." *Ulster Journal of Archaeology* 23 (1960): 89–96.

Index